1807
WILEY
2007
BICENTENNIAL · BICENTENNIAL · BICENTENNIAL

THE WILEY BICENTENNIAL—KNOWLEDGE FOR GENERATIONS

*E*ach generation has its unique needs and aspirations. When Charles Wiley first opened his small printing shop in lower Manhattan in 1807, it was a generation of boundless potential searching for an identity. And we were there, helping to define a new American literary tradition. Over half a century later, in the midst of the Second Industrial Revolution, it was a generation focused on building the future. Once again, we were there, supplying the critical scientific, technical, and engineering knowledge that helped frame the world. Throughout the 20th Century, and into the new millennium, nations began to reach out beyond their own borders and a new international community was born. Wiley was there, expanding its operations around the world to enable a global exchange of ideas, opinions, and know-how.

For 200 years, Wiley has been an integral part of each generation's journey, enabling the flow of information and understanding necessary to meet their needs and fulfill their aspirations. Today, bold new technologies are changing the way we live and learn. Wiley will be there, providing you the must-have knowledge you need to imagine new worlds, new possibilities, and new opportunities.

Generations come and go, but you can always count on Wiley to provide you the knowledge you need, when and where you need it!

WILLIAM J. PESCE
PRESIDENT AND CHIEF EXECUTIVE OFFICER

PETER BOOTH WILEY
CHAIRMAN OF THE BOARD

Selling

Tom Hopkins, Douglas J. Dalrymple,
William L. Cron, *Texas Christian University*
Thomas E. DeCarlo, *Iowa State University*

with *Terri Horvath*

BICENTENNIAL
1807
WILEY
2007
BICENTENNIAL

Credits

PUBLISHER
Anne Smith

PROJECT EDITOR
Beth Tripmacher

MARKETING MANAGER
Jennifer Slomack

SENIOR EDITORIAL ASSISTANT
Tiara Kelly

PRODUCTION MANAGER
Kelly Tavares

PRODUCTION ASSISTANT
Courtney Leshko

PROJECT MANAGER
Shana Meyer

CREATIVE DIRECTOR
Harry Nolan

COVER DESIGNER
Hope Miller

COVER PHOTO
Jurgen Reisch/Stone/Getty Images

Wiley 200th Anniversary Logo designed by: Richard J. Pacifico

This book was set in Times New Roman by Techbooks and printed and bound by R.R. Donnelley. The cover was printed by R.R. Donnelley.

This book is printed on acid free paper. ∞

To order books or for customer service please, call 1-800-CALL WILEY (225-5945).

ISBN-13 978-0-470-11125-3

Printed in the United States of America

10 9 8 7 6 5 4 3 2 1

College classrooms bring together learners from many backgrounds with a variety of aspirations. Although the students are in the same course, they are not necessarily on the same path. This diversity, coupled with the reality that these learners often have jobs, families, and other commitments, requires a flexibility that our nation's higher education system is addressing. Distance learning, shorter course terms, chunked curriculum, new disciplines, evening courses, and certification programs are some of the approaches that colleges employ to reach as many students as possible and help them clarify and achieve their goals.

Wiley Pathways books, a new line of texts from John Wiley & Sons, Inc., are designed to help you address this diversity and the need for flexibility. These books focus on the fundamentals, identify core competencies and skills, and promote independent learning. The focus on the fundamentals helps students grasp the subject, bringing them all to the same basic understanding. These books use clear, everyday language, presented in an uncluttered format, making the content more accessible and the reading experience more pleasurable. The core competencies and practical skills focus help students succeed in the classroom and beyond, whether in another course or in a professional setting. A variety of built-in learning resources promote independent learning and help instructors and students gauge students' understanding of the content. These resources enable students to think critically about their new knowledge, and apply their skills in any situation.

Our goal with *Wiley Pathways* books—with its brief, inviting format, clear language, and core competencies and skills focus—is to celebrate the many students in your courses, respect their needs, and help you guide them on their way.

Wiley Pathways Pedagogy

To meet the needs of working college students, all *Wiley Pathways* texts explicitly use an outcomes and assessment-based pedagogy for the books: students will review what they have learned, acquire new information and skills, and apply their new knowledge and skills to real-life situations. Based on the recently updated categories of Bloom's Taxonomy of Learning, *Wiley Pathways Selling* presents key topics in selling (the content) in easy-to-follow chapters. The text then prompts analysis, synthesis, and evaluation with a variety of learning aids and assessment tools. Students move efficiently from reviewing what they have learned, to acquiring new information and skills, to applying their new knowledge and skills to real-life scenarios.

With *Wiley Pathways Selling* students not only achieve academic mastery of selling *topics*, but they master real-world *skills* related to that content. The books help students become independent learners, giving them a distinct advantage in the field, whether they are starting out or seek to advance in their careers.

Organization, Depth and Breadth of the Text

▲ **Modular format.** Research on college students shows that they access information from textbooks in a non-linear way. Instructors also often wish to reorder textbook content to suit the needs of a particular class. Therefore, although *Wiley Pathways Selling* proceeds logically from the basics to increasingly more challenging material, chapters are further organized into sections that are self-contained for maximum teaching and learning flexibility.

▲ **Numeric system of headings.** *Wiley Pathways Selling* uses a numeric system for headings (for example, 2.3.4 identifies the fourth sub-section of section 3 of chapter 2). With this system, students and teachers can quickly and easily pinpoint topics in the table of contents and the text, keeping class time and study sessions focused.

▲ **Core content.** Topics in the text are organized into thirteen chapters.

Part I: The Art of Selling

Chapter 1, The Life and Career of a Professional Salesperson, focuses on the universal need for sales, the advantages in improving sales skills, and the characteristics and tools needed for success in this profession. The chapter also examines ideas on continual improvement for the professional.

Chapter 2, Ethical and Legal Issues in Selling, examines ethical standards in sales by individuals and businesses. Advice on how to make ethical decisions is provided along with factors influencing those decisions. The chapter also reviews some of the common ethical problems facing salespeople in today's business world.

Part II: Preparing for the Sale

Chapter 3, Why People Buy, focuses on understanding buyer behavior and the importance of uncovering the needs and wants of customers. The chapter provides tips on how to uncover these consumer needs and steps for developing the individual's sales strategy.

Chapter 4, Communication Skills for Relationship Building, reviews the importance of good communication skills for the professional salesperson. The chapter also outlines advice on improving communication skills and the elements necessary for building a salesperson/buyer relationship.

Chapter 5, Prospecting, examines how to find prospects, the most important step in a sales strategy for a novice. Sources for prospecting, factors involved in qualifying the prospect, and organizational tips are provided. The chapter also looks at the elements comprising prospecting and sales forecast plans.

Chapter 6, Planning a Sales Call, emphasizes the need to prepare before making sales calls. Sources for obtaining needed information, the elements necessary for an effective marketing strategy, and the development of sales presentation objectives are examined. Information on the purchasing process is also provided.

Part III: The Selling Process

Chapter 7, Making a Sales Call, presents advice in contacting and meeting customers. The chapter focuses on tips for getting an appointment and on presentation and style during the sales call. Plus, advice on leaving a positive impression is also provided.

Chapter 8, Elements of a Great Sales Presentation, describes the components of a successful presentation. The chapter outlines necessary tools and the structure of an effective presentation.

Chapter 9, Responding to Objections, is a practical guide in negotiating buyer concerns and problems. Common sources of buyer concerns and strategies for negotiating are reviewed.

Chapter 10, Closing a Sale, focuses on how the salesperson helps customers make a decision that is right for their circumstances. The chapter examines guidelines for closing the sale, closing techniques, and dealing with common stalling tactics.

Chapter 11, After the Sale: Service to Build a Partnership, reviews the keys to the long-term sales relationship. Focus is on developing and maintaining methods and strategies that strengthen the partnership. The chapter concludes with steps for getting referrals.

Part IV: Managing Yourself and Your Career

Chapter 12, Time and Territory Management: Keys to Success, explains the importance of the salespersons' self-management skills.

The chapter focuses on advice for developing and maintaining good time and territory management skills. It concludes with a look at how territories are designed.

Chapter 13, Managing and Training Others, summarizes the activities involved in sales management. These include recruiting and selecting salespeople, training employees, motivating a sales force, developing compensation plans, and assessing sales force productivity.

Pre-reading Learning Aids

Each chapter of *Wiley Pathways Selling* features the following learning and study aids to activate students' prior knowledge of the topics and orient them to the material.

▲ **Pre-test.** This pre-reading assessment tool in multiple-choice format not only introduces chapter material, but it also helps students anticipate the chapter's learning outcomes. By focusing students' attention on what they do not know, the self-test provides students with a benchmark against which they can measure their own progress. The pre-test is available online at www.wiley.com/college/hopkins.

▲ **What You'll Learn in this Chapter.** This bulleted list focuses on *subject matter* that will be taught. It tells students what they will be learning in this chapter and why it is significant for their careers. It will also help students understand why the chapter is important and how it relates to other chapters in the text.

▲ **After Studying this Chapter, You'll Be Able To.** This list emphasizes *capabilities and skills* students will learn as a result of reading the chapter. It focuses on the *execution* of subject matter to shows the relationship between what students will learn in the chapter and how the information learned will be applied in an on-the-job situation.

Within-text Learning Aids

The following learning aids are designed to encourage analysis and synthesis of the material, support the learning process, and ensure success during the evaluation phase:

▲ **Introduction.** This section orients the student by introducing the chapter and explaining its practical value and relevance to the book as a whole. Short summaries of chapter sections preview the topics to follow.

▲ **"For Example" Boxes.** Found within each chapter, these boxes tie section content to real-world examples, scenarios, and applications.

▲ **Figures and tables.** Line art and photos have been carefully chosen to be truly instructional rather than filler. Tables distill and present information in a way that is easy to identify, access, and understand, enhancing the focus of the text on essential ideas.

▲ **Self-Check.** Related to the "What You'll Learn" bullets and found at the end of each section, this battery of short answer questions emphasizes student understanding of concepts and mastery of section content. Though the questions may either be discussed in class or studied by students outside of class, students should not go on before they can answer all questions correctly.

▲ **Key Terms and Glossary.** To help students develop a professional vocabulary, key terms are bolded in the introduction, summary, and when they first appear in the chapter. A complete list of key terms with brief definitions appears at the end of each chapter and again in a glossary at the end of the book. Knowledge of key terms is assessed by all assessment tools (see below).

▲ **Summary.** Each chapter concludes with a summary paragraph that reviews the major concepts in the chapter and links back to the "What You'll Learn" list.

Evaluation and Assessment Tools

Each *Wiley Pathways* text consists of a variety of within-chapter and end-of-chapter assessment tools that test how well students have learned the material. These tools also encourage students to extend their learning into different scenarios and higher levels of understanding and thinking. The following assessment tools appear in every chapter of *Wiley Pathways Selling:*

▲ *Summary Questions* help students summarize the chapter's main points by asking a series of multiple choice and true/false questions that emphasize student understanding of concepts and mastery of chapter content. Students should be able to answer all of the Summary Questions correctly before moving on.

▲ *Applying this Chapter Questions* drive home key ideas by asking students to synthesize and apply chapter concepts to new, real-life situations and scenarios. Asks student to practice using the material they have learned in contrived situations that help reinforce their understanding, and may throw light on important considerations, advantages, or drawbacks to a specific methodology.

▲ *You Try It Questions* are designed to extend students' thinking, and so are ideal for discussion, writing assignments, or for use as case studies. Using an open-ended format and sometimes based on Web sources, they encourage students to draw conclusions using chapter material applied to real-world situations, which fosters both mastery and independent learning.

▲ *Post-test* should be taken after students have completed the chapter. It includes all of the questions in the pre-test, so that students can see how their learning has progressed and improved.

Instructor and Student Package

Wiley Pathways Selling is available with the following teaching and learning supplements. All supplements are available online at the text's Book Companion Website, located at www.wiley.com/college/hopkins.

▲ **Instructor's Resource Guide.** Provides the following aids and supplements for teaching an Introduction to Selling course:

- *Sample syllabus.* A convenient template that instructors may use for creating their own course syllabi.

- *Teaching suggestions.* For each chapter, these include a chapter summary, learning objectives, definitions of key terms, lecture notes, answers to select text question sets, and at least 3 suggestions for classroom activities, such as ideas for speakers to invite, videos to show, and other projects.

▲ **PowerPoints.** Key information is summarized in 15 to 20 PowerPoints per chapter. Instructors may use these in class or choose to share them with students for class presentations or to provide additional study support.

▲ **Test Bank.** One test per chapter, as well as a mid-term, and two finals: one cumulative, one non-cumulative. Each includes true/false, multiple choice, and open-ended questions. Answers and page references are provided for the true/false and multiple choice questions, and page references for the open-ended questions. Available in Microsoft Word and computerized formats.

Taken together, the content, pedagogy, and assessment elements of *Wiley Pathways Selling* offer the career-oriented student the most important aspects of the sales field as well as ways to develop the skills and capabilities that current and future employers seek in the individuals they hire and promote. Instructors will appreciate its practical focus, conciseness, and real-world emphasis. We would like to thank the reviewers for their feedback and suggestions during the text's development. Their advice on how to shape *Wiley Pathways Selling* into a solid learning tool that meets both their needs and those of their busy students is deeply appreciated.

BRIEF CONTENTS

Part I: The Art of Selling 1

1. The Life and Career of a Professional Salesperson 1
2. Ethical and Legal Issues in Selling 23

Part II: Preparing for the Sale 45

3. Why People Buy 45
4. Communication Skills for Relationship Building 65
5. Prospecting 93
6. Planning a Sales Call 124

Part III: The Selling Process 146

7. Making a Sales Call 146
8. Elements of a Great Sales Presentation 164
9. Responding to Objections 187
10. Closing a Sale 204
11. After the Sale: Service to Build a Partnership 223

Part VI: Managing Yourself and Your Career 241

12. Time and Territory Management: Keys to Success 241
13. Managing and Training Others 263

Endnotes 295
Glossary 301
Index 312

CONTENTS

Part I: The Art of Selling 1

1   **The Life and Career of a Professional Salesperson** 1

Introduction 2

1.1   Understanding the Universal Need for Sales 2
     1.1.1   Using Sales Skills 2
     1.1.2   The Concept of Selling 3

     Self-Check 4

1.2   Using the Approaches of the Trade 4
     1.2.1   Person-to-Person 4
     1.2.2   Telemarketing 5
     1.2.3   Direct Mail 5
     1.2.4   E-Mail 5
     1.2.5   The Internet 6

     Self-Check 6

1.3   Experiencing the Learning Curve 6
     1.3.1   Unconscious Incompetence 6
     1.3.2   Conscious Incompetence 7
     1.3.3   Conscious Competence 7
     1.3.4   Unconscious Competence 7

     Self-Check 8

1.4   Describing the Ideal Sales Professional 8
     1.4.1   Creating the Selling Triangle 8
     1.4.2   The 10 Characteristics of a Successful
            Sales Professional 8

     Self-Check 10

1.5   Shifting into High Gear: Professional Sales 11
     1.5.1   Preparing Before the Sales Pitch 11
     1.5.2   Maintaining Professionalism in Your
            Presentation 12
     1.5.3   Communicating Effectively 13
     1.5.4   Having Realistic Expectations 14
     1.5.5   Maintaining Your Discipline and Commitment . . . 15
     1.5.6   Evaluating Yourself 15

     Self-Check 16

1.6   Using Technology in Sales 16

     Self-Check 18

     Summary 18

     Key Terms 19

Summary Questions 20

Applying This Chapter 21

You Try It 22

2   **Ethical and Legal Issues in Selling** 23

Introduction 24

2.1   Making Ethical Decisions 24
2.1.1   The Role of a Job Description in Ensuring Ethics . . . 26
2.1.2   The Role of the Business Environment in Ethics . . . 27
2.1.3   Ethics Training 29

Self-Check 29

2.2   Factors That Influence the Ethics of Salespeople 30
2.2.1   Relativism and Idealism 30
2.2.2   Machiavellianism 30
2.2.3   Conventional Morality 31

Self-Check 32

2.3   Ethical Problems Salespeople Face 32
2.3.1   Hiring and Firing 32
2.3.2   House Accounts 33
2.3.3   Expense Accounts 33
2.3.4   Gifts for Buyers 34
2.3.5   Bribes 34
2.3.6   Entertainment 35
2.3.7   Sexual Harassment 36
2.3.8   Whistle-blowing 37

Self-Check 38

2.4   Relying on Government Regulation for Sales Ethics 39
2.4.1   Reasons for Regulations 39
2.4.2   Problems with Regulation 39

Self-Check 40

Summary 40

Key Terms 40

Summary Questions 42

Applying This Chapter 43

You Try It 44

Part II: Preparing for the Sale 45

3   **Why People Buy** 45

Introduction 46

3.1   Uncovering Needs and Wants 46

Self-Check 48

3.2   Developing the Seven Steps of the Sales Strategy 49
     3.2.1   Step 1: Prospecting 49
     3.2.2   Step 2: Original Contact 50
     3.2.3   Step 3: Qualification 50
     3.2.4   Step 4: Presentation 51
     3.2.5   Step 5: Addressing Concerns 51
     3.2.6   Step 6: Closing the Sale 51
     3.2.7   Step 7: Getting Referrals 52
     Self-Check 52

3.3   Buying Motives 52
     3.3.1   Task Motives vs. Personal Buying
           Motives 53
     3.3.2   Transactional Relationship vs. Consultative
           Relationships 54
     Self-Check 56

3.4   How Customers Make Buying Decisions 56
     3.4.1   The Standardized Model 56
     3.4.2   The Need-Satisfaction Model 57
     3.4.3   The Problem-Solution Model 58
     3.4.4   Thinking Outside the Models 58
     Self-Check 59
     Summary 60
     Key Terms 60
     Summary Questions 62
     Applying This Chapter 62
     You Try It 64

4   **Communication Skills for Relationship Building** 65
     Introduction 66
4.1   The Importance of Communication Skills in Sales 66
     Self-Check 67
4.2   Developing Communication-Style Flexibility 67
     4.2.1   Believers 67
     4.2.2   Wheeler-dealers 67
     4.2.3   No-Nonsense Buyers 68
     4.2.4   Evaders 68
     4.2.5   Complainers 68
     4.2.6   Analyzers 69
     4.2.7   Power Seekers 69
     4.2.8   Disorganized and Controlling Buyers 69
     4.2.9   Cynics 70
     Self-Check 70

4.3   Communication Do's and Don'ts 71
       4.3.1   Positive Nonverbal Messages 71
       4.3.2   Negative Nonverbal Messages 72
       Self-Check 72
4.4   Vocabulary of a Great Salesperson 72
       Self-Check 73
4.5   Listening to Your Clients 73
       Self-Check 75
4.6   Cultural Considerations 75
       4.6.1   Unique Cultural Needs 75
       4.6.2   Getting Names Right 76
       4.6.3   Making an Appointment 77
       4.6.4   Presenting Your Business Card 77
       4.6.5   Respecting Personal Space 78
       4.6.6   Meeting and Greeting People 78
       4.6.7   Giving Gifts 78
       4.6.8   Choosing Your Words Wisely 80
       Self-Check 80
4.7   Relationship Building 80
       4.7.1   The Evolution of a Relationship 81
       4.7.2   Relationship Binders 81
       4.7.3   Relating Skills 85
       Self-Check 86
       Summary 87
       Key Terms 87
       Summary Questions 89
       Applying This Chapter 90
       You Try It 92
5 Prospecting 93
   Introduction 94
5.1   Prospecting: An Introduction 94
       Self-Check 95
5.2   Where to Find Prospects 95
       5.2.1   Current Customers 95
       5.2.2   Chambers of Commerce and Public
               Libraries 96
       5.2.3   The Internet 97
       5.2.4   List Brokers 97
       5.2.5   Your Current Contacts 97
       5.2.6   The Yellow Pages and Toll-Free Directories . . . 99
       5.2.7   Your Colleagues and Other Professionals 99

	5.2.8	The Newspaper	101
	Self-Check		101
5.3	Qualifying a Prospect		101
	5.3.1	Following the NEADS Formula	102
	5.3.2	Questioning Your Way to Success	103
	Self-Check		106
5.4	Organizing Your Prospect Information		106
	5.4.1	An Organized Workspace	107
	5.4.2	Technological Tools	107
	5.4.3	Organization in Contacting Prospects	109
	Self-Check		112
5.5	Developing a Prospecting and Sales Forecasting Plan		112
	5.5.1	Qualitative Methods	113
	5.5.2	Data Needed in Order to Use Qualitative Methods	113
	5.5.3	Quantitative Techniques	117
	Self-Check		118
	Summary		118
	Key Terms		119
	Summary Questions		121
	Applying This Chapter		121
	You Try It		123

6	**Planning a Sales Call**		**124**
	Introduction		125
6.1	Obtaining Knowledge		125
	6.1.1	The Product	127
	6.1.2	Your Customers	128
	6.1.3	Your Organization	130
	6.1.4	The Competition	130
	6.1.5	The Environment	131
	Self-Check		132
6.2	Developing a Marketing Strategy		133
	6.2.1	Market Segmentation	133
	6.2.2	Target Marketing	135
	6.2.3	Positioning Strategy	136
	6.2.4	Understanding the Purchasing Process	137
	Self-Check		138
6.3	Establishing Sales Presentation Objectives		138
	Self-Check		140

6.4   Advocating Skills 140

       Self-Check *140*

       Summary 140

       Key Terms 141

       Summary Questions 143

       Applying This Chapter 143

       You Try It 145

Part III: The Selling Process **146**

7   **Making a Sales Call** **146**

    Introduction 147

    7.1   Getting an Appointment 147

       7.1.1   Telephone Calls 147

       7.1.2   In-Person Calls 150

       7.1.3   Letters 150

       7.1.4   Third-Party Introductions 151

       Self-Check *151*

    7.2   Making a First Impression 151

       Self-Check *152*

    7.3   Approaching a Customer 152

       7.3.1   Managing Sales Call Anxiety and Motivation . . . 154

       7.3.2   Courtesy and Common Sense 155

       7.3.3   Being Observant 156

       Self-Check *156*

    7.4   Before Opening the Presentation 157

       Self-Check *158*

    7.5   Using Attention-Getters 158

       Self-Check *159*

    7.6   The Biggest Sales Mistakes 159

       Self-Check *160*

       Summary 160

       Key Terms 160

       Summary Questions 161

       Applying This Chapter 161

       You Try It 163

8   **Elements of a Great Sales Presentation** **164**

    Introduction 165

    8.1   The Importance of the Sales Presentation 165

       Self-Check *165*

8.2   Components of a Successful Presentation 165
       8.2.1   Finding the Power Players 166
       8.2.2   Keeping the Presentation as Brief as Possible . . . 166
       8.2.3   Handling Breaks 167
       8.2.4   Preparing Beforehand 167
       8.2.5   Customizing Your Materials 169
       8.2.6   Developing Your Selling Vocabulary 169
       8.2.7   Deciphering Body Language 173
       8.2.8   Being Comfortable with Long-Distance
                Presentations 174
       8.2.9   Establishing Trust 175

       Self-Check 176

8.3   Solution Presentations 176

       Self-Check 177

8.4   Adjuncts to a Presentation 177
       8.4.1   Product Specifications 177
       8.4.2   Written Proposals 177

       Self-Check 179

8.5   Proof Devices for Effective Sales Presentations 179
       8.5.1   The Product 179
       8.5.2   Visual Aids 180
       8.5.3   Demonstrations 182

       Self-Check 182

       Summary 183

       Key Terms 183

       Summary Questions 184

       Applying This Chapter. 185

       You Try It 186

9   **Responding to Objections** **187**
    Introduction 188

9.1   Negotiating Buyer Concerns and Problems 188

       Self-Check 189

9.2   Common Sources of Buyer Concerns 189
       9.2.1   Fear of Salespeople 190
       9.2.2   Fear of Failure 191
       9.2.3   Fear of Owing Money 191
       9.2.4   Fear of Deception 192
       9.2.5   Fear of Embarrassment 192
       9.2.6   Fear of the Unknown 193
       9.2.7   Fear of Repeating Past Mistakes 193

9.2.8   Fear Generated by Others 194

Self-Check 194

9.3   General Steps for Negotiating Buyer Concerns 194

Self-Check 194

9.4   Specific Steps in Negotiating Buyer Concerns 195

9.4.1   Listening to the Client's Feelings 195

9.4.2   Share the Concerns Without Judgment 196

9.4.3   Clarifying the Real Issue by Asking Questions . . . 196

9.4.4   Problem-Solving by Presenting
Options and Solutions 197

9.4.5   Asking for Action to Determine Commitment . . . 200

Self-Check 200

Summary 201

Key Terms 201

Summary Questions 202

Applying This Chapter 202

You Try It 203

10   Closing a Sale **204**

Introduction 205

10.1   Guidelines for Closing a Sale 205

10.1.1   Focusing on Buying Motives 206

10.1.2   Using Trial Closes to Gauge Interest 206

10.1.3   Asking a Reflex Question 208

10.1.4   Knowing What You Can Deliver 208

10.1.5   Displaying Self-Confidence 208

10.1.6   Asking for the Order More Than Once 209

10.1.7   Recognizing Closing Cues 209

Self-Check 210

10.2   Closing Techniques 211

10.2.1   The Basic Oral Close 211

10.2.2   The Basic Written Close 211

10.2.3   The Alternative Choice Close 211

10.2.4   The Porcupine Method 211

10.2.5   The Summary Close 212

10.2.6   Sharp Angling 212

10.2.7   The Higher Authority Close 213

10.2.8   Advanced Closing Techniques 214

Self-Check 217

10.3   Dealing with "I Want to Think It Over" 217

Self-Check 218

Summary 218

Key Terms 218
Summary Questions 220
Applying This Chapter 221
You Try It 222

11   **After the Sale: Service to Build a Partnership** **223**
Introduction 224
11.1   Building Long-Term Partnerships 224
    11.1.1   Creating More Value for the Customer 225
    11.1.2   Achieving Successful Sales 226
    Self-Check 227
11.2   Customer Service Methods That Strengthen
    a Partnership 227
    11.2.1   Cross-Selling and Up-Selling to Grow Sales 228
    11.2.2   Following Up 228
    11.2.3   Sending Thank-You Notes 230
    Self-Check 231
11.3   Preplanning Your Service Strategy 232
    Self-Check 234
11.4   Getting Referrals 234
    Self-Check 236
    Summary 236
    Key Terms 236
    Summary Questions 238
    Applying This Chapter 239
    You Try It 240

Part VI: Managing Yourself and Your Career **241**

12   **Time and Territory Management: Keys to Success** **241**
Introduction 242
12.1   Managing Yourself 242
    12.1.1   Self-Discipline 242
    12.1.2   Good Habits 244
    Self-Check 245
12.2   Time Management 245
    12.2.1   Time Traps 246
    12.2.2   Professional Selling Efficiency 250
    12.2.3   Productivity Gains 250
    Self-Check 251
12.3   Suggestions for Time Management 252
    Self-Check 255

12.4   Territory Management 255
        12.4.1   What Territory Management Involves 256
        12.4.2   Territory Design 256
        12.4.3   Sales Call Plans 257
        Self-Check 258
        Summary 258
        Key Terms 258
        Summary Questions 260
        Applying This Chapter 261
        You Try It 262

13   Managing and Training Others 263
     Introduction 264
     13.1   Sales Management Functions 264
             Self-Check 265
     13.2   Recruitment and Selection of Salespeople 265
             13.2.1   The Planning Process 266
             13.2.2   Recruiting Salespeople 266
             13.2.3   Selecting Salespeople 267
             13.2.4   Interviewing Salespeople 269
             13.2.5   Avoiding Nine Common Recruiting Mistakes . . . 270
             13.2.6   Validating the Hiring Process 272
             Self-Check 273
     13.3   Orientation and Training 273
             13.3.1   The Benefits of a Training Program 273
             13.3.2   Planning for Training 275
             Self-Check 276
     13.4   Team Building 276
             Self-Check 277
     13.5   Sales Force Motivation 277
             13.5.1   Individual Needs 278
             13.5.2   Career Stages 280
             13.5.3   Incentive and Recognition Programs 280
             Self-Check 283
     13.6   Compensation Plans 283
             13.6.1   Expense Reimbursement 285
             13.6.2   Benefits 285
             Self-Check 285
     13.7   Assessing Sales Force Productivity 286
             13.7.1   Six Insights for Evaluation and Control Systems . . 287
             Self-Check 288

Summary 289

Key Terms 289

Summary Questions 291

Applying This Chapter 292

You Try It 294

Endnotes 295

Glossary 301

Index 312

1

THE LIFE AND CAREER OF A PROFESSIONAL SALESPERSON

Developing Skills for Success

Starting Point

Go to www.wiley.com/college/hopkins to assess your knowledge of the characteristics of a professional salesperson and the needed skills. *Determine where you need to concentrate your effort.*

What You'll Learn in This Chapter

▲ The universal need for sales
▲ The benefits of improving your sales skills
▲ The definition of selling
▲ The five primary approaches of a salesperson
▲ The definition and four phases of the learning curve
▲ The three sides of the sales triangle
▲ The 10 characteristics of a successful salesperson
▲ Characteristics you need to advance in your career

After Studying This Chapter, You'll Be Able To

▲ Understand the foundational knowledge necessary to build a career in sales

INTRODUCTION

Sales are part of everyday life. Waiters, actors, politicians, mothers—we all practice sales in some form to get something we want or need. Some people, however, practice sales as their primary occupation. This chapter focuses on defining the profession of sales, characteristics of top sales professionals, and the skills necessary for success in this occupation. The chapter concludes with a look at ideas for continual improvement for the professional.

1.1 Understanding the Universal Need for Sales

Everyone sells something. Whether the sales pitch involves a refrigerator to a newly wed couple or an idea for a refrigeration improvement to a board of directors, selling occurs all around, everyday, in one form or another. Salespeople are everywhere. At some point nearly every day, you're involved in a selling situation of some kind.

According to the U.S. Department of Labor's Bureau of Labor Statistics, people working in sales number close to 12 million, or about 10 percent of the total workforce in the United States.

1.1.1 Using Sales Skills

In some form or another, we start selling at a very early age. In time, some of us become more attuned, either unconsciously or consciously, to the advantages of selling.

Selling skills can do for you what a way with words did for William Shakespeare. They can do for you what sex appeal did for Marilyn Monroe. They can do for you what powerful communication skills did for historical greats such

FOR EXAMPLE

Saving Daylight

Ten-year-old Jason knows his bedtime is 9 p.m. on weekdays. But when summer rolls around, it's still light at 9 p.m. He could use that extra hour of daylight for baseball practice. Jason wants to extend bedtime to 10 p.m. during the summer. He presents his case to his mother, including the fact that there is no school to attend, so he no longer has an early-morning schedule. In response, Jason's mother sees an opening to get something she wants—no more delaying tactics at bedtime. Jason's mother agrees to the bedtime extension as longer as Jason will come quickly and quietly at the appointed hour. Both are using a sales skill to get something they want.

as Abraham Lincoln, Franklin D. Roosevelt, and Martin Luther King, Jr. Selling skills can make or break you in whatever endeavor you choose. They can mean the difference between obtaining your goal and needing to settle for less.

Having selling skills is like having an inside track on what the next batch of winning lottery numbers will be. All you have to do is invest a bit of your time and effort to understand and apply these tried-and-true, proven-effective skills to your everyday life. Before you know it, they'll be such a natural part of you that no one, including yourself, will even recognize them as selling skills.

Writers, actors, and politicians have used sales skills in a seemingly unconscious manner. These are people who recognize their art or idea as a product and set about to sell it to a segment of the population. Then there are people who choose to list "sales" as their primary occupation—professional salespeople.

1.1.2 The Concept of Selling

So what does *selling* mean? For our purposes, we'll concentrate on **personal selling,** which is defined as direct communications between paid representatives and prospects that lead to transactions, customer satisfaction, account development, and profitable relationships. Personal selling is critical to the sale of many goods and services, especially major commercial and industrial products and consumer durables.

Marketing programs are designed around four elements of the marketing mix:

▲ Products to be sold.
▲ Pricing.
▲ Promotion.
▲ Distribution channels.

The promotion component includes advertising, public relations, personal selling, and sales promotion (e.g., point-of-purchase displays, coupons, sweepstakes). Note that advertising and sales promotions are not personal communications. Whereas salespeople talk directly to customers, advertising and sales promotions "pull" merchandise through the channel, and personal selling provides the "push" needed to get orders signed. With public relations, the message is perceived as coming from the medium rather than directly from the organization. Personal selling involves two-way communication with prospects and customers that allows the salesperson to address the special needs of the customer.

It is often the job of a salesperson to uncover the special needs of the customer. When customers have questions or concerns, the salesperson is there to provide appropriate explanations. Plus, personal selling can be directed to qualified prospects. Perhaps the most important advantage of personal selling is that it is considerably more effective than advertising, public relations, and sales promotions in identifying opportunities to create value for the customer and gaining customer commitment.

Professional selling is the process of moving goods and services from the hands of those who produce them into the hands of those who benefit most from their use. Selling involves persuasive skills on the part of the person doing the talking. It's supported by print, audio, and video messages that sell the item, service, or idea as being desirable.

It's been said that nothing ever happens unless someone sells something to someone else. Without selling, products that have been manufactured would sit in warehouses for eternity, people working for those manufacturers would become unemployed, transportation and freight services wouldn't be needed, and we would all be living isolated little lives, striving to eke out livings from whatever bit of land we owned. Or would we even own the land if no one were there to sell it to us?

SELF-CHECK

1. Explain how selling is a universal concept.
2. Define **selling** in a professional context.

1.2 Using the Approaches of the Trade

The primary approaches used in sales today are:

▲ Person-to-person.
▲ Telemarketing.
▲ Direct mail.
▲ E-mail.
▲ The Internet.

Although these approaches can be as varied as the individuals using them, there are some important considerations in using each one. Each of these areas is explored in more depth in subsequent chapters, but here are some tips to introduce you to the life of a sales professional who works in one or all of these areas.

1.2.1 Person-to-Person

Person-to-person selling, conducted worldwide, is the single largest type of selling. Retail stores abound with sales opportunities, and millions of salespeople sit at desk, conference table, or kitchen table, turning prospects into clients. The message in China may be presented differently than one in Germany, but the goal is the same—to make a sale.

A sales professional talking to a client in a face-to-face fashion has the advantage of being able to use many different senses. You can have the client possibly touch, taste, smell, and hear the product that is on sale. The person-to-person approach has the advantage of actively engaging the customer in the sales process.

1.2.2 Telemarketing

Telemarketing is an approach that a salesperson can use to contact a prospect by phone. The telephone can connect a salesperson with nearly any other person on the planet. That's a clear advantage. You can reach a much large market in less time than by using the person-to-person approach. The primary disadvantage of telemarketing is that the prospect has to answer the phone, and you then have to quickly engage the prospect.

In some industries, you actually try to sell the product on the first call (referred to as a **one-time close**). In other industries, you're selling enough interest that the person to whom you speak gets out of her home and down to your store or lets you come visit her in her home or place of business. Either way, you're selling what your business is all about, leaving the person on the other end with a very distinct impression of you and your company—good or bad.

1.2.3 Direct Mail

Much of the mail you receive is designed to sell you something. This is referred to as **direct mail.** The following are some examples:

▲ A coupon for a local restaurant is designed to get you into the eatery, with the hope of you becoming a regular customer.
▲ A clothing catalog is sent to entice you to try shopping at home.
▲ A flyer from a politician encourages you to get out and vote.

Companies and individuals play the odds that enough people will respond to their direct mail pieces.

A 1 percent response rate for direct mail is considered average. Based on that percentage, only 1 out of 100 catalogs sent may actually produce an order. Companies are willing to spend the money on production and postage in the hope of obtaining regular customers who continue to place orders.

Another factor that affects the response rate is that a direct mail piece doesn't always reach the intended recipient. A well-intentioned secretary or spouse may consider the item junk mail and discard it.

1.2.4 E-Mail

Many companies have found the **e-mail approach** to work well because e-mail solicitations are more likely to reach the intended recipient than other telemarketing or direct mail pieces.

So far, business e-mail appears to be deemed personal territory. Secretaries and receptionists may receive copies of e-mails, but they aren't likely to delete e-mail messages from their bosses' computers.

1.2.5 The Internet

Like selling via the telephone, **the Internet approach,** or selling via Web sites, has global opportunities. Your headquarters could be located anywhere, and you could still reach millions who use the Internet every day. The primary advantages to having an Internet presence are immediacy and convenience. A prospect can visit a company's web site at any time to view a product. The customer doesn't even have to change out of his bathrobe, if he prefers. The sale may be only a click away.

A salesperson who knows how to use the Internet to his or her advantage has a wealth of global opportunities—not just those available locally.

SELF-CHECK

1. Discuss the advantages and disadvantages of person-to-person selling.
2. Discuss the advantages and disadvantages of telemarketing.
3. Discuss the advantages and disadvantages of direct mail.
4. Discuss the advantages and disadvantages of selling via e-mail.
5. Discuss the advantages and disadvantages of selling via the Internet.

1.3 Experiencing the Learning Curve

Knowing the various sales approaches is part of the selling equation. In order to succeed, a professional salesperson passes through a **learning curve**—the time needed to progress from being a complete beginner to an expert. The learning curve consists of four major phases or levels of competency:

▲ Unconscious incompetence.
▲ Conscious incompetence.
▲ Conscious competence.
▲ Unconscious competence.

1.3.1 Unconscious Incompetence

During **unconscious incompetence,** the first stage of the learning curve, you are unaware of the amount of knowledge needed to accomplish a task. In this most elementary phase, you may be a complete novice or someone with some product knowledge but still needing more knowledge in sales techniques.

You are at the unconscious incompetence level of learning when you first try something new. You could define this stage as the first part of the learning curve in which a person is unaware of the amount the knowledge needed to accomplish a task.

1.3.2 Conscious Incompetence

People abandon unconscious incompetence when they realize their incompetence. At this second stage, the **conscious incompetence** level, they may choose to move forward or not. If they move forward, they choose to learn more. This conscious acknowledgement leads to the next level, and you choose to learn the skills needed.

1.3.3 Conscious Competence

New challenges and new victories await a professional who chooses to move into the third level of the learning curve, **conscious competence.** In this phase of the learning curve, a person chooses to learn specific skills and knowledge. A professional in this third phase is growing and learning new material.

At this level, you are practicing and honing the skills you've decided you need. You might want to practice these skills with your friends and associates before testing new strategies on qualified clients.

1.3.4 Unconscious Competence

At the fourth and final level of competence, **unconscious competence,** you apply all your previous knowledge without making a conscious effort to do so. As an unconsciously competent salesperson, the strategies are now a natural part of your presentation.

FOR EXAMPLE

Taking Baby Steps

Think of how a baby learns to walk. The inexperienced toddler doesn't know he doesn't know how to walk. He just tries it because everyone else is doing it. When he learns, by falling, that it's not as easy as it looks, he reaches for helping hands. The instant he reaches for help, he moves to the next level of competency. The baby eventually moves through and completes the learning curve.

SELF-CHECK

1. List and describe the four levels of the learning curve.

1.4 Describing the Ideal Sales Professional

By taking this course and reading the assigned material, you are well on your way through the learning curve. You know you need to learn about sales skills. You want to learn more. You already possess one of the characteristics of the ideal sales professional: the desire to become one. In most surveys of successful sales professionals, they generally agree that the number-one factor in their success is that they enjoy their job. Studies have proven that attitude is one of the traits that separate so-so salespeople from their highly successful colleagues.

1.4.1 Creating the Selling Triangle

Optimally, a sales professional is one who has mastered all three sides of a selling triangle consisting of

▲ Product knowledge.
▲ Selling tactics and strategies.
▲ Attitude and goal setting.

The three sides of the selling triangle are equally important. A professional who doesn't develop each side of the triangle fails to meet her full potential. If product knowledge were the only necessary element, then the product's designers or manufacturing team would be the best salespeople. Being able to describe the product doesn't necessarily mean being able to meet the client's needs. That's an important aspect of sales. Likewise, a professional salesperson must have an enthusiastic attitude for the job and set specific goals in terms of sales quotas.

1.4.2 The 10 Characteristics of a Successful Sales Professional

Aside from the factors we've already discussed, what else do you need to be a good salesperson? People who are successful at persuading, convincing, or selling others on their ideas, products, or services, have 10 characteristics in common[1]:

▲ **Desire and passion to succeed:** A professional persuader has a strong reason for wanting to succeed.
▲ **Interest in others:** Top sales professionals show an interest in providing the right solution for a client's needs. They know how to engage people.

▲ **Confidence and strength:** Professional persuaders radiate confidence and strength, which become evident in their body language, speech, and overall presence.

▲ **Empathy:** A sincere interest in the prospects' needs creates a bond of trust and openness.

▲ **Goal setting:** Professional salespeople have set their goals and put them in writing. They know exactly what they're striving for and when they expect to accomplish it.

▲ **Persistence:** They know how to plan their time effectively and take steps toward achieving their goals. They rely on proven systems for planning their time and have discovered effective time-management strategies.

▲ **Enthusiasm through difficult situations:** Even with the most careful planning and preparation, your career path may have a few bumps along the journey. Top professionals recognize this and work through difficult times.

▲ **A positive attitude:** Professional persuaders keep themselves in a positive shell and avoid jealousy, gossip, anger, and negative thinking. They don't allow negativity to steal their energy or tempt them to stray from their chosen course.

▲ **An understanding that people come before money:** They understand the old adages that you have to spend money to make money and that persuasion is a people business. And they invest wisely in things for the good of the people they serve.

▲ **An investment in their minds:** Professional persuaders are lifelong learners. They know their product lines and prospects and remain up-to-date on the latest news affecting their business.

These traits are more than just sales skills. They are also people skills. A top sales professional recognizes that knowing how to get along well with others is vital. To be successful, top sales professionals:

▲ Know they must learn cooperation and good listening skills.
▲ Tend to be curious and interested in others.
▲ Take satisfaction in fulfilling someone's need and love meeting the challenge of serving the next customer.
▲ Make money doing something, or at least part of something, they enjoy.

In addition to having these characteristics, it is important to develop a mental image of who you want to become. You should visualize yourself as a person who uses selling skills effectively. Visualization is an effective technique used by many successful people, including professional athletes. For example, a basketball

---

FOR EXAMPLE

My Passion for Selling

A merging of passion and profession has occurred in my life with selling. For me, selling began as a career opportunity that would fulfill a need— the need to make money. When I failed miserably at first, I knew I needed help, and I started a journey of study. I knew that some people made huge incomes in sales, so I assumed that they must have known something I'd not yet discovered. It was at that point that I chose to turn selling into my hobby, my passion. When I started to educate myself—by watching everyday people and looking for little nuances of selling that worked for them and by reading up on the subject. I also started making a lot of money. Believe me when I say that, at first, money was my motivation for keeping up my selling hobby. But since then, I've managed to transform my job-turned-hobby into something much more: It has become a way of life. Selling now pervades every communication I have with others, and I thoroughly enjoy my life these days.

---

player develops a clear picture in his mind's eye of just how the basketball will leave his hands for a three-point shot. He pictures his fingers releasing the ball and sees nothing of the crowd—only the net. When he first begins visualizing this, his body may not be up to speed with the picture. If he plays the picture often enough, though, chances are good that his body will get the idea and soon perform accordingly.

Everyone can use this technique. When you act like the person you want to become, you try to say and do what you think this "new" person would say and do. Eventually, you begin having small success with the material, and soon you are that person.

SELF-CHECK

1. Discuss the three-sided triangle and how each side is as important as the other two.
2. List and describe the 10 characteristics of a successful sales professional.

1.5 Shifting into High Gear: Professional Sales

You've probably encountered professional salespeople. Being a professional sales-person means the person has learned how to:

▲ Sell more and in a more efficient manner.

▲ Find and qualify prospects quickly and smoothly.

How did this person achieve this status? What are the steps you need to learn to get there? You will examine these steps in detail throughout this book. This section discusses some of the general steps necessary in your journey toward becoming and remaining a sales professional.

1.5.1 Preparing Before the Sales Pitch

You need to prepare yourself both mentally and physically for the challenge of persuading others. In your sales approach, you need to:

▲ Dress appropriately.

▲ Maintain a positive attitude toward the product, yourself, and your client.

▲ Concentrate on the needs of your customer and the best presentation you can give.

▲ Review any notes or information that may be vital within a few hours of meeting with your prospects.

You need to particularly take note of the importance of a good first impression. You don't hear too many winning stories about people who overcame bad first impressions to go on to land a major account or persuade an important person to their way of thinking. Going in confident and handling the initial rapport-setting stage properly goes a long way toward winning.

Another aspect of preparation is learning the necessary skills and details to complete a specific task. Before you enter into any new experience, you should adopt an attitude of positive anticipation and enthusiasm. Remember that a master salesperson was once an excellent student. Here are some tips to help you obtain that attitude:

▲ **Discover your best learning environment:** You need to figure out where and how you can most effectively focus on learning. For some, sitting in the family room with the family as they watch football may be the appropriate place, while others require silence and isolation to best comprehend what they read. Whatever your personal needs, if you plan to study, memorize, and adopt the sales techniques in this book, you need to make the most of the time you set aside for that purpose.

▲ **Study at a pace that fits you:** Some people learn better when they read little bits of information and give themselves a chance to internalize what they've learned. Others like to take big clumps of information at one sitting so they can see the bigger picture and understand the full concept of what is being presented.

▲ **Limit your interruptions:** It's important to set up a regular time to study and limit interruptions. The average person needs about 10 minutes after being interrupted to regain the previous concentration. That's why staying in study mode when people interrupt you is so difficult. Getting 30 minutes of uninterrupted reading and studying time is better than patching together four or five interrupted periods that equal an hour of study time. If you can't hide out for a long period of time, you should cut your time or break it into two sessions in order to maximize your learning.

By analyzing your optimum learning patterns and working with them, your attitude about the material being studied will be positive. You'll be more relaxed and learn at a faster pace.

1.5.2 Maintaining Professionalism in Your Presentation

By making every presentation as though it's the most important thing in your life at that moment, you show the decision makers that you're sincere about their needs and that they're important to you. Generally, people are whatever you expect them to be, so you should expect your prospects to be vital to your overall success in life and treat them with the proper respect.

Prospects also want to know that you believe in your product. If you believe in what you're doing, you must personally be a part of it. If you're selling Fords, you don't want to be seen driving a Chevy. If you sell home-security systems, you better have one in your home. If you market freelance graphic design, your business cards better be creative. If you can talk personally about your own experiences with your product, service, or idea, you'll win over a lot more people than if you can't.

As with any other endeavor, you need practice and critique to perfect your new skills. In addition to rehearsing your sales pitch, you also need to experiment with the nuances of body language and voice intonation and inflection. You should rehearse by yourself until you feel confident enough to practice in front of your family, friends, or peers who can give you some important pointers. You need to listen to their comments and incorporate them into your presentation.

When performing before a prospect, you need to give yourself permission to be a rookie, but be sure to follow the rookie rules:

▲ Find and use many opportunities to perfect your new selling techniques.

▲ Reflect on your presentations and examine how to improve.

▲ Persist until you become a polished sales professional.

> ## FOR EXAMPLE
>
> ### Preparing for the First Client
>
> Ted is a recently hired pharmaceutical sales representative. The company leads him through training that concentrates on product knowledge as well as tips on approaching his prospects. Ted studies all the manuals and then follows Bill, an experienced sales representative, on his sales calls. After a few days, armed with product and company knowledge, Ted begins to see how to incorporate the information into his own style. He practices his presentations before a mirror and then in front of his wife and then in front of Bill. Each notes the good and bad of his presentation. Ted assesses how to adjust and then approaches his first client.

Sometimes you may need to memorize concepts and specific words in a presentation. To succeed, you need to look like you don't have a canned message. The worst habit you can develop is to memorize phrases and then shut off your personality and resort to a robot imitation whenever you get desperate. Remember, as you sell, you need to be genuine and personable: Look for ways to make the memorization reflect your personality. Practice how you will say them. Think about how you will carry yourself and how you will stand or sit when you utter those words. Use your sense of humor, your previous knowledge, and your natural speech and mannerisms to make your new selling skills sound spontaneous.

1.5.3 Communicating Effectively

Selling is a two-way communication process. Here are some important steps in effective sales communication:

1. **Qualify the prospect:** By asking a few simple questions, you can determine quickly whether the person you're meeting with is right for your offering. By doing this, you maximize your efforts by continuing presentations only with someone who can make a decision. Making a quick determination also shows that you respect the prospect and extend the courtesy of not wasting time.

2. **Address the client's concerns:** If and when your prospect voices a concern about something, you shouldn't ever glide over it. Instead, you should let it stop you momentarily and think about what was said and what you may have said or done to trigger the comment. Then you can carefully and thoughtfully address the concern.

> ┌─ **FOR EXAMPLE** ─┐
>
> ### Shifting to Meet the Client's Needs
>
> During a visit to a local auto dealer, Mr. Friedman revealed to John, the sales representative, many items he wanted for his new car. Mixed in among the list was Mr. Friedman's need for a large trunk, which he specified as needing to haul his sales samples. John understood that a large trunk was a major selling point for Mr. Friedman. "What I understand from your comment, Mr. Friedman," John said, "is that you're particularly concerned about the size of the trunk in your new vehicle, is that correct?" Mr. Friedman agreed that it was a major issue. John looked for a vehicle with a large trunk and made the sale.

3. **Confirm everything:** Miscommunication costs people money, time, and effort every year. Missed appointments, flights, or phone calls can destroy in minutes what may have taken months to build. Inattention to details, wrong orders, and wrong people handling important tasks take their toll as well. It's important to take the time to confirm (and reconfirm) the details.

4. **Ask for the decision:** You have nothing to lose by asking a prospect for a decision. The client may or may not be ready to make a decision, and you need to learn the right time to let go and try another time.

Few people want to be guinea pigs, so sharing the experiences of others who bought your product, use your service, or are committed to the same project is a good tactic. Your prospects will recognize that they're not going into uncharted waters. Overcoming their fears will take you far in convincing or persuading people, especially if you can use examples of people they know.

1.5.4 Having Realistic Expectations

You are experiencing the learning curve now, and professionalism in sales takes some time and knowledge. You need to be patient with yourself and not expect to be a winner 100 percent of the time. On the other hand, you should be honest with yourself and recognize times when inadequate knowledge or an inaccurate application of new selling techniques has kept you from giving your best performance.

It's important to know your limitations but not be bound by them. You should do what you know you should do, do it the best way you know how, and stay on the lookout for ways to improve your selling skills.

You should also try to be flexible. Change isn't necessarily easy, and learning and adapting require change. Sometimes you may need to change some of your hàbits. It's normal to feel anxiety and confusion during this period of change or improvement. As you become a more effective salesperson, you'll find yourself applying what you've discovered to your personal relationships and decisions. But there's lag time between the practice and the perfection, so you should allow yourself and others time to adjust to the new and improved version of you. Flexibility also applies to being aware of the new technology and practices that will improve your practice.

1.5.5 Maintaining Your Discipline and Commitment

One of the greatest pitfalls of great success in a short period of time is a failure to continue. People have a tendency to want to rest on their laurels when they know they're good. Slowing down after achieving success quickly is a dangerous mistake. The fact that you've tasted some success doesn't mean that you can stop and fall back into the same old methods that crippled your sales career. The real trick is to remain balanced during your successes.

You can think of every technique you read in this book as one link in the chain of your success in sales. If you have a weak chain, you may need to review a chapter or two. If you don't go back and make the weak link stronger, your career chain will never carry the weight it needs to carry in order to haul you up to top-producer status.

1.5.6 Evaluating Yourself

In order to accurately evaluate results, you need to know the point of origin. You should take time to record your journey with a success journal, starting with Day 1. You use a **success journal** to record specific instances and details of when you successfully used new selling techniques; by doing so, you not only immediately reinforce the benefits to your career but also provide encouragement when reviewing and reliving a positive selling experience.

In reviewing your success journal, you should compare what you did right in a given situation to what you did when you did not get a sale. When you

FOR EXAMPLE

Journaling for Success

Allison started a success journal the first day she became a salesperson for a real estate firm. First, she recorded her sales pitch. Then she wrote about her first sale, including the details that helped her land the deal. Two specifics were that she remembered to ask about her client's needs and wants and that she asked for the decision. Allison decided those were key points in making this particular sale, and she made a notation for future reference.

make such a comparison, the reasons for not getting the sale should become obvious. By comparing an unsuccessful experience to a successful one, you see what you left out or skimmed over and why you failed to convince the customer of the benefits of your offering. When such negatives occur, you can adjust your presentation or sales techniques.

Keeping a success journal is also a way to remain alert to various situations that may become sales opportunities. When you witness a good job of selling, you should make a note of it in your success journal. When a master sells you on something, you should jot down the details. Make specific notes of things the professional did that especially impressed or influenced you. Observe, listen, and take time to reflect on the situation. Observe the expressions and actions of the other party as a result of the selling methods being used. Indicate which techniques have negative or positive effects on the prospect. Sometimes the negative lessons have a stronger impact than those that look smooth and effortless.

The definition of *success* is as individual as you are. The definition could reflect a desire for financial gain, love and security, adventure, or a score of other goals. Here's a definition that could help you visualize a definition of *success* for yourself: Success is the continuous journey toward the achievement of predetermined, worthwhile goals. This encompasses the idea that the journey is never over and that it is part of human nature to continually strive toward a goal. You've made a choice and set a course. The commitment to follow through is up to you.

SELF-CHECK

1. Outline and describe the habits or characteristics you must learn to become an effective sales professional.

1.6 Using Technology in Sales

Computer literacy is no longer just a business skill—it's a life skill as important as knowing how to add, subtract, or drive a car. Using the Internet, mobile phones, handheld planning devices, and certain common computer software programs all fall under the umbrella of computer literacy.

If you're new to some of the technological tools that are available for you to use, you may think of all those gadgets as time-consuming things you have to spend hours figuring out. To some degree, you're right. Anytime you use a new product or service, you have to spend a little time up front, learning how to use it. But the reward is definitely worthwhile if you have the right tool for the job.

Gone are the days of 3-by-5 index cards with handwritten notes about clients. Also gone are the giant wheels of name and address information. In the 1990s, computers and the Internet took off to such a degree that if you didn't jump on that wave, you may have been left floating along, wondering how you missed it. But don't worry: It's never too late to use technology to your advantage. A salesperson has plenty of opportunities to do exactly that. Technology skills can make your daily life easier and your selling more efficient.

Let's look at some of the key technology tools that make a salesperson's work easier and more effective:

▲ **Laptop computers:** Giving presentations is a key element in selling, and Microsoft's PowerPoint software program makes it easy for you to tell your prospective clients about yourself, your product, or your service. You can also easily and quickly customize a slide presentation for each prospect. You can easily store and transport PowerPoint presentations via laptop computers. This is one reason some companies supply their salespeople with these portable computers. In addition to presentation software, these devices allow fast and easy access to a multitude of programs, including e-mail, shared files within the company, calendars, and address books.

▲ **Digital cameras:** Digital cameras have become more popular—with good reason. You can easily take a photo, review it immediately on the camera's screen, pop the disk into your computer, and add the photo to your presentation. Salespeople can include photos of the company buildings, staff, products, services in use, and, of course, the company logo. All these features can help create a truly customized sales training session.

▲ **Address book software:** Software designed specifically for maintaining your address book is extremely helpful. Simple address book programs are easy to find and accompany programs such as Microsoft Outlook and Lotus Notes. Your business may demand extra attention, however, and you might want to use contact management software, which includes a database of information about your present and future clients. This is discussed further in Chapter 5.

▲ **Personal digital assistants (PDAs):** A PDA is an electronic device that is smaller than a videocassette tape and works like a computer. It has a screen display and works using a touchpad system. A PDA is useful for keeping track of your contact lists, merging your personal and business calendars into one organized program, and getting connected to the Internet for current information. The downside of a PDA is that data entry is done primarily using a stylus, which means you hunt and peck on a keyboard display. However, some PDAs can be plugged into a standard keyboard for easy data entry.

▲ **Mobile phones:** Mobile phones have almost become miniature computers. Features that make your life easier vary in the vast number of phone offerings. E-mail, Internet access, and more are available with the right mobile phone. All these services are available for a fee, and these fees vary widely, depending on the types of service you need.

- ▲ **The Internet:** The Internet has made it particularly easy to arrange travel plans. Most airlines have their own Web sites, where you can check availability and purchase tickets. Plus, many other web-based services help with travel plans. If you need to travel by car, you can find road maps online. Several sites give you estimated travel times, all the turns you need to take, and the total mileage of your trip. You can print out the information or download it into your computer or PDA. The directions are provided in step-by-step text form, along with maps of the area. You can also find the nearest hotels and restaurants along your route.

SELF-CHECK

1. Describe how a laptop computer can improve the daily life of a salesperson.
2. Describe how a PDA can improve the daily life of a salesperson.
3. Describe how a mobile phone can improve the daily life of a salesperson.
4. Describe how the Internet can improve the daily life of a salesperson.

SUMMARY

For a professional salesperson, selling is the process of moving goods and services from the hands of those who produce them into the hands of those who will benefit from their use. A successful salesperson understands the skills necessary to move these goods. This chapter provides a general overview of those skills and how and when to apply them.

Salespeople use five primary selling approaches: person-to-person, telemarketing, direct mail, e-mail, and the Internet. In using one or a combination of these approaches, they learn the skills they need to show sensitivity toward and respect for their customers. Selling success increases at a significant pace when satisfying the needs of their clients is a top priority. Top salespeople also know the importance of goal setting, professionalism in their presentation, effective communication, realistic expectations, flexibility, and discipline.

A vast array of technological aids, from laptop computers to online services, assist modern-day salespeople in achieving their goals.

KEY TERMS

Conscious competence	The third phase of the learning curve, in which a person realizes the skills he or she has acquired.
Conscious incompetence	The second phase of the learning curve, in which a person chooses to learn specific skills and knowledge.
Direct mail	Mail, such as catalogs and flyers, sent for sales purposes.
E-mail approach	An electronic sales approach for reaching prospects.
Internet approach	Use of Web sites to sell to a global audience.
Learning curve	The time needed to progress from being a complete beginner to an expert.
One-time close	A technique used in telemarketing to sell a product during the first call.
Person-to-person selling	A sales method in which the salesperson has face-to-face contact with the prospect.
Personal selling	The direct communications between paid representatives and prospects that lead to transactions, customer satisfaction, account development, and profitable relationships.
Professional selling	The process of moving goods and services from the hands of those who produce them into the hands of those who benefit from them.
Success journal	A tool in which a salesperson records specific instances and details of successfully using new selling techniques. A success journal reinforces successful sales habits.
Telemarketing	A sales method in which the salesperson contacts a prospect by phone.
Unconscious competence	The fourth stage of the learning curve, in which the person has learned specific skills and knowledge and applies them in an unconscious manner.
Unconscious incompetence	The first stage of the learning curve, in which a person is unaware of the amount of knowledge needed to accomplish a task.

ASSESS YOUR UNDERSTANDING

Go to www.wiley.com/college/hopkins to evaluate your knowledge of the elements necessary for the career of a professional salesperson.
Measure your learning by comparing pre-test and post-test results.

Summary Questions

1. Few people practice sales in their jobs. True or false?
2. One definition of selling is the process of moving goods and services from the hands of those who produce them into the hands of those who benefit from their use. True or false?
3. Which of the following is not considered a primary approach used in sales?
   (a) direct mail
   (b) person-to-person
   (c) diplomacy
   (d) telemarketing
4. The time needed to progress from being a complete beginner to an expert is referred to as the:
   (a) learning compendium.
   (b) learning curve.
   (c) learning tree.
   (d) learning experience.
5. When you are able to apply all your previous knowledge naturally and easily, you are experiencing:
   (a) conscious incompetence.
   (b) unconscious incompetence.
   (c) unconscious competence.
   (d) conscious competence.
6. The selling triangle consists of product knowledge, selling tactics and strategies, and:
   (a) a high IQ and vocabulary.
   (b) politics and referrals.
   (c) risk taking and entrepreneurship.
   (d) attitude and goal setting.
7. Professional salespeople recognize that their primary focus should be on making money. True or false?
8. Professional salespeople show confidence and strength in their body language, speech, and overall presence. True or false?

9. The optimal way to adopt an attitude of discovery is to:
   (a) discover your best learning environment.
   (b) study at a pace that fits you.
   (c) limit your interruptions during study.
   (d) incorporate all of the above.
10. A master salesperson does all the talk during a conference with a prospect. True or false?
11. The purpose of a success journal is to help you learn your strengths and adjust in order to overcome any weakness. True or false?
12. Computer literacy is an essential life skill in today's business environment. True or false?

Applying This Chapter

1. Describe how you've encountered sales techniques used by waiters, actors, politicians, doctors, and lawyers. Describe the benefits of improving sales skills in each of these professions.
2. Discuss the four phases of your own learning curve as you continue on your journey to becoming a professional salesperson. How should you progress from one stage to the next?
3. Think about the possibility of selling a large parcel of farm land. Outline and discuss the primary approaches of selling and how a sales professional might use each approach to sell this land.
4. List the characteristics of a professional salesperson that you currently have. What are some of the areas you need to improve? How could you adopt improvements in your routine?
5. Think about a recent experience with a sales representative. Did this person persuade you to make a decision? If so, what did the salesperson do to affect your decision? If the salesperson did not persuade you to make a decision, what might he or she have done differently?
6. Decide on a product that you would like to sell. Prepare a short sales pitch on the benefits of the product and present it to a friend or fellow student. What did you do or say during the sales pitch that you would qualify as one of your strengths? Describe this strength in your success journal.
7. Visualize yourself as a successful sales professional. Describe the characteristics you possess. What do you visualize as the environment where you work and where you live?
8. Describe the current technology that you use every day to assist in achieving your goals. Which device or system that you currently use could you visualize using in your role as a salesperson?

Getting the Job

You just made an appointment for a job interview, which is an opportunity for you to sell the benefits of hiring you. Based on the material in this chapter, outline

1. how you should prepare for the job.
2. how you should act and react during the interview.
3. what you should do after the interview.

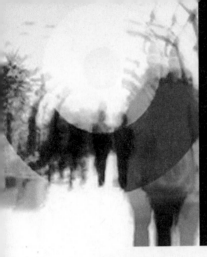

2

ETHICAL AND LEGAL ISSUES IN SELLING
Understanding the Importance of Ethics in Sales

Starting Point

Go to www.wiley.com/college/hopkins to assess your knowledge of ethical and legal issues related to a career in sales.
Determine where you need to concentrate your effort.

What You'll Learn in This Chapter

▲ The importance of ethical standards in sales
▲ How to make ethical decisions
▲ The roles of employers and government in ethical guidelines
▲ Factors that influence the ethics of salespeople
▲ Common ethical problems that salespeople face

After Studying This Chapter, You'll Be Able To

▲ Evaluate your own ethics standards and reconcile them with those of an employer
▲ Balance decision making and ethical standards in solving problems in the workplace
▲ Recognize when you are placed in an ethical dilemma

INTRODUCTION

Ethics refers to a code of moral behavior that governs the conduct of an individual or a group. In business, sometimes the code of business conflicts with that of an individual. This chapter helps you understand how to evaluate your own standards of ethics and understand the roles of companies and government in providing ethical guidelines. In this chapter, you'll also examine common ethical problems that salespeople face.

2.1 Making Ethical Decisions

Sales ethics provides a moral framework to guide salespeople in their daily contacts with customers. Ethical dilemmas are common in selling because salespeople often have to make decisions in the field in response to customers' demands and competitive offers. How a salesperson deals with these dilemmas reflects not only the person's character but also the company's profile.

Sometimes these decisions raise difficult and deeply personal questions. In these situations, you might wonder if you have a different set of values at work than at home. You might be asking yourself, "How much do I have to sacrifice of myself to get ahead?" Your answer is often a matter of right vs. right, not right vs. wrong. In other words, you may have to choose between two ways of resolving a difficult issue, where each alternative is the right thing to do, but it is impossible to do both.

A salesperson might find himself in a "defining moment," for example, when the lure of an easy commission tests his ethical resolve. And there are plenty of examples of bad ethical decisions by salespeople.

FOR EXAMPLE

Insuring Trouble

Some salespeople for Prudential Insurance Company of America told clients that the new policies were no more expensive than the policies they replaced. However, the new policies did indeed cost more and could not be paid for with future dividends. These deceptive sales practices that encouraged customers to trade in old life insurance policies for new ones led to major legal troubles for Prudential. A report prepared by insurance regulators from 30 states revealed that Prudential management knew of sales abuses by agents and in many cases failed to adequately investigate and impose effective discipline. The report cited cases in which agents with "significant complaint histories" were promoted to sales and general managers, with supervisory and training responsibility over agents. Regulatory agencies reacted. As a result, Prudential had to take a $2.6 billion charge against earnings to pay policyholders damages.[1]

FOR EXAMPLE

"Just Say Anything?"

Sometimes a fat commission check has its price. For Matt Cooper, the cost of earning up to $150,000 per sale was spending every day lying to his customers. Matt worked for a New York–based startup company as a major account rep and sold multimillion-dollar advertising campaigns to some of the world's largest companies. He did whatever it took to close those deals. Almost 100 percent of the time, that meant stretching the truth and, at times, lying to the client. "If you didn't lie, you were fired," Matt says. "It always came down to careful wording and fudging numbers."

Among various other deceptive tactics, Matt would book $2 million deals, promising a certain number of impressions on the client's banner ads for the first million dollars and guaranteeing a certain level of sales for the second million dollars. "You really can never guarantee somebody sales," Matt says. So, he reneged on his promises a lot.

Renewals were, of course, out of the question, which might explain the eventual demise of this and thousands of other dot-com companies. Matt began to feel the pressure of this sell-at-any-cost culture, especially after he had to begin screening his calls to avoid irate customers. Finally, he just couldn't take it anymore. "I started selling only what I knew worked because I couldn't lie anymore. So my managers told me to either close more deals or find another job," he says.

Eventually, he quit, but he now works at another startup in New York—one that holds him to a higher ethical standard. Matt is finding that building relationships with clients is a better long-term sales strategy—not only for his own financial and emotional well-being but also for the long-term financial health of the company.

Selling is rife with ethical dilemmas. The ethics in some businesses may create situations that test a sales professional's personal values.

As you could probably surmise by now, ethics is concerned with the effect of actions on the individual, the firm, the business community, and society as a whole. Figure 2-1 is a hierarchical diagram that shows the order in which ethical decisions evolve.

Notice that the ethical values and standards of the business firm are derived from the general values and norms of society. Business decisions represent a synthesis of the moral and ethical principles embraced by the various entities. Conflict is common because the values of the firm, as interpreted by its executives, may not match the values held by the individual. The difficult choice for salespeople in solving problems is whether they should adhere to their own moral

Figure 2-1

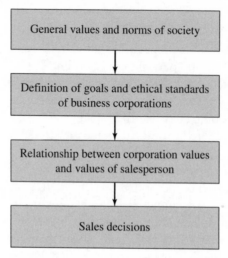

Making decisions on ethical problems.

standards, rely on company policy, or do what is expedient to maximize the short-run profits of the firm.

When faced with ethical problems, executives too frequently choose what is expedient rather than what is morally correct. In one exercise, for example, 47 percent of 400 top executives directed employees to avoid write-offs that would hurt profits.[2] The presence of a company ethics policy did not change the results. In a different ethics survey, almost half of the 316 sales managers who participated in the survey reported that they had heard their salespeople lie about promised delivery times to secure deals.[3] This tendency to sell out personal ethical standards for a chance at corporate glory means that organizations need to foster a business climate that reinforces ethical behavior and to establish ombudsmen who train and provide salespeople with guidance on ethical dilemmas. A good starting point is to develop a job description that includes moral and ethical guidelines.

2.1.1 The Role of a Job Description in Ensuring Ethics

A **job description** is a set of rules or practices that define the role of an employee. It resembles a legal contract because it specifies the number of hours of work, starting and stopping times, and the goals that are to be accomplished. If an employee fails to live up to the legal rules of his or her job description, there are grounds for dismissal. When an accurate and complete job description is available, employees are in a better position to resolve any ethical problems that occur.

A comprehensive job description is a good first step, but individuals often need practical guidelines in making difficult moral decisions. Some companies suggest using a simple checklist, similar to the following, when confronted with an ethical dilemma:

1. Recognize the dilemma.
2. Get the facts.
3. List your options.
   - Are they legal?
   - Are they right?
   - Are they beneficial?
4. Make your decision.

2.1.2 The Role of the Business Environment in Ethics

The moral climate of a business reflects the words and actions of its top executives. If management tolerates unethical behavior in the sales force, then there is little a member of the organization can do about it. Superiors set the moral climate and provide the constraints within which business decisions are made. The moral philosophies held by the executives in companies are important in maintaining an ethical workforce because managers are the ethics teachers of their organizations. They select field salespeople, provide ethical training, and enforce the moral codes of the firm. Both their actions and omissions send moral signals.

A strong sales ethics program, therefore, must have the backing of the board chairperson and the president of the company. When this support is not available, ethical violations are likely. The following are eight considerations for managers in developing an ethical environment:

▲ Get support from top management, showing that they expect you to follow the spirit and letter of the law.
▲ Develop and distribute a sales ethics policy.
▲ Establish the proper moral climate. If the bosses follow the rules, the troops are apt to do likewise.
▲ Assign realistic sales goals. People who try to meet an unfair quota are more likely to rationalize unethical behavior.
▲ Set up controls when needed. Watch people who live beyond their income.
▲ Suggest that salespeople call for help when they face unethical demands.
▲ Get together with your competition if payoffs are an industry problem.
▲ Report any unethical behavior.

With the support of top management, the next step is to have a written sales **ethics policy statement** that indicates to the sales force that the company believes in playing fair with customers and competitors. Research has shown that salespeople employed in organizations that have codes of ethics perceived their work environments to have more positive ethical values than do other sales professionals.[4] In addition, a survey of 218 salespeople indicated that field reps want written policies that help them perform their jobs ethically.[5]

The advantage of having a written ethics policy is that it allows the firm to be explicit about what activities are permissible and what actions violate company standards. This can be useful when customers, suppliers, or your boss ask you to participate in unethical activities. If your company has a code of ethics, you can reply, "I'm sorry, but company policy forbids that" and graciously end a conversation about a shady deal. The vast majority of firms that have been involved in foreign payoff scandals had no written policies on commercial bribery. Today, most firms claim to have formal ethics codes, but only half ask employees to acknowledge or sign them.[6] This suggests that some firms need to make personnel more aware of the company's ethical standards. General Motors (GM) has a code of ethics that is a 12-page document, complete with instructional scenarios featuring fictional characters.[7]

An ethics policy needs to be monitored regularly to ensure that it is relevant to the current selling arena. Management should also be prepared to enforce company policies on bribery. It is therefore important to keep tabs on salespeople who appear to live beyond their income. It also means setting reasonable sales goals so that salespeople will not be tempted to cheat to reach unfair quotas. Salespeople should be encouraged to ask for assistance when they encounter unethical situations. If payoffs become too widespread, management should meet with the competition to work out a set of standards for the industry.

FOR EXAMPLE

Looking Inside GM's Policy Manual

One scenario in the GM ethics policy manual shows a purchasing employee visiting the home office of a possible supplier. In this scenario, the employee is offered a ticket to a football game and a chance to mingle with top executives. According to GM policy, this opportunity should be turned down. In another scenario, an investment banking firm that helped with an acquisition for GM invites several GM employees to New York for a dinner and a gift of a mantel clock. In this case, the dinner and the clock should be refused. GM's policy provides some wiggle room for employees outside the United States. Workers in certain other countries may accept meals, gifts, or outings to comply with local business practices and to avoid being placed at a competitive disadvantage. Also, GM employees can continue providing gifts and meals to their customers, but only within limits. Taking clients to the most expensive restaurant in town is no longer appropriate.

2.1.3 Ethics Training

Ethics training should be a part of company policy. In a variety of competitive situations, field salespeople may be tempted to engage in unethical behavior to reach company or personal goals. However, research has revealed that only 44 percent of firms include ethics as a topic in their sales management training programs.[8] This suggests that more attention to ethics training is needed to help salespeople function in today's business environment. Companies should offer classes to make sure employees know what to do in morally ambiguous situations. For example, at one training session, a salesperson asked, "When I check in at a motel, I get a coupon for a free drink; can I use it?" The correct answer was that it would be acceptable to use the coupon, but it would be wrong to accept $50 to stay there in the first place.

Research has shown that pharmaceutical salespeople should stress the importance of long-term relationships with doctors and develop training classes that enhance product and customer knowledge. Salespeople who have the greatest expertise tend to act most ethically in their relationships with doctors.[9]

Research has also confirmed that younger sales managers are less idealistic and more relativistic in their ethical decision making.[10] This finding suggests the importance of adjusting training program content to meet the needs of different age groups. New hires, for example, should be given material that emphasizes the importance of company ethical norms and values as well as examples of specific behaviors to avoid. For example, Honeywell recently replaced its vague employee policy manual with a detailed handbook. Some of the unacceptable practices spelled out in the handbook involve catcalls and sexual jokes.

Ethics training can be used to find solutions to simulated moral dilemmas. By working through a number of scenarios, salespeople can learn how to recognize problems, assemble facts, consider alternatives, and make decisions. For example, what should women do when a male customer makes a pass and puts his hand on a saleswoman's knee? In this case, she should firmly remove his hand and say, "Let's pretend this didn't happen." Men should be offered advice on how to avoid crude jokes and other forms of intimidation when dealing with female buyers. The idea behind ethics training is to make sure employees are equipped to handle real-world issues they are likely to encounter when calling on customers.

SELF-CHECK

1. Define **ethics**.
2. Discuss the order in which ethical decisions evolve.
3. Describe how companies play a role in helping their employees regarding ethical situations.

2.2 Factors That Influence the Ethics of Salespeople

Many times, there are no laws or court decisions to guide people in specific situations, so people must take actions in an area between the clearly right and the clearly wrong. Salespeople also have to deal with an ambiguous area between clearly right and maybe-not-so right. Obviously, many ethical problems are due to the poor decisions made by salespeople. Even the best salesperson can go wrong if forced to operate under policies that promote misdeeds.

In describing the moral philosophies of individuals, scholars have labeled four patterns of moral reasoning:

▲ Relativism.
▲ Idealism.
▲ Machiavellianism.
▲ Conventional morality.

2.2.1 Relativism and Idealism

A relativist tends to reject universal moral rules and makes decisions on the basis of personal values and the ramifications of each situation. An idealist accepts moral codes and believes that positive outcomes for all can be achieved through morally correct actions. In general, **idealism** leads to better ethical decisions than **realism,** which is more of an "it all depends" approach.

When 602 marketers were asked 20 questions to assess their relativism and idealism, the scores of sales managers were not significantly higher on relativism or lower on idealism than those of other marketing personnel. This contradicts the popular myth that sales personnel have lower ethical standards than those in other business occupations. This study also showed that relativism declines with age and that idealism scores increase with age. Also, female idealism scores were significantly higher than those for males. When sales managers were asked to evaluate unethical sales scenarios, idealistic managers were more sensitive to the moral problems exhibited than were relativistic managers.[11] These findings suggest that basic moral philosophies such as relativism and idealism may have some influence on how an ethical sales force is built and maintained.

2.2.2 Machiavellianism

Although the dictionary may define **Machiavellianism** as the principles and methods of craftiness, duplicity, and deceit, the namesake himself would employ such practices only for self-preservation.

Niccolo Machiavelli, secretary of state in the Florentine Republic in the 16th century, is best known for his observations on human behavior and the workings of power. Many consider him to have been basically a **realist**—a person who focused on what is rather than on what ought to be. Machiavelli's political doctrine denied the relevance of morality in public life and regarded expediency as the guiding principle. He was prepared to manipulate people and bend the laws of business to achieve his own goals. The opportunism that characterized Machiavelli's philosophy is reflected in the following quote:

> *Any person who decides in every situation to act as a good man is bound to be destroyed in the company of so many men who are not good. Wherefore, if a Prince desires to stay in power, he must learn how to be not as good as the occasion requires.*[12]

Machiavelli might ask today's sales professional: "Are you playing to win?"

One survey of salespeople revealed that those with Machiavellian tendencies were less ethical than other salespeople.[13] These results suggest that sales managers may not want to hire people who score high on Machiavellian surveys and should teach their current salespeople how Machiavellian tendencies could influence ethical decisions in the field.

2.2.3 Conventional Morality

Another ethical standard that can guide the actions of salespeople is known as **conventional morality** (or situation ethics). This philosophy is reflected in the familiar phrase "When in Rome, do as the Romans do." The emphasis shifts from the individual to what society thinks about the ethical issue. The standard of morality becomes what is acceptable to others at a particular time and place. Thus, with conventional morality, social approval is the ultimate test of right and wrong, and relationships with others are more important than end results.

The conventional morality approach has no absolute ethical standards to guide actions. Rather, morality is based on social convention and group consensus. The problem with this approach is that the majority might conflict with your personal moral standards.

FOR EXAMPLE

Padding an Expense Account

James is a recently hired sales representative for a sporting goods manufacturer. After training, he started to follow Alex, an experienced salesperson for the company, on sales calls to clients. James and Alex took one client out to lunch one day. James noticed that Alex had the waitress present him with a blank receipt, which he then padded with extra expenses. When James asked Alex about the padded expense, Alex replied, "Everybody does it." James decided to just ignore Alex's advice because he felt like he was abusing his new employer's trust.

Another problem with conventional morality is that it is difficult for salespeople to adapt to changing contexts or cultures. Whereas $10 given to a headwaiter is a tip, $10 given to a customs official to get a perishable product moving is a bribe. Although both transactions represent payment for extra services rendered, one is socially acceptable and the other is not—in the United States at least. Often, in fact, what is moral, ethical, or common in one country is unacceptable or even illegal in another. For example, the hiring or favoring of relatives is called **nepotism** in the United States. In South America, the practice is viewed as an honorable family duty.

SELF-CHECK

1. Define **relativism.**
2. Define **idealism.**
3. Define **Machiavellianism.**
4. Define **conventional morality.**

2.3 Ethical Problems Salespeople Face

Salespeople and their managers must make decisions in a wide variety of situations that have ethical dimensions. These include relationships with superiors, other salespeople, customers, competitors, and dealers, as well as issues such as sexual harassment. As discussed earlier, there are no well-defined guidelines for moral conduct in every situation because what is right often depends on the particular circumstances. This section, however, raises some questions about business ethics for you to consider and points out some potential problem areas.

2.3.1 Hiring and Firing

Various federal and state laws prohibit discrimination in hiring practices. For instance, firms that hire only white male Christians between the ages of 25 and 30 are breaking the law rather than operating unethically. An ethical problem, in contrast, usually requires considerable judgment as to the proper course of action.

Here's one example: hiring candidates who are relatives of officers of the firm. Suppose a sales manager must choose between a man and a woman for a field representative position. Both candidates are well trained, but the man has somewhat more experience. Assume further that the woman is the daughter of a vice president of the company. If the decision were based strictly on qualifications, the man would get the position. However, the firm is under pressure from the federal government to hire women, so maybe she should get the position even though she has somewhat lower qualifications. Although nothing has been said, the sales manager knows there could be personal advantages in hiring the vice president's daughter. Some would contend that hiring the woman instead of the man would be reverse discrimination and unethical. In this example, the sales manager must make a moral choice between what is best for the firm and what might enhance his or her own position in the firm.

Another sticky ethical question relates to hiring salespeople from competitors. The main advantages are that these people are trained and are likely to bring along some customers from their former employers. However, securing salespeople from competitors can increase selling costs and may lead to lawsuits if trade secrets are involved. Despite these risks, raiding competitors is common in the insurance, real estate, and stock brokerage fields. These firms operate on the premise that it is easier to hire successful agents than to train new ones. To prevent such practices, some firms have unwritten agreements that local competitors will not hire salespeople from each other. Although this arrangement helps to control selling costs, it often precludes salespeople from improving their positions by moving to another firm in the local area.

With so many firms concerned about reducing selling costs to boost profits, some companies are tempted to fire older salespeople who are paid high wages and replace them with younger people who earn less. This approach is clearly illegal if it is part of a general plan to discriminate against older employees. However, the courts have ruled that it is legal to fire older employees if the decision is based solely on the need to reduce costs.

2.3.2 House Accounts

A touchy problem for businesses is how to handle major customers. These larger accounts often require special attention that exceeds the time and skills available from the salesperson assigned to the territory. Should these accounts be left with the district salesperson or shifted to headquarters as house accounts? This is not an easy decision because the accounts often generate high commission income. The designation of a customer as a house account is usually defended on the grounds that it results in better service. However, the district salesperson who developed the account is likely to feel a proprietary interest because of the historical relationship with the client. A transfer to house account status, therefore, is sure to be viewed as unfair by the salesperson losing the account. House accounts are clearly one area where firms need specific and well-publicized policies in order to avoid misunderstandings and resentment.

2.3.3 Expense Accounts

Most ethical abuse in a sales organization takes place with expense accounts. Salespeople are expected to spend money contacting customers and are then reimbursed for their expenses. Those who abuse the reimbursement policy often claim higher expenditures than the amounts spent, keep the difference, and then don't report it to the Internal Revenue Service (IRS).

Sales managers must decide how tight to make the controls on expense accounts. Tight control on expense accounts could result in salespeople not traveling to contact out-of-the-way customers. However, liberal repayment for expenses invites investigations by the IRS and results in selling expense ratios that are higher than they should be.

To solve the problem, a sales manager might monitor the actual expenses of some reliable salespeople for a month each year and then use those figures to set reimbursement amounts for all field reps. This approach greatly reduces the costs of processing expense accounts and keeps expense payments in line with actual expenses.

2.3.4 Gifts for Buyers

U.S. businesses have a tradition of giving small **gifts** for buyers to express appreciation for past and future business. Salespeople typically give novelties and samples as well as seasonal gifts, such as gift-wrapped bottles of liquor at Christmas. The problem is that the gift giving may start out with a pair of hockey tickets and end up as a television set for the customer's den. So how can a gift be distinguished from a bribe?

A recent survey of sales executives revealed that 64 percent of those surveyed considered a bribe to be a personal gift worth more $100 to a buyer.[14] In the same survey, however, 89 percent of the sales executives had witnessed colleagues offer potential clients personal gifts valued at more than $100 in exchange for their business. One way to differentiate a gift from a bribe is when the item is unexpected (gift) rather than part of an agreed-upon payment for business (bribe).

Today, purchasing managers appear to be willing to accept gifts of clothing, pens, and calendars. However, management guidance on gifts has typically been a gray area, so it is increasingly difficult for salespeople to know what is right or wrong in the changing business environment. Some firms have policies that prohibit buyers from accepting any gifts, meals, or favors that might compromise their integrity. Although these polices appear to solve the problem, they are difficult to enforce. Another guideline is the IRS ruling that only $25 can be deducted each year for company business gifts to any one person. In the absence of explicit rules, sales management and salespeople must judge what is a reasonable gift and what others could interpret as a bribe.

2.3.5 Bribes

As just discussed, the use of **bribes** to obtain business is widespread, so you must know what to do when you feel compelled to engage in this practice. Bribery is fairly easy to spot in its most blatant forms. If a customer says that an order will be placed if a $20,000 commission is paid to a third party, then the salesperson can be sure that someone is being paid off. Bribes of this size are not only unethical, they can be illegal.

Foreign payoffs are so common that the U.S. Congress passed the **Foreign Corrupt Practices Act** in 1977, making it a criminal offense to offer a payment to a foreign government official to obtain or retain foreign business. However, other industrialized nations have been slow to follow. France, Italy, Belgium, and the Netherlands have yet to pass laws prohibiting bribery and the deduction of bribes as business expenses for tax purposes. The United States lost more than $100 billion in international contracts in the 1990s where bribery influenced the awarding of the contracts. The U.S. government has obtained information indicating that bribes were used to influence the outcome of 239 international contracts. About 70 percent of the bribes were offered or paid to ministry or executive branch officials. As you can see, different rules in different countries can create ethical problems.

Because of the difficulties caused by the Foreign Corrupt Practices Act in bidding on overseas contracts, the law has been amended so that now U.S. companies break the law only if they knowingly make an illegal payment. In addition, "grease payments" are now permitted to facilitate routine matters such as getting a visa or a permit. It is also proper to make payments allowed under the written laws of a foreign country. Although these changes have helped, U.S. firms can't engage in many of the activities their local competitors carry out every day.

Unfortunately, much of the bribery and extortion in business dealings is disguised to make it even more difficult for a businessperson to choose right from wrong. Some examples of these ethical problems are bribes disguised as gifts to hospital building funds, scholarships for relatives, memorial contributions, trips to professional meetings, and golf outings.

2.3.6 Entertainment

Providing entertainment for potential customers is standard practice in U.S. business, but it can lead to ethical problems. The issue is often how much is too much? Most would agree that taking a customer to lunch is fair, reasonable, and expected. Few would argue against occasionally taking a client and his or her spouse to dinner and a nightclub. But what about the use of a company car or a weekend on the company yacht? On big orders, it is not unusual to fly personnel from the customer's plant to the supplier's headquarters in order to include plant tours and introductions to corporate executives as part of the sales presentation. Should the expenses of spouses taken on such trips be covered? Is it ethical to offer customers free use of the company's hunting lodge in Canada? What legitimately and ethically constitutes business entertainment?

An example of a difficult entertainment issue is customers asking to be taken to topless bars. A survey revealed that 49 percent of male reps and 5 percent of female reps had taken customers to topless bars.[15] The survey also revealed that

FOR EXAMPLE

Federal Fines Levied Against Unethical Practices

The sales managers at TAP Pharmaceutical Products, Inc., fostered a culture based on gift giving and parties for their customers, who were primarily doctors. For example, TAP offered every urologist in the country a wide-screen TV, as well as computers, fax machines, and golf vacations. TAP's culture did little to earn doctors' trust through good science and product development. Plus, sales representatives were not encouraged to keep track of their samples, even though losing track of a single dose could have resulted in a fine of up to $1 million. There were numerous cases of kickbacks and bribes. Finally, the federal prosecutors took action and slapped the company with a record $875 million fine. The government calculates that TAP bilked federal and state medical programs out of $145 million over a 10-year period.

customers suggested 72 percent of the visits. Most women reps do not like topless bars and believe that entertaining customers at these places gives men an unfair advantage over female salespeople. Although 40 percent of the surveyed firms do not allow reps to entertain at topless bars, many firms simply look the other way. This example suggests that it is hard to solicit business on the basis of product quality and service features when your competition is "buying" customers with exotic entertainment.

2.3.7 Sexual Harassment

The Equal Employment Opportunity Commission defines **sexual harassment** as unwelcome sexual advances, requests for sexual favors, and other verbal or physical conduct of a sexual nature. It further states that an act constitutes sexual harassment when any of the following occurs:

▲ Submission to such conduct is made either explicitly or implicitly a term or condition of an individual's employment.

▲ Submission to, or rejection of, such conduct by an individual is used as the basis for employment decisions affecting such individual.

▲ Such conduct has the purpose or effect of substantially interfering with an individual's work performance or creating an intimidating, hostile, or offensive working environment.

Title VII of the 1964 Civil Rights Act prohibits workplace sexual harassment. Although sexual harassment is against the law, salespeople may encounter it. In particular, salespeople are vulnerable to what is known as **third-party harassment,** which is harassment by someone outside the boundaries of the firm, such as a customer, vendor, or service person. A typical situation could involve a male buyer at a key account asking a female salesperson for sexual favors in exchange for an order. In this case, the salesperson may want the order to help make her quota and may fear that the contract will be given to a competitor if she refuses. She may also believe that if she complains to her boss, she will be seen as lacking the selling skills needed to resolve the harassment problem. Another worry is that efforts to reform the buyer could sour relations between the two firms. Unfortunately, many employees are unaware that their own firms could be held liable for third-party harassment and that third-party harassment is prohibited behavior.[16]

Every firm should have a formal policy on harassment within the organization and by those outside the organization. It should also provide a process for salespeople to remove themselves from a harassing situation perpetrated by an outsider without sanctions. Third-party harassers can be dealt with by writing them a letter or by asking them to stop. These actions attract attention because they imply that the victim may take further, more public action. Some firms try a more passive response and simply reassign accounts with harassing buyers to new salespeople. Although this approach does not stop harassment, it may help the seller retain the account.

2.3.8 Whistle-blowing

Whistle-blowing is a last-resort action that is justified when an employee has the appropriate moral motive to inform the public about an employer's or a supervisor's immoral or illegal behavior. Before whistle-blowing takes place, the person who has observed the unethical behavior should have exhausted all the internal channels for dissent. This means talking to a supervisor or the company ombudsman if one is available.

Another test of whistle-blowing is that the evidence should be strong enough to convince the average person that a violation is taking place. Furthermore, the observed moral violation should be serious enough to require immediate attention. Finally, the act of telling the public must have some chance for success. From a practical standpoint, it makes no sense to complain to the public unless something is going to be done about the problem. Why expose yourself to hardship if there is no moral gain?

Whistle-blowing should not be taken lightly because employees know they may suffer if they "go public" with a moral problem.

Why are whistle-blowers treated so badly for simply following high personal moral standards? The problem seems to be that by speaking up, they violate **role morality**, which demands that employees be loyal and keep their mouths shut. Whistle-blowing will probably embarrass company managers, so they often try to get rid of people they feel can't be trusted.

To help encourage whistle-blowers to come forward, federal laws have been modified to pay rewards of 15 to 25 percent of any recovery, plus attorneys' fees.

> ## FOR EXAMPLE
>
> ### Inside the Life of a Whistle-Blower
>
> A West Virginia bank manager was fired for complaining about illegal over-charges for certain classes of his customers. The manager sued the bank and won an unfair firing judgment, but he received only $18,000 after paying his legal fees. Even worse, he was unable to find another bank job, even after applying to all the other banks in the state. The former banker was eventually forced to take a lesser job as a state bank examiner.

As a result of this change, whistle-blowers have received an average of $1 million in recent cases. In one case, a whistleblower won $77 million for exposing to federal prosecutors a scheme to bribe doctors to prescribe a particular company's drugs over the competition.[17]

Whistle-blowing displays the classic conflict between the high ethical standards of individuals and the often lower morality found in the business world. The ultimate elimination of whistle-blowing may occur when more firms set up formal internal mechanisms so that employees with moral problems to report are not ignored or punished.

SELF-CHECK

1. Describe the primary ethical problems salespeople face today in hiring and firing.
2. Describe the primary ethical problems salespeople face today in house accounts.
3. Describe the primary ethical problems salespeople face today in expense accounts.
4. Describe the primary ethical problems salespeople face today related to gifts for buyers.
5. Describe the primary ethical problems salespeople face today related to bribes.
6. Describe the primary ethical problems salespeople face today in entertainment.
7. Describe the primary ethical problems salespeople face today in sexual harassment.
8. Describe the primary ethical problems salespeople face today in whistle-blowing.

2.4 Relying on Government Regulation for Sales Ethics

When business fails to operate in an ethical manner, there is usually a public outcry for more government regulation. Thus one of the basic roles of government is to set minimum standards of business morality and then to enforce the rules. The judicial branch of government settles disputes over the interpretation of the regulations, and Congress writes new rules as they are needed. Some of the first government regulations in the United States affecting business were designed to protect the public from noncompetitive activities.

2.4.1 Reasons for Regulations

A number of federal laws have been passed to set ethical standards for transactions between manufacturers and consumers. The following are some examples:

▲ The common practice of dealers inflating the prices of new cars came to an end when the Automobile Information Disclosure Act required manufacturers to attach labels to car windows, showing the suggested price for the car, accessories, and transportation.

▲ Deceptive packaging has been attacked with the Fair Packaging and Labeling Act, which calls for standard package sizes and disclosure of the manufacturer's name or the distributor.

▲ Attempts by loan companies and retailers to mislead consumers on interest rates led to the enactment of the Consumer Credit Protection Act.

▲ Truth-in-lending laws require full disclosure of annual interest rates and other charges on loans and credit sales.

▲ The Magnuson-Moss Warranty Act has increased the Federal Trade Commission's (FTC's) power to regulate product warranties. New FTC rules require full disclosure of warranty terms and reduce the use of warranties as promotional gimmicks.

Government often gets involved in business ethics when the problem is too big for individual firms to handle. For example, automobile exhaust is a major cause of air pollution, but it is difficult for an individual firm to solve the problem. If one company feels it is morally correct to install air pollution equipment on its cars, its costs will be higher than those of the competition. Thus, the cars of the ethically lazy firm will be less expensive and more powerful, and that company will literally run off with the market. In this situation, government regulation allows the well-intentioned business to be the good citizen it wants to be.

2.4.2 Problems with Regulation

Many argue that there is too much government regulation of business. Businesspeople generally dislike government controls because they rob them of the

FOR EXAMPLE

Regulating Prices

The U.S. government got into the regulation of natural gas prices because gas is often shipped through interstate pipelines. As might be expected, the government tended to set low gas prices for maximum political gain. However, the drillers were more rational, and they slowed their search for new gas. As a result, the supply of natural gas declined until the price controls were removed.

This example helps illustrate both the frustration with and the purpose of government intervention. It also provides a good case for the need for government officials to learn to balance too little government intervention with too much regulation in which business is strangled by endless rules and red tape.

flexibility needed to respond to changing conditions. In addition, government rules established to solve problems in one decade are often obsolete by the next decade.

SELF-CHECK

1. Describe the advantages and disadvantages of government regulation on business.

SUMMARY

Ethics in sales sometimes presents unique challenges for a salesperson. Individuals have a responsibility to evaluate and develop their own moral codes of ethics. But a business also has a duty to set guidelines that help salespeople deal with ethical problems they encounter in the workplace and with clients. This chapter examines the moral bases for business ethics, ethical decision making, issues of common sales ethics, corporate expectations for ethics in business, and the role of government regulation.

KEY TERMS

Bribe	An agreed-upon payment to obtain a customer's business.
Conventional morality	A standard in which emphasis shifts from the individual to what society thinks about the ethical issue. Also known as *situation ethics*.

Ethics	A code of moral behavior that governs the conduct of an individual or a business community.
Ethics policy statement	A document prepared by a company that indicates to the sales force that the company believes in playing fair with customers and competitors.
Foreign Corrupt Practices Act	U.S. legislation that makes it a criminal offense to offer a payment to a foreign government official to obtain or retain foreign business.
Gift	An unexpected item given to a customer, primarily to thank the client for his or her business.
Idealism	A pattern of moral reasoning that accepts moral codes and believes that positive outcomes are possible through morally correct actions.
Job description	A set of rules or practices that define the role of an employee.
Machiavellianism	A pattern of moral reasoning that is usually defined as the principles and methods of craftiness, duplicity, and deceit. Machiavellianism is based on realism.
Nepotism	A practice in which relatives are favored or hired.
Realist	A person who focuses on what is rather than on what ought to be.
Relativism	A pattern of moral reasoning that rejects universal moral rules and makes decisions on the basis of personal values and the ramifications of each situation.
Role morality	A code that demands the loyalty of employees and their silence when faced with unethical situations.
Sexual harassment	Unwelcome sexual advances, requests for sexual favors, and other verbal or physical conduct of a sexual nature.
Third-party harassment	Harassment by someone outside the boundaries of a firm, such as a customer, vendor, or service person.
Whistle-blowing	A last-resort action to inform the public about an employer's or a supervisor's immoral or illegal behavior.

ASSESS YOUR UNDERSTANDING

Go to www.wiley.com/college/hopkins to evaluate your knowledge of the ethical standards and legal issues that a professional salesperson faces.
Measure your learning by comparing pre-test and post-test results.

Summary Questions

1. Business decisions represent a blending of a salesperson's and a company's moral and ethical principles. True or false?

2. Part of the purpose of a job description formulated by a company is to help guide an employee's ethical choices. True or false?

3. Research has shown that salespeople employed in organizations that have codes of ethics perceive their work environments to have:

   (a) a strong drive for employees to make money.

   (b) a strong religious background.

   (c) strong ethical values.

   (d) strong and strict rules.

4. A chief executive officer has no effect on the ethical decisions made by an employee in the field. True or false?

5. In ethical decision making, there is only one right answer to a particular situation. True or false?

6. The pattern of moral reasoning in which a person accepts moral codes and believes that positive outcomes for all can be achieved through morally correct actions is known as:

   (a) relativism.

   (b) idealism.

   (c) Machiavellianism.

   (d) conventional morality.

7. There is no difference between a gift and a bribe to a client. True or false?

8. The Foreign Corrupt Practices Act applies to all U.S.-based businesses regarding all overseas contracts. True or false?

9. Whistle-blowing for public acknowledgement is the first step an employee should take after learning of a supervisor's immoral or illegal behavior. True or false?

10. The government has no role in establishing guidelines for ethical decision making. True or false?

Applying This Chapter

1. Many people believe there is a benefit in telling their children that the Easter Bunny is real. Describe the advantages and disadvantages of deceiving someone for a reason that you believe is justified and ethical.

2. Describe the ethical climate of your ideal place of employment.

3. Before declaring bankruptcy and going out of business, a dry cleaner fills a vat with a toxic cleaning solution. The dry cleaner is supposed to pay for pickup by a certified toxic disposal service. The dry cleaner doesn't arrange for such a service. Another tenant leases the space and discovers the vat. Describe how the new tenant might react to this situation using each of these moral patterns:

   (a) relativism.

   (b) idealism.

   (c) Machiavellianism.

   (d) conventional morality.

4. Gasoline prices have increased tremendously within the past few years. Many U.S. consumers find it difficult to afford even enough gasoline to travel to and from work. Yet the industry continually posts billions of dollars in quarterly profits. Do you see any ethical dilemma in this situation? Explain your answer.

5. Discuss the advantages and disadvantages of government regulation of gasoline prices.

Managing Ethical Decision Making

Visualize yourself as the sales manager for a sales team. You notice that the sales volume of a team member named Edward is slipping. Edward was formerly a good employee, and he has been employed by the company for five years. Until recently, he has never had a complaint from customers about his performance and service. An example of a recent problem is that Edward promised a one-week delivery for a customer without first checking with the production department, which couldn't fulfill the order. You learn through other team members that Edward may have a drug problem that is interfering with normal sales-call patterns. You know that you have to do something about the current situation. How would you handle the situation? What ethical issues do you think you face?

Making a Tough Decision

Imagine that you have been working as a sales representative for the same company for the past five years. It has been common practice for the sales staff to give small gifts, such as tickets to a ball game, to customers on occasion. The company's new CEO just introduced a no-gift policy. At the same time, the CEO announced even higher sales quotas for each representative than in the past. One of your colleagues, who knows that his clients truly enjoy and expect the gifts, plans to ignore the no-gift policy and work his gift-giving practice into his expense account. You want to follow the company policy but are anxious about your customers being displeased. What would you do? Do you think you would lose your customers because of the new policy?

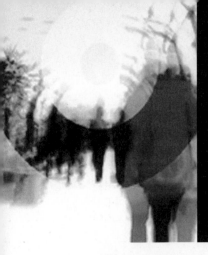

3

WHY PEOPLE BUY
Understanding Buyer Behavior

Starting Point

Go to www.wiley.com/college/hopkins to assess your knowledge of the behavior patterns of consumers.
Determine where you need to concentrate your effort.

What You'll Learn in This Chapter

▲ The importance of uncovering the needs and wants of customers
▲ Tips on researching customers
▲ The steps to develop a sales strategy
▲ How and why buying decisions are made

After Studying This Chapter, You'll Be Able To

▲ Understand the fundamental knowledge necessary for a successful career in sales
▲ Choose appropriate sales methods for working with customers
▲ Begin to develop a sales strategy

INTRODUCTION

You can think of selling as a cycle because, if it's done properly, the last step in the cycle leads you back to the first. A satisfied customer refers you to other prospects that would benefit from your product or service. You now have your next prospect, and the cycle begins again. This cycle depends heavily on understanding buyer behavior. This chapter examines the importance of understanding the needs and wants of the buyer and how to appeal to specific decision makers' buying preferences.

3.1 Uncovering Needs and Wants

Sometimes the hardest part of starting something new is breaking through established teachings or beliefs that you once felt were acceptable for successful living. You probably remember the old adages "Ignorance is bliss" and "What you don't know can't hurt you." Although living by these sayings may have worked in people's personal lives in simpler times, such maxims were never sage advice for people who were trying to sell or persuade others. In fact, the loss of sales and the personal career damage caused by ignorance can be so disastrous that some people give up on selling altogether. A key to success in sales lies in uncovering the needs and wants of your customers.

Obviously, knowing everything is impossible. As discussed in Chapter 1, learning is a lifelong habit. To be successful, you have to continue the learning process. Therefore, true professionals know that they can still learn a lot after they supposedly know it all. The enemy of learning is knowing, and admitting that you need to find out some things is the first step to achieving anything.

How can you prepare for selling in the best manner possible? In fact, why do you need to research your prospective clients and their businesses? The answer to both questions is two-fold:

▲ To show that you understand how to fulfill clients' needs.
▲ To look as professional and knowledgeable during your sales presentation as possible.

You do all your research simply to build for that final moment when your prospect gives you the okay to deliver your product and to start building a long-term relationship. The more you know about a prospect, the more competent you will appear and the stronger you will be when you present your case.

In fact, **prequalification,** or the behind-the-scenes activity of learning all you can about a prospect, is one of the most important aspects of sales. Successful salespeople understand the importance of planning and preparation before those few minutes of face-to-face selling begin.

FOR EXAMPLE

Airing Out a Sales Pitch

Eduardo is a sales representative for a manufacturer of residential and commercial air-treatment systems. He discovers that one small manufacturer in his area just received a huge contract and needs to hire more employees to manufacture more products. However, the company's expanded workforce will be confined to the same space until a new facility is completed. Eduardo's research shows that employees in close proximity to each other have an increased likelihood of spreading germs rapidly. The employer can't afford to have its employees take a lot of sick time. Based on his research, Eduardo knows that his company's air-treatment system could help. He calls the manufacturers' purchasing agent for an appointment, makes his sales pitch, and gets the order.

The same principle that you use when you sell to business applies when you sell to individuals or families: The more you know about their background, the better. You warm people up faster when you talk about their hobbies, jobs, and kids than if you know nothing other than their address and phone number. You can a use a variety of methods to find information on individuals, families, or companies. One way is to rent a list from a list broker that could include such information as the families in the area who purchase certain supplies related to your business. List brokers often have enough information about a potential client that you can find out what types of pets they have, cleaning products they purchase, and whether they make a lot of long-distance phone calls. List brokers get their information in a variety of ways, including surveys and collected material from manufacturers and organizations.

To be successful at selling, you must be constantly on the prowl for information—everything and anything about your product, your company, your competition, and (most importantly) your prospect. The most important thing to remember is the customer's needs and wants. You can't be of any help to a prospective client with what you're offering her until you truly understand what she needs. All you need is the commitment to locate and internalize the information you uncover.

Chapter 6 covers obtaining details on researching prospective clients, their businesses, and their goals. The following, however, is a quick guide:

▲ **Gather as much literature and other information as possible on a company before approaching it with your offering:** You want to be as prepared as possible before you make that first approach.

▲ **Visit the business's Web site:** Pay particular attention to the business's online product catalog, if it has one. Look for press releases posted on the site so you're up to date on the most recent news related to the business. Plus, always look for an "About Us" link on the website. The information you find there will give you valuable insight into the management team and their backgrounds. You may find out that you know someone who works there or that you know someone who knows someone there.

▲ **Get copies of the company's product brochures and/or catalogs:** Talk with a customer service representative about what the company offers. If you're familiar with the products your prospect sells, you'll be better able to better relate how your product fits within the client's environment.

▲ **Go to the library or surf the Web and look up past news articles on the business:** If you're familiar with what's been happening in the business in the past few months, you'll be able to work that information into your conversations with the people who work there. The prospect will get the sense that you've done your homework about them and about your own products. That's exactly the impression you want to make.

▲ **Check out the business's financial report, if it's available:** Get the names of the company president and other key people and find out how to pronounce and spell their names. For the pronunciation, simply call the company and ask the receptionist for that information.

Although doing your research and gathering information about your prospective client is essential, knowing when you have enough information is often difficult. In the end, it's up to you, of course. When you think you know enough to get the job done and make the sale, you've probably researched enough. If a question comes up during your presentation that you don't know how to answer, and if what you don't know might hurt your chances of closing the sale, you don't know enough. Experience will tell you how much you need to prepare, but you're better off erring on the side of preparing too much than not preparing enough.

Remember that knowledge is power and your key to success in sales.

SELF-CHECK

1. Discuss the importance of researching a prospective client to determine the customer's needs and wants.
2. List three ways to research a prospective client.

3.2 Developing the Seven Steps of the Sales Strategy

One way to better understand buyer behavior is to gather information for your sales strategy. Developing a sales strategy connects all the pieces you need. For example, in the prospecting stage, you study the people who either need or want your product. You may even ask your prospects what might tempt them to buy. During the qualification phase, you delve into great depth about what it takes to get your client to buy.

You've already examined one of the most important aspects of sales—prequalifying your prospect. That's actually part of step 1—prospecting—in a successful sales strategy. Take a look at how selling breaks down neatly into seven steps:

Step 1: Prospecting
Step 2: Original contact
Step 3: Qualification
Step 4: Presentation
Step 5: Addressing concerns
Step 6: Closing the sale
Step 7: Getting referrals

Each step is equally important in uncovering the prospect's needs and then fulfilling them. In fact, a major reason for developing a sales strategy is to provide a systematic way to uncover buyers' motives. The steps are interrelated with each other. You can rarely skip a step and still make the sale. If done properly, your strategy leads you to the next step in a natural, flowing manner. These steps are covered in more detail in subsequent chapters, but this section outlines the basics.

3.2.1 Step 1: Prospecting

Before you begin to develop your sales strategy, you should visualize yourself as a customer. What would motivate you to invest your time and money in learning more about your product or service? If you can't come up with solid answers, you may not have done enough product research or you might not know enough about your potential audience. You need to do more product and market research before attempting the first step—prospecting.

Prospecting means finding the right potential buyer for your product or service. When considering your product or service, you should ask yourself, "Who would benefit most from this?" If the end user is a corporation, you need to make contacts within the corporation. Usually, a purchasing agent is assigned to make buying decisions on behalf of the company, so you need to find a way to get in touch with that person. If your end user is a family with school-aged

---

FOR EXAMPLE

Graduating at the Head of the Class

Valerie has just graduated and chooses a career as an insurance salesperson. The first thing she learns is that she needs to develop her network of contacts. So she starts with the area in which she has the most contacts—recently graduated alumni of her university. She is able to obtain a list of local alumni to contact. After she has completed the proper research and prequalification steps, she makes some appointments with her fellow alumni.

---

children, you need to find a source where families tend to gather. For example, you could make contact with the local parents and teachers organization. You might also acquire a list from a credible source and start contacting those prospects at home.

3.2.2 Step 2: Original Contact

You've found the people. Now you need to go out and meet them. The **original contact** refers to the first time you spend with a prospect.

To persuade another person to spend valuable time with you, you need to offer something of value in return. To gain entrance to someone's home, for example, you need to offer a free estimate or gift in exchange for the person's opinion on the demonstration of your product. With a business-to-business appointment, getting an appointment may be a bit easier because you often work with purchasing agents whose job it is to meet with and gather information from people like you. If you offer anything remotely like a product the agent's company may use, a purchasing agent should be responsible for learning more about it.

3.2.3 Step 3: Qualification

In selling, **qualification** means finding out details about the prospect and determining how your product can fulfill a need. When you meet a prospect, you need to find out if she's qualified to be your client of choice. You need to uncover

- ▲ who the prospect is.
- ▲ what the prospect does.
- ▲ what the prospect has.
- ▲ what the prospect needs.

If you've done your homework and looked up information about the prospect, you know what questions to ask. If you get the account, you'll eventually have to know a lot of information about the prospect. If you're convinced that this is a good match, you should ask questions now. The more specific your questions, the more impressed your potential client will be with your expertise. Asking pertinent questions now shows that you're interested in more than just a closed sale and that you're looking into the future as a valued business partner with your client.

3.2.4 Step 4: Presentation

During the fourth step, **presentation,** you need to show the benefits of your product or service to a prospect. Your presentation of a product, a service, or an idea requires more preparation than in any other step, possibly excluding prequalification. Here are some general guidelines for presentation:

▲ Be sure to incorporate any visual aids you might need. Referring to charts or brochures helps reinforce your message, and it serves as a memory aid.

▲ Practice your answers to common questions with a family member or close friend and ask for feedback.

▲ Make a list of the benefits you think are your strongest persuaders in placing your product. Then try to figure out a way to work those points into responses to the common questions.

3.2.5 Step 5: Addressing Concerns

Addressing concerns of a prospect is likely to be part of your presentation. Addressing concerns involves knowing how to answer the prospect's questions satisfactorily and fulfill any needs. You also have to have prepared and satisfied the first four steps in detail.

How do you handle any negative comments or qualifications that your prospect raises during or after your presentation? You should answer in simple, unemotional terms and have recommendations in mind. For example, if your product is available in only certain colors, and none of them quite fit the decor of your prospect's office, you should be prepared to recommend the least offensive color suggestion.

3.2.6 Step 6: Closing the Sale

Closing the sale means that you've met the prospect's needs and concerns. It also means you've

▲ researched your prospect properly.

▲ given yourself enough preparation time.

▲ handled all the previous steps in a professional manner.

If you've accomplished these steps, you'll likely close the sale. Closing the sale should follow naturally and smoothly after you address your prospect's concerns. But if your prospect doesn't automatically pick up a pen to approve your paperwork or write a check, you shouldn't panic. You don't have to apply pressure to get what you want. Getting your prospect's business can be as simple as saying, "How soon do we start?" At this point, if you're confident about meeting the prospect's needs, you should begin taking verbal ownership of your future business relationship by using assumptive statements and questions.

When it comes time to close, you've hopefully reduced any sales resistance this person had early on and increased the prospect's level of sales acceptance so that it's just a matter of agreeing on the details of startup or delivery dates and/or financing arrangements.

3.2.7 Step 7: Getting Referrals

Getting a **referral** from a customer is ideal. This means one satisfied customer is recommending another prospect for business with you.

After you close a sale with a client, you should take a moment to ask for referrals. This can be as simple as asking, "Because you're so happy with this decision today, would you mind if I ask you for the names of other people you know who might also be interested in learning about this product?" In a corporate situation, you should ask about other departments within the company that might need your service. Then you should ask about any other office locations the same company has. Finally, you can ask about associates of the purchasing agent who may work at noncompeting companies.

SELF-CHECK

1. List and discuss, in order, the seven steps of a successful sales strategy.

3.3 Buying Motives

Developing a sales strategy is an important step in understanding prospects' buying motives. Great salespeople try to understand what's on a prospect's mind rather than strictly focus discussion on the product and its benefits. Remember that customers do not buy products or services; they buy solutions that address their problems or enhance opportunities. Contractors don't want bulldozers; they want dirt moved quickly and at low cost. Plant managers do not buy computer-controlled milling machines; they are interested in reduced setup time, closer tolerances, and fewer defects. A salesperson's job is to discover the true needs of a prospect and then inform her of the characteristics, capabilities, and availability of goods and services that can address those needs.

Research has shown that there is a direct relationship between the number of needs a salesperson uncovers and selling success. A study by Xerox of more than 500 sales calls revealed that successful sales calls contained three times more identified needs than failed calls.

What you perceive as being a good relationship and a distinct set of customer needs is not enough to make a sale. The customer must also perceive the same needs. Recommending a solution that the buyer does not perceive or does not rank high in importance falls on deaf ears. In fact, this recommendation is likely to delay further progress toward a profitable relationship because the client may conclude that you do not really understand the situation.

Needs discovery is about understanding clients' perceptions of their most important needs and helping them to fully understand these needs. It's not easy to do, but when you really help customers understand the total cost of their problem and the extent of their opportunities, it's easier for them to choose the best solution.

3.3.1 Task Motives vs. Personal Buying Motives

In selling to organizations, both task and personal motives influence the purchasing decision. **Task motives** can be defined as the logical, practical, or functional reasons for buying. These motives usually involve either money or productivity. Typical financial motives may include cost savings or profit increases. Productivity motives may focus on increasing output, increasing quality, or reducing effort. Organizations tend to emphasize different task issues in their cultures, so it is important for salespeople to understand these tendencies.

Personal motives are the individual preferences that spur a person to buy. They are generally psychological in nature and involve relationships with other people. Successful salespeople know that customers' personal needs may be just as important as their business needs in making a decision. If a vice president is choosing among several proposals that would benefit her division, she is most likely to go with the one that lightens her workload or increases the chances of her own promotion.

Personal motives include the need for respect, approval, power, and recognition. Respect-oriented clients want to demonstrate and prove their expertise. People focusing on approval want to be sure that those affected by the decision to buy will be pleased. People interested in power seek ways to gain greater control over some real, practical aspect of their situation. For some people, the desire for recognition is the dominant personal motive: They are interested in products or services that give them greater visibility and provide opportunities to demonstrate their leadership ability.

3.3.2 Transactional Relationships vs. Consultative Relationships

Relationships with different customers differ. Your sales skills should be flexible for use in either a transactional relationship or a consultative relationship.

A **transactional relationship** involves less time and fewer resources than a consultative relationship and concentrates on explaining product features. Often, a transactional relationship involves a personal relationship between the buyer and seller. This type of relationship is based on such nurturing elements as a history of building trust, creating value, and meeting or exceeding customers' expectations.

What types of firms are likely to emphasize transactional customer relationships? One study of companies from four countries showed that 68 percent of firms focus on transactional relationships with at least some of their customers. In particular, consumer goods firms and large organizations are most likely to have this type of relationship.[1]

Consultative relationships involve great investment in time and resources, and they take a problem-solving approach. This type of relationship is based on the customer's demand and willingness to pay for a sales effort that creates new value and provides additional benefits outside the product itself. The success of this relationship depends on the salesperson's ability to get very close to the customer and grasp the client's business issues. Experience indicates that a consultative relationship is most appropriate when one or more of the following conditions are present:

- ▲ The product or service can be differentiated from competitive alternatives.
- ▲ The product or service can be adapted or customized to the needs of the customer.
- ▲ The customer is not completely clear about how the product or service provides solutions or adds value.
- ▲ The delivery, installation, or use of the product or service requires coordinated support from the seller.
- ▲ The benefits of the product or service justify the relatively high cost of consultative relationships.

Figure 3-1 shows some of the general differences between the interaction practices in transactional relationships and those in consultative and enterprise relationships.

In today's business environment, 80 percent of the selling process focuses on discovering and matching customer needs. Indeed, this is one of the goals of consultative relationships. You should become intimately knowledgeable

Figure 3-1

Transactional Relationship	Consultative and Enterprise Relationship
Focuses on closing sales	Focuses on customer's bottom line
Makes limited call planning investment	Considers call planning a top priority
Spends most contact time telling account about products	Spends most contact time attempting to build a problem-solving environment
Conducts product-specific needs assessment	Conducts discovery in the full scope of the account's operations
Uses "lone wolf" approach to the account	Uses a team approach to the account
Makes proposals and presentations based on pricing and product features	Makes proposals and presentations based on profit impact and on strategic benefits
Adopts short-term sales follow-up, focused on product delivery	Adopts long-term sales follow-up and focuses on long-term relationship enhancement

Key differences in practices between types of relationships.

about a customer's business, such as knowing the most important organizational opportunities, openings for improvement, and barriers to change. Achieving this degree of intimacy may go beyond the capabilities of one person. When this is the case, some companies assign the task to a team of salespeople.

The nuances of the different relationships can be quite subtle. To better understand this point, consider the following research findings:

▲ In most successful transactional relationships, the seller can make a solution presentation immediately after uncovering a customer problem. However, presenting solutions too early is one of the most common mistakes in consultative and enterprise relationships.

▲ Listing features and advantages often leads to success in transactional relationships. In consultative relationships, however, these types of presentations often lead to more objections and raise barriers to commitment.[2]

These are just a couple of ways in which the type of customer relationship can influence successful use of selling skills.

SELF-CHECK

1. Discuss how buyers' motives differ.
2. List the differences between transactional relationships and consultative relationships.

3.4 How Customers Make Buying Decisions

Sales consultants have devised numerous titles or labels for the selling approaches they teach. Most approaches, however, are based on variations of the three basic models that appeal to different kinds of buyers:

▲ Standardized.

▲ Need-satisfaction.

▲ Problem-solution.

Each model requires a salesperson to take a specific approach. Your delivery style must be flexible enough to relate to all the different personality types. You should never settle for having one presentation style or using one approach because doing so severely limits the number of people you can serve.

3.4.1 The Standardized Model

In the **standardized model,** the buyer responds most positively to a series of statements constructed about an offering, so as to stimulate a positive response by the customer. This is often referred to as **benefitizing** an offering. Benefitizing means translating features of a product into benefits believed to be of value to the customer. A benefit of a new software package, for example, might be the ease with which employees could learn to use it.

At the extreme with the standardized model, specific statements are developed using phrases that tend to elicit positive responses, including words and phrases such as *user friendly, productivity improvement, satisfaction guaranteed,* and *no money down.*

Buyers also respond to highly structured sales presentations, often referred to as **canned presentations** because the same basic presentation is given to each customer. Not much time and effort are put into preparing for any single customer interaction after the basic presentation has been mastered.

The standardized model is most appropriate in situations where a product is standardized or when the benefits are generally the same for all customers. In such a situation, the sales pitch can be studied and refined to such a degree that even voice tone can be studied for its impact on sales. This type of selling

> ## FOR EXAMPLE
>
> ### A Good Place to Start
>
> Jane is a new representative for a cosmetics company that specializes in selling at-home parties. The company advises her to stick to its standardized or canned sales presentation as much as possible. The company says that this version is easy to learn and ideal for beginners. Jane follows that advice for her initial presentations. She believes that, with enough practice, the presentation will become a natural exchange of ideas with her prospects.

approach is most appropriate for transactional relationships where customers are concerned about the lowest cost and convenience.

Because standardized sales presentations are easiest to learn, they are also used in cases where the sales force is relatively inexperienced and employee turnover is high. This also helps to ensure uniform, high-quality presentations.

Although there are a number of advantages to the standardized model for selling purposes, there are also disadvantages in some situations. If the buyer's decision making is complex, a standardized selling approach is at a disadvantage primarily because the salesperson is not trained to uncover this complexity. As a result, the salesperson and the customer are out of sync in their discussions. In a business-selling situation, a standardized sales presentation is likely to be perceived as a "vendor" rather than a problem solver.

3.4.2 The Need–Satisfaction Model

The **need-satisfaction model** is oriented to discovering and meeting customers' needs. In general, the customers who probably best fit the need-satisfaction model are those who want to invest more time and resources in the buyer–seller relationship than those in a typical transactional relationship. The need-satisfaction type of selling approach is most appropriate for consultative customer relationships. Both the customer and the supplier invest more time and resources in the relationship than is typical of transactional relationships.

Needs discovery is achieved by skillfully asking questions that elicit customer-buying needs. This type of selling requires more selling skill than the standardized model because, if it is not tactfully handled, customers may become irritated by the questions or find them intrusive. Needs discovery takes place early in the selling cycle, often during the first call, and it is the most important step in the selling process.

The general-line sales forces of most consumer goods and office products companies are trained to use this model. As with each of the other sales models, it must be used in certain situations. The needs-satisfaction model is most appropriate when customer needs vary in important ways from one another.

The profits generated from a sale using this model must be significant to cover the costs of training a sales force in this selling method and to justify the longer selling cycle that is involved compared to the standardized model. Likewise, customers are likely to see you and your company as being good at resolving specific client issues but perhaps not capable of resolving the larger issues of the company.

3.4.3 The Problem-Solution Model

Generally, customers who positively respond to the problem-solution model are looking at extensive or complicated modifications. The **problem-solution model** is similar to the need-satisfaction model in that both involve an analysis of each customer's circumstances. The primary difference is that with the problem-solution model, this process is based on more formal studies of the customer's operations. Instead of identifying the customer's needs on the first sales call, the early selling objective is to get the customer's permission to conduct a formal study. The sales rep or sales team typically conducts the study and submits a written proposal based on the study. A formal presentation, perhaps by a team including a salesperson, management, and technical personnel, often accompanies the proposal.

This selling model usually involves significant monetary expenditures, and the selling cycle may be quite long. Examples of products involved include computer systems, advertising campaigns, telecommunications systems, and information systems. The problem analysis study may be so involved that the customer may be asked to pay to have it performed. For instance, a customer shopping for an electronic data system (EDS) might be asked to pay several hundred thousand dollars for a study of its computer system to determine whether an EDS can help the company. It is not unusual for clients to pay several advertising agencies to research and prepare a proposed ad campaign before deciding which agency will be awarded the account. As is probably obvious from this description and the EDS example, a problem-solution selling approach is most appropriate for a consultative or enterprise type of relationship in which both the seller and client organizations have a great investment in the relationship.

The problem of identifying customer relationships of sufficient value to cover the high investment involved in problem-solving selling is an important stumbling block to the success of using this model. Another is the development of the capabilities of the company's sales effort to effectively solve problems better than the competition. The institutional knowledge management that is necessary is often daunting.

3.4.4 Thinking Outside the Models

Which sales model is the best approach? There is no unequivocal answer to this question. The most appropriate approach depends on factors such as the offering, the professionalism of the sales force, the dollar value of the transaction,

FOR EXAMPLE

"I Saw It on Oprah"

Oprah Winfrey's TV show has had a tremendous impact on book publishing. If Ms. Winfrey selected a book for discussion on her show, it nearly guaranteed best-seller status. An example is Elie Wiesel's Holocaust survival memoir *Night*. The week after the show on Wiesel's book aired, *Night* sold 49,000 copies, up from 13,000 the week before. It jumped from 20th on the U.S. chart to 3rd, its highest position since charting.

and the type of customer relationship involved. Sometimes none of the models are appropriate.

A logical series of reasons might explain why buyers make their purchases; other times, there is no logic. The reason may be as simple as the product making the buyer feel good or the right people promoting it.

A basic motive of buyers is that they want a product because a respected person recommended it. However, it's also important to understand the market and the factors that influence it. In addition, people may simply react on emotions. It's your job as a salesperson to understand those emotions, the factors influencing them, and how to deal with them.

FOR EXAMPLE

Living the Fresh Life

Today's mothers are increasingly looking for healthy fast food they can prepare for their children. Baja Fresh recognized this fact and sought to revitalize its market with a new tagline—Live Fresh—and association with soccer star Mia Hamm. The tagline is designed to emphasize healthy food for an active family. The company also sponsored a contest featuring playing time with Ms. Hamm for budding soccer stars. The company attributes its healthier bottom line to the new campaign.

SELF-CHECK

1. List and describe the three basic buyer models.

SUMMARY

Success in sales depends greatly on learning why your client will buy your product or service. A great salesperson learns how to uncover the needs and wants of a customer. This chapter discusses many of the tools and strategies used in discovering these needs and wants. You've examined how to develop a sales strategy, which is necessary for learning how to meet these needs and wants. You've also studied the various factors that affect buyers' motives and how to build relationships suitable for different clients.

KEY TERMS

Addressing concerns	The sales strategy's fifth step, in which the salesperson answers the prospect's questions satisfactorily and fulfills any needs.
Benefitizing	Translating features of a product into benefits believed to be of value to the customer.
Canned presentation	The same basic presentation given to every customer.
Closing the sale	The sales strategy's sixth step, in which the salesperson meets the prospect's needs and concerns.
Consultative relationship	A high-investment approach to relationship building that focuses on problem solving for the client.
Original contact	The sales strategy's second step, in which the salesperson first spends time with a prospect.
Need-satisfaction model	An approach used for buyers who best respond to an investment of more time and resources in the buyer–seller relationship and discovery process.
Personal motives	An individual's preferences that spur that person to buy.
Prequalification	Behind-the-scenes activity of learning about a prospect.
Presentation	The sales strategy's fourth step, in which a salesperson shows the benefits of a product or service to a prospect.
Problem-solution model	An approach that is similar to the need-satisfaction model but that is based on more formal studies of the customer's operations.

Prospecting	The sales strategy's first step, in which a salesperson finds the right potential buyer.
Qualification	The sales strategy's third step, in which a salesperson meets with a prospect, learns details about the prospect, and determines how the product can fulfill a need.
Referral	The sales strategy's seventh step, or a satisfied customer's recommendation of another prospect for the salesperson.
Standardized model	An approach for a buyer who responds most positively to a series of statements constructed about an offering.
Task motives	The logical, practical, or functional reasons for buying.
Transactional relationship	A low-investment approach to relationship building that concentrates on explaining product features.

ASSESS YOUR UNDERSTANDING

Go to www.wiley.com/college/hopkins to evaluate your knowledge of the buying patterns of consumers.
Measure your learning by comparing pre-test and post-test results.

Summary Questions

1. The behind-the-scenes activity of learning all you can about a prospect is called:
   (a) prospecting.
   (b) pitching.
   (c) prequalification.
   (d) partying.

2. Which of the following is *not* a way to research a client?
   (a) visiting the client's website
   (b) finding copies of the company's annual report
   (c) talking to other salespeople within your company
   (d) all of the above

3. The first action a salesperson should take in developing a sales strategy is to create and practice a winning presentation. True or false?

4. Individual preferences that spur a person to buy are referred to as task motives. True or false?

5. Presenting solutions too early in a consultative relationship is a common mistake. True or false?

6. An approach to selling that illustrates a buyer responding most positively to a series of statements constructed about an offering is known as the:
   (a) need-satisfaction model.
   (b) standardized model.
   (c) problem-solution model.
   (d) hybrid model.

Applying This Chapter

1. Describe a recent incident in which someone sold you a product. Can you visualize how that salesperson might have had a seven-step sales strategy? If not, which steps were excluded?

2. Describe a sales experience in which you expressed a concern or problem about buying a product. What was the concern? Did the salesperson adequately address your concern?

3. Describe a product that you want to buy. Describe the type of information that a salesperson might find pertinent about you to persuade you to buy that product. Which of the buyer models should the salesperson use?

4. Describe a product or service that you have referred to someone. Why did you make the referral? What do you consider the benefits of that product?

5. Visualize yourself as a real estate agent. Your company has a listing of 80 acres currently used for farming in an area that is beginning to see suburban growth. Your customers are both farmers wanting a lot of acreage and companies looking to develop housing communities. Discuss the commonalities and differences of selling this property to individuals and families and to businesses.

6. Describe your motivation in buying the following items:

    (a) formal attire for a party

    (b) a 16-piece set of china

    (c) a lawnmower

7. Explain your preferences for transactional relationships and consultative relationships in your purchasing decisions.

YOU TRY IT

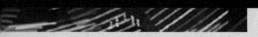

The Strategy for Success

You've accepted a job as a sales representative for the educational toy manufacturer Play Right, which specializes in toys for children in kindergarten through fifth grade. The company is introducing a new toy for the Christmas season. The toy is designed primarily for children in kindergarten through third grade. Your job is to help introduce the toy to the market. Outline and explain your sales strategy.

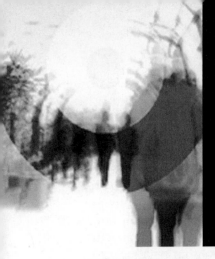

4

COMMUNICATION SKILLS FOR RELATIONSHIP BUILDING
Laying the Foundation for Sales

Starting Point

Go to www.wiley.com/college/hopkins to assess your communication skills. *Determine where you need to concentrate your effort.*

What You'll Learn in This Chapter

▲ The importance of good communication skills
▲ How to develop flexibility in communicating with different people
▲ Unique cultural considerations in communication
▲ The stages of building a relationship
▲ The factors necessary to build a salesperson/buyer relationship

After Studying This Chapter, You'll Be Able To

▲ Apply proper communication techniques to build a salesperson/client relationship

INTRODUCTION

In order to be successful in sales, you need to be able to present your product or service in the best manner possible. You need to communicate about the benefits of doing business with you. But communication is more than you doing all the talking. It is an exchange of ideas, preferably one that works in your favor. For this exchange to occur, you need to understand the dynamics of communications. This chapter explores those dynamics, which include flexibility in how you communicate with different personalities, listening skills, and cultural considerations. You'll also learn about the importance of relationship building to a salesperson.

4.1 The Importance of Communication Skills in Sales

Great salespeople are also great communicators. They understand when to talk and when to listen. Both skills are needed for good communication to occur. There also has to be openness and honesty in order to uncover the needs of the customer. Unfortunately, this is often difficult.

In a benchmark study by the consulting firm Meritus-IBM, suppliers and customers recognized and emphasized the importance of openness, honesty, good communications, and mutual strategy creation. But the study found that in reality, suppliers and customers were rarely entirely open and honest with each other and often didn't even try. To understand why this is the case, consider the example of a retailer who planned a special promotion but refused to tell the beverage bottler which of its products was involved. Why would the retailer not share this information? Because he was concerned that details would leak out to other retail competitors. Probably every grocery retailer can readily recall an instance in which a competitor sabotaged a special promotion after finding out about it ahead of time. So the bottler had to build up inventory levels of several possible products and be prepared to incur extra costs of fulfilling late-breaking orders. Naturally, after the promotion was launched, the bottler ended up with excess inventory for several weeks in those products not selected for the promotion.

Let's look at the beginning of the selling relationship. You have to be able to communicate to determine who is the true **decision maker.** This is the person who has the ability or power to make decisions about the products or services you sell. That's the person you want to meet. At companies, the decision maker may be an office manager, a purchasing agent, or a department head. You can usually find out simply by asking the receptionist who is responsible for the area of business to which your products or services apply. When you get an answer, you should ask a confirming question, such as, "So, Ms. Carter has the responsibility of authorizing purchase orders, is that right?"

When you have the name and position of the person responsible for purchasing in your area, you need to know a little about that person's style. If you recognize the personality type of the person you want to sell to, you'll be able to respond appropriately. Knowing how to respond appropriately is key.

SELF-CHECK

1. Discuss the importance of communication skills for a salesperson.
2. Define **decision maker**.

4.2 Developing Communication-Style Flexibility

Your delivery style must be flexible enough to relate to the different personality types. You should never settle for having one presentation style. Having only one style severely limits the number of people you can serve. Even if you don't like the personality of the decision maker, you can learn to like the opportunity the person is offering for business with you.

Let's take a look at some personality types you might encounter on-the-job. They are purposely exaggerated here to demonstrate various characteristics of buyers.

4.2.1 Believers

Believers are buyers who are already sold on your company or brand. They know what to expect from your company and like its reliability. They are easy to work with and, after you convince them of your personal competence, they remain loyal to you and your product. If they are not convinced that you're competent, they won't hesitate to call your company and request another representative.

How do you appeal to this personality type? You shouldn't short-sell the product or service just because a believer is already sold on its quality. You need to exhibit great product knowledge to garner trust and belief in your ability to meet the buyer's needs. Providing dependable service and follow-up will help you close the sale and gain the repeat business of a believer.

4.2.2 Wheeler-dealers

Buyers considered **wheeler-dealers** don't settle until they think they have an advantage over you and you've agreed to give them something extra. Today's market is full of these types of buyers. If you give wheeler-dealers any extras in order to consummate the sale, they'll probably brag to and upset others who may not have received the same benefit.

So how do you handle this type? You should let them know that they are important and special. They need to believe that they are skilled in negotiation and purchasing. If their business is worth providing extra service or a price cut, you should consult with your management about the possibilities. The enticement may be as simple as sending thank-you notes or making a few extra calls to let the wheeler-dealers know how important they are.

4.2.3 No-Nonsense Buyers

No-nonsense buyers are distant, matter-of-fact types who carry a high level of responsibility. They may have little personal contact throughout the day besides contact with outside salespeople. They can't risk liking you too much because they may have to replace you with the competition at any time.

When you're dealing with a no-nonsense type, you should give a no-fluff presentation. You shouldn't try to become too familiar but should stick to the facts and figures. By being low key, you'll be different from the other all-too-typical salespeople they encounter—a fact they will remember. It's important to let them know that you understand how important and challenging their position can be. You should send thank-you notes to no-nonsense buyers, present all figures to them in the most professional manner possible, and do everything in writing. They need the certainty of documentation.

4.2.4 Evaders

The most challenging buyers are the **evaders.** They refuse to return your phone calls, postpone appointments or reschedule at the last minute, like to shop around, and keep you waiting. In other words, they test your patience at every turn.

If you find yourself up against evaders, you should enlist the aid of their secretaries and other support staff, who may be able to tell you how to get and keep the evaders' business. You need to work on creating urgency in your presentations so these buyers can see the benefit of a speedy decision quickly and, just as important, the loss if they wait to make the decision. For example, you could offer an evader a special reduced investment or closeout on a product that you can offer only for a short period of time.

4.2.5 Complainers

Obviously, the **complainers** are buyers who always have something to complain about or something negative to say. To deal with complainers, you have to decide whether the income their business generates for you is worth all the energy they steal from you. If their business doesn't rate high on your priority list, you might want to consider finding other clients who don't exhaust you.

To limit your exposure to complainers' negativity, you should call them a few minutes before their normal lunch hour or just before the end of the day, when they won't want to talk long. If they call you at other times and cost you valuable selling time, you need to find polite ways to get off the line. The best you can do for a complainer is listen and be empathetic and stay pleasant and helpful. That's why they give you their business. If complainers get to be too much to handle, the easiest and least costly thing to do may be to refer them to someone else in your organization. The person receiving these new clients may not be as strongly affected and able to handle their constant complaining.

4.2.6 Analyzers

People who act as **analyzers** know what they want. They want everything in writing, go over every detail, and need to feel in control.

With these buyers, you must be extremely organized, handle every detail in writing, be punctual, and double-check everything and let them know that you've done so. When they are able to recognize your dependability, analyzers rely on you. You should confirm appointments with analyzers, reconfirm details of your meetings in writing, and provide a recap of every meeting you have with them. Before your next appointment, you should let an analyzer know what information you plan to discuss. It's important that you not be a source of disorder for an analyzer.

4.2.7 Power Seekers

A **power seeker** usually aspires to a more powerful position in the company. Power-seekers often hide their needs because they expect you to have done your homework. Their philosophy is that if you have done the proper research, you already know their needs.

In talking to power-seekers, perhaps the most important thing you can do is to compliment them on their importance and remind them of the value of their abilities to their company. They may be difficult to handle, but an advantage of working with power-seekers is that if they believe in you and your product, they'll be staunch supporters.

4.2.8 Disorganized and Controlling Buyers

Disorganized and controlling buyers are usually self-proclaimed experts but poor at delegating authority. They want everyone and everything reported to them. They may also be rude and interrupt your presentation by taking calls or giving directions to someone else.

When dealing with these buyers, you need to be extremely polite, prepared, and concise. You shouldn't make any assumptions. Instead, you should let disorganized and controlling buyers know that you value their time. If the interruptions

---

FOR EXAMPLE

Flexing the Sales Procedure

Evan knows that the person he usually sells his machinery tools to at a major manufacturer is a true believer. This decision maker, named Peter, has believed in Evan and the machinery tools for the past five years. However, Peter is retiring and being replaced by Deanna, who wants to reexamine all the vendors Peter hired. From information provided by Peter, Evan knows that Deanna falls into the analyzer category. Evan will have to deal with this analyzer much differently that he has with Peter. Evan determines that in order to keep the manufacturing company's business, he needs to provide all details in writing to Deanna, keep organized, and give her control over the details.

---

with this type of buyer become too distracting, you can offer to reschedule your meeting off the premises so that you can have that person's undivided attention. Or you can, simply by asking, enlist the aid of the buyer's secretary in keeping interruptions to a minimum during your appointment. Depending on the buyer's instructions on visitors and calls, you're likely to get the assistance you want just by making a polite request.

4.2.9 Cynics

Buyers in the **cynics** category fight change, are suspicious, and question your every move. Many of them have been working at their companies for many years.

You need to know how to overcome the doubts of a cynic. You can try dropping the names of people and companies the cynic trusts. But, in fact, the cynic's hesitancy can become the best thing for you because it'll be hard for your competition to persuade this person to change loyalties after you establish the value of becoming your client. Loyalty like that is your goal.

SELF-CHECK

1. Discuss the importance of flexibility in your communication style.
2. List and describe the personalities of buyers. How should you communicate with each personality type?

4.3 Communication Do's and Don'ts

Probably the most important communication "do" is to believe in yourself, your product, and your company. The most convincing tool you have at your disposal is the statement "I truly believe in what I am saying." The human being is an intuitive creature, and customers can tell whether you are merely interested in quick sales or whether you care about finding a solution to their problems. A client can see it in your body and hear it in your voice.

With sincerity comes enthusiasm. Both are hard to fake, so if you find that your communication efforts lack sincerity and enthusiasm, you need to uncover the problem and fix it.

Your sincerity and enthusiasm also help to keep your presentations—one-on-one or to groups—from boring people. When you are enthusiastic about your product, your tone is contagious. Other people get caught up in your enthusiasm and enjoy listening to your message.

You can also bore people by talking too much or giving too much information. When your customers tune out, you've lost the communication link. One way to maintaining interest is to include personal stories whenever possible. When you tell your own story, you tend to evoke more enthusiasm.

Another tip to improve your communication effort is to maintain control over the sound of your voice. The tone you use and your vocal variation allow you to project your personality and to elicit a positive response.

Do you need to improve your diction? One way to improve your enunciation is to practice speaking slowly. Or, you could practice repeating those tongue-twisters you learned in grade school, such as "Sally sells seashells by the seashore."

4.3.1 Positive Nonverbal Messages

In addition to sending messages with your speech, you send out nonverbal messages as well. Here are five top positive body language gestures to make yourself more exciting, more attractive, and, therefore, more successful in sales:

▲ **Smiling:** Your smile is one of the most effective nonverbal gestures you can use to create a positive image. Smile when you are listening and even speaking. Make it a sincere smile, however, not an ear-to-ear fake one.

▲ **Eye contact:** When you make eye contact with an individual, you are expressing interest. The combination of smiling and eye contact is powerful.

▲ **Nodding:** When someone is speaking, it might not be possible to verbally confirm and assure that person that you are listening and understanding. Head nodding is an important nonverbal gesture that can do both.

▲ **Lean forward:** When sitting, use your own back, not the back of the chair, to sit up straight. This effort demonstrates enthusiasm, work ethic, and interest in your customer.

▲ **Open-handed gestures:** These reflect honesty and increase your credibility.

4.3.2 Negative Nonverbal Messages

Just as positive body language sends positive messages, negative body language sends negative ones. Be aware of your posture and stance at all times. Here are three of the biggest body language errors that most salespeople make:

▲ **Folded arms:** Even though you just may be cold, folding your arms across your chest can communicate to others that you are closed or defensive.

▲ **Hands in pockets:** Hands in the pockets are often interpreted as a sign of insecurity or suspicious behavior. When your hands are in your pockets, they are not open and visible. It probably also causes you to slouch.

▲ **Hiding behind barriers:** When you are working on making a connection with someone, if possible come out from behind the counter or desk. Sit or stand next to the individual, almost face to face, but slightly offset (depending whether the other person is sitting or standing).

SELF-CHECK

1. Discuss the importance of the following in communication efforts:
   (a) Sincerity and enthusiasm
   (b) Personal stories
   (c) Vocal variation
   (d) Diction
2. What are five nonverbal gestures you can use to make your presentations more interesting?
3. Name and describe the three biggest body language errors made by most salespeople.

4.4 Vocabulary of a Great Salesperson

As with any profession, sales has certain words that are heard frequently in the industry. Unfortunately, many of the common terms used by salespeople bring about negative images in the minds of potential clients. The word "pitch" is one of many negative words used within the sales profession.

Negative words and phrases lead to the reduction of respect and credibility to an individual as well as the overall profession of sales. We suggest you use words that create respect and positive images in the minds of our clients.

Pitch is defined in the dictionary[1] as "To attempt to promote or sell, often in a high-pressure manner." Instead of using the word pitch, true professionals call this process a presentation or an exchange of information based on the customer's desires.

Another negative word is "spiel." A spiel[2] is defined as "as talk or harangue; harangue defined as a 'long, blustering speech; a tirade.'"[3] Great salespeople do not want to harangue their customers, so they avoid the word "spiel" and replace it with "discussion."

By replacing demeaning, unprofessional words with professional vocabulary, we garner more respect from our potential clients, satisfied clients, and coworkers, and we feel better about ourselves. Regardless of whether your client uses slang, the use of slang by a salesperson gives that client an indication of a low level of professionalism.

Last, be careful not to use trade or industry talk when speaking with someone outside of or not familiar with your industry. Clients might not understand or appreciate it, and you *never* want to cause confusion in the mind of the potential client. We talk more about jargon and other words to avoid—and use—in Section 8.6.2.

SELF-CHECK

1. Why are "pitch" and "spiel" considered negative words?
2. List three negative words and their positive replacements.
3. Why should a salesperson never use slang or jargon when speaking with a customer?

4.5 Listening to Your Clients

For communication to occur, in addition to expressing yourself, you need to listen to your clients. A good rule of thumb is to listen twice as much as you talk, and you'll succeed in persuading others nearly every time. When you do most of the talking,

▲ You aren't finding out about either your customer or your customer's needs.
▲ You aren't hearing buying clues or concerns.

▲ You may be raising concerns the prospect may not have had in the first place.

▲ You're shifting your prospect's attention from your offering.

▲ You're giving your prospect more opportunity to disagree with you, to distrust one of your statements, or both.

▲ You're taking center stage away from the customer.

▲ You aren't able to think ahead.

▲ You aren't able to guide the conversation.

▲ You aren't able to convince the other person of the best decision for him or her.

To develop your listening skills, you should try these two simple exercises:

▲ **Listen to a salesperson selling others or trying to sell you:** While you're listening, ask yourself these questions:

- Do the salesperson's words paint positive or negative mental pictures?
- Do the words say anything that may raise a new objection to the product or service?
- Are all these words necessary?
- Does the salesperson ask questions and then carefully listen to the prospect's answers?
- Does this person move forward with questions or get diverted by talking about features and benefits that are of no interest to the customer?

▲ **Record yourself when you're talking with a customer:** You may be shocked at how much chatter you can cut out. To detect what you need to cut, ask yourself these questions:

- What is the quality of the questions I ask?
- Am I asking information-gathering questions to help myself move forward with my sale, or am I just asking questions to fill a sound void? Questions don't mean much unless the answers are helping you get the information you need to help you serve your customer better and keep the sale moving forward.

You should watch and listen to others and to yourself more carefully than you're used to listening in everyday conversation. It's important that you acquaint yourself with what good listening really "sounds" like: It should sound like the voice of others, not your own voice.

Fortunately, you can develop good listening skills by focusing on and not interrupting the speaker, paraphrasing questions, answering at the appropriate time, and using complete sentences instead of saying simply yes or no.

1. Why is listening important to communication?
2. List and describe ways to improve your listening skills.

4.6 Cultural Considerations

Communication happens on many levels in both verbal and nonverbal ways. You communicate through your words, gestures, and actions. All these work together to convey your messages. You therefore need to keep in mind that the communication methods you use in one country may have insulting results in another. This section looks at some of the considerations in working with a diverse client list.

4.6.1 Unique Cultural Needs

If you're planning to do business in another country, you need to invest as much time understanding your prospects' culture as you do understanding their needs in terms of your products and services. The same rule holds true even if you do business within cultural groups different from your own in the country in which you live. Even if you're just building a Web site that may be viewed by people from many different countries or cultures, you need to be aware of words and phrases that just don't translate well or may be offensive when a translation is made.

Here are a few general tips for communicating well with those from other cultures[4]:

▲ **Be patient when building trust and establishing relationships:** People from countries other than the United States generally need more time to build trust. Observing a greater degree of formality while becoming acquainted is important.

▲ **Speak more slowly than you normally do, but don't raise your voice:** Volume doesn't usually increase comprehension.

▲ **Avoid slang, buzzwords, idioms, jargon, and lingo:** These can all be easily misunderstood by those who don't speak your language as natives would.

▲ **If you're using an interpreter, make sure you meet the interpreter ahead of time:** This will allow the interpreter to learn your language patterns as well as special terminology and numbers used, such as product identifiers or other codes specific to your company or industry. These details affect the whole dimension of the conversation.

▲ **Pay attention to nonverbal interaction cues:** For example, the word "yes" or an affirmative nod often means, "Yes, I hear you," in Asian cultures, not, "Yes, I agree."

> ## FOR EXAMPLE
>
> ### Speaking Up
>
> Lori was born in and now works in the Southern states of the United States. She is a sales representative for a major textile company and must travel to New York City frequently. She was born in an environment where people speak in a manner very different from the clipped, fast-paced speech pattern of native New Yorkers. She found she had to learn to talk faster than she was used to speaking to keep her New York clients' attention. Plus, she had to put all her listening skills into practice because they talked faster than people in her hometown. She found that adapting to her clients' way of conversing put them more at ease, and they focused more on her message.

Culture influences people as much as their personal experiences. Knowing your clients' customs and traditions makes sense. That way, neither you nor your client will be made to feel uncomfortable.

Even if you're doing business within your native country, you may need to pay attention to differences among various regions. Your customers may speak the same language but with different accents or using different dialects. People in nearly every region of the United States, for example, have accents or certain ways of saying particular words. These accents can be charming or irritating to others, depending on their existing assumptions.

4.6.2 Getting Names Right

Pronouncing or spelling a client's name correctly goes a long way toward earning the person's respect and trust. If you forget a client's name or mispronounce it, you'll have extra work to remedy the situation and earn or regain the client's respect.

In some cultures, a person's surname (i.e., last name) is given before the given name (i.e., first name). For example, suppose you greet Mao Ling as Mr. Ling. That may be the same as addressing Mr. Ling as Mr. Bob. Hispanic names usually include both the father's and mother's family names. The father's name comes first and should be used as the term of address. Suppose you meet Luis Mendoza Trujillo. Luis is his first name, Mendoza is his father's family name, and Trujillo is his mother's family name. You should address him as Señor Mendoza.

In Germany, the preference is to be addressed by job title as opposed to the German equivalent of Mr. or Ms. For example, addressing Otto Schmidt as Vice President Schmidt is considered appropriate. In Italy, including someone's profession when introducing or referring to him is considered more appropriate. For example, you might meet "our engineer, Mr. Puccini."

In any culture, including your own, you should never use a customer's first name unless that person specifically asks you to do so. And you should never abbreviate a name unless instructed to do so.

4.6.3 Making an Appointment

Getting together with people on neutral, or at least acceptable, territory can be a difficult aspect of selling to someone from another culture. Knowing your client's customs is critical. So is remembering the importance of making a good first impression.

When you're planning to sell to a client from a culture other than your own, you need to determine the best way to approach someone for an appointment. In India, for example, mail delivery can be unreliable, so you convey important messages by fax, telephone, or e-mail. You should find out whether your client's country requires any similar considerations.

After you determine the best method to use to reach your client, you need to decide which environment would be most conducive for business. Although many businesspeople prefer formal settings, such as a corporate conference room, others prefer more relaxed locations, such as restaurants or clubs. In the Chinese culture, for example, the feng shui of a location can play an important part in how the business goes. *Feng shui* is the placement and arrangement of space to achieve harmony with the environment. It is an ancient discipline with guidelines compatible with many decorating styles. Paying attention to details such as those may be the key to your success with Chinese clients.

When you have an appointment, it's important to confirm all the details and do your homework on what to wear, what to bring with you, and how to give your presentation. In addition, you should always be punctual, but you shouldn't expect the other person to be. In many cultures, relationships are much more important than time clocks. You should value the time your client gives you but not count the minutes.

4.6.4 Presenting Your Business Card

Having some business cards with your contact information in the language of the recipient is a good idea. You might want to put the information in your language on one side and in another language on the other. You always present your card with the client's language facing up to make your client most comfortable in understanding the information. You should allow the client a moment to read the card before talking or moving on to the next aspect of your presentation.

If you're in charge of printing your own cards, you need to seek out the advice of a protocol professional to ensure that you present your cards properly. Some countries have specific etiquette surrounding the use of business cards. For example, if you're going to Japan, you need to take plenty of business cards and give one to every person you meet. Academic degrees are also important in

Japanese culture, so if you have a master's degree, you should be certain to show that on your card. In addition, you should pull out only one card at a time; holding a stack of business cards in your hand is considered bad manners in Japan.

In any culture, taking the time to read the card of each person who gives you one before accepting another card is wise. You should not set the cards aside quickly. That would be like dismissing the person to move on to someone else. Putting the cards in a business card case shows respect for the person who gave it to you. Shoving it in your pocket or notebook does not.

4.6.5 Respecting Personal Space

All people, regardless of their country, have a need for **personal space**, which could be defined as the distance between you and another person during a conversation. But in each culture, the amount of personal space a person needs is different. For example, the British want more personal space than people from the United States. Russians and Arabs, on the other hand, need less personal space than most Americans.

If you want to be sure that people feel comfortable around you (a necessity in the world of selling), you shouldn't invade their space. On the other hand, if you're working with people from cultures where less personal space is required, you should be sure not to back away when they step into your larger personal space. That can be construed as a sign that you are fearful or hesitant about the other person. Neither is good with potential business clients.

4.6.6 Meeting and Greeting People

Some countries, such as most of the Middle Eastern nations, include embraces or handshakes when meeting and departing. You should determine in advance whether a potential client would be likely to welcome or expect an embrace or a handshake. When the relationship becomes closer, a kiss on the cheek may be appropriate.

Inquiring about a person's health is a positive gesture in Arab culture. However, you should not extend your hand to shake an Arab woman's hand unless she extends hers first.

Learning the small details of how people meet and greet one another in a particular country makes a huge difference in the balance of your contact time with each client.

4.6.7 Giving Gifts

The decision makers at most companies understand the value of appropriate gift giving and usually establish parameters for gift giving by their staff. If your company doesn't have specific guidelines for you to follow, you should ask management for their preferences or suggest some appropriate parameters based on the potential value of each client to the company. If you're the sales representative who is the main source of contact with a client, you should ensure that the client thinks well of you when he or she receives a gift. So you shouldn't be afraid to jump in with some solid suggestions.

The stronger your relationship with your client, the more personalized your gift should be. For a long-term client, you should know what that person likes and gear your gift to the client's highest level of enjoyment.

Beware that some cultures find the giving and receiving of gifts a personal matter, not a business matter. For example, in France, business gifts aren't given. If you're invited to a French business associate's home, however, you should be certain to bring flowers, chocolates, or a bottle of high-quality spirits, such as vodka or Scotch. The host or hostess will have already chosen the proper wine for the meal.

It's important to realize that gifts that would be considered very appropriate in your country may be offensive to people in the country you're visiting. For example, in Japan or Latin America, a gift of a letter opener may imply that you are severing the relationship because the letter opener looks like a knife. A Hindu would not appreciate a gift made of leather because the cow is considered sacred in that religion. In Japan, white is used in funeral services, so you want to make sure that you don't wrap gifts in white or send white flowers. In Germany, red roses are given only in personal relationships, never in business ones. And in many Asian cultures, singling someone out with a gift or a compliment may be considered offensive rather than polite. You need to be sure to read up on the country in which you'll be selling so you can avoid offending your clients and so everyone's attention is focused on what you're selling instead of on an unfortunate faux pas.

Be sure that the recipient doesn't construe the gift as being inappropriate. Giving a Rolex watch to a client who only purchased $500 worth of product from you is probably not a wise move. If the client is uncomfortable at all with the gift, he or she may wonder whether you're offering a bribe for future business. That's exactly the opposite of the reaction you want.

FOR EXAMPLE

Selling Overseas

As a sales representative for a U.S. grain exporter, Alexander usually sent a nice pen to his customers as a token of appreciation for their business. He opened up new territory in Malaysia. He sent a pen to one of the purchasing agents at one firm, who was his first customer in that territory. The other firm's agents, however, learned of his gift and resented the fact that they didn't receive anything, so they refused to work with him.

Before you give a gift to a client, you need to determine whether the recipient's company has a policy on receiving gifts. Many companies don't allow their employees to accept gifts. If you offer one, your client may be in the uncomfortable position of having to decline or return your gift. If the company doesn't allow the receiving of gifts, ask the person with whom you have the best relationship in the company what you can do. Maybe you can send a box of candy or a basket of fruit for the department to share, but not a pen-and-pencil set for an individual.

Some countries also require duties or other fees to be paid on shipments from outside that country. You should therefore find out whether this applies in the country you're visiting and pay any duty in advance. You can get this information from the nearest consulate for that country. Or you can simply order the gift from a major supplier within that country.

4.6.8 Choosing Your Words Wisely

When you're getting to know your clients, you need to think about the effective power of language. Every word you utter creates a picture or symbol in the mind's eye of the listener. Each symbol often has emotions attached to it as well. Words, such as *spring, summer, autumn,* and *winter,* can generate positive or negative emotions in a person. If you love gardening, the warm spring air may bring to mind beautiful blossoms, the opportunity to get your fingers in the dirt, and preparing your soil for a summer crop. If you are a hay fever sufferer, the picture painted by the word *spring* may be totally different.

You don't know in advance which words about you, your product, and your company will generate positive feelings in your clients. So you need to become extra-sensitive to the way you use words.

SELF-CHECK

1. Describe how learning various cultural differences can benefit a salesperson.
2. Outline the areas that a salesperson should consider in learning about cultural differences.

4.7 Relationship Building

Most salespeople would like to establish long-term relationships with their customers to ensure a stream of purchases and an upgrading of the equipment a client purchases over time. Therefore, it's important to understand how to build and enhance professional relationships at all levels in an organization. This section reviews important elements in building a relationship, including the evolution of a relationship, relating skills, and tips to ease relationship anxiety.

4.7.1 The Evolution of a Relationship

According to research in social psychology,[5] growing relationships evolve through five general stages:

1. Awareness
2. Exploration
3. Expansion
4. Commitment
5. Dissolution.

Although it may be difficult to determine exactly when a relationship progresses from one stage to the next, each stage represents a major shift in the relationship. Salespeople should be aware of these changes and proceed accordingly. These five stages of **relationship evolution** and the objectives associated with each stage are summarized in Figure 4-1. All relationships are dynamic and changing, but they don't necessarily proceed in steps. There is often a recycling through the different general stages shown in Figure 4-1.

4.7.2 Relationship Binders

Certain factors drive individuals or organizations to progress to a fully committed relationship. Salespeople should be aware of these factors. This section discusses three important factors that a salesperson should understand:

▲ Creating value.
▲ Meeting expectations.
▲ Building trust.

Creating Value

The term **value** refers to the perception that the rewards exceed the costs associated with establishing and/or expanding a relationship. Value to a buyer is not always the lowest list price. It may involve the opportunity to save time and labor, or it may result in higher sales of the customer's products. Value must ultimately reach the client's customers in the form of better-quality or less-expensive products, wider choices, and/or quicker access to those choices. This individualized product development, however, requires a considerable investment of time and effort when you assess the client's needs.

Figure 4-1

Relationship Stage	Description	Key Selling Objectives
Awareness	Recognition that a supplier may be able to satify an important need.	1. Gain customer's attention 2. Demonstrate how the product/service can satisfy a need.
Exploration	A tentative initial trial with limited commitments by both parties. This trial period may go on for an extended period of time.	1. Gain initial acceptance. 2. Build a successful relationship.
Expansion	Expansion of rewards for each party in the relationship.	1. Get to know customers and their business better. 2. Expand ways to help the customer.
Commitment	The commitment by both the buyer and seller to an exclusive relationship.	1. Interaction at levels between the buyer's and seller's organizations. 2. Early supplier involvement in development processes. 3. Long-term focus to the relationship.
Dissolution	Total disengagement from the relationship. This may occur at any point in the relationship.	1. Look for warning signals. 2. Attempt to reinitiate the relationship.

Stages in a buyer/seller relationship.

Meeting Expectations

In any relationship, the involved parties develop **expectations**, sometimes referred to as *rules* or *norms,* with respect to acceptable conduct and performance. Acceptable behavior varies, depending on individual preferences, company policies, and national cultures.

Sometimes buyers and sellers derive a mutually agreed-upon set of team values. These values are sometimes put in writing in order to remind all members that these are the accepted standards of conduct of the relationship to which every individual must subscribe. It is especially important to ensure that new members of the team are aware of and comply with these values.

Salespeople must be careful not to encourage unfavorable buyer expectations as a result of present behaviors. If a salesperson agrees to a special price discount at the buyer's request, for example, the buyer may think this is standard practice and expect some sort of discounting in the future. Because of this behavior, many companies do not give their salespeople the flexibility to discount prices.

Expectations also develop with respect to performance. Customer performance expectations include expectations about the performance of the product as well as a number of service activities, such as frequency of sales calls, notification of price changes, lead time in delivery, order fill rate, emergency orders, and installation. Studies comparing the performance perceptions of salespeople and buyers in a wide variety of industries show that there is considerable inaccuracy in salespeople's perceptions of buyers' performance expectations. Plus, accuracy in identifying the buyer's performance rules is related to high sales performance. Interestingly, more experienced salespeople tend to be less accurate in their buyer performance expectations.

To encourage accuracy in customer assessment, some companies require their salespeople to provide a yearly written assessment of their key customers. This assessment process involves answering a series of questions. Writing the answers helps to identify key assumptions, inconsistencies, and missing information. Figure 4-2 lists the type of questions that should be answered about an account. The objective is to have superior customer intelligence, which means having better information than any competitor has about the account.

Building Trust

Trust refers to the opinion that an individual's word or promise can be believed and that the long-term interests of the customer will be served. Trust in salespeople and their companies is essential to buyers' evaluation of the quality of a relationship and to establishing working partnerships. Indeed, customer surveys often find that it is difficult for customers to distinguish between their feelings toward a supplier and their feelings toward a salesperson.[6] Customer trust in the supplier's salesperson is particularly important in growing the customer/supplier relationship beyond the exploration phase.

Trust takes time to develop. Research indicates that the length of tenure of a salesperson is important to partnering with customers and to the profitability of customer/partner relationships.[7] How does a salesperson earn a buyer's trust? Studies of buyers and sellers have shown that salespeople buyers trust possess the following five attributes:

▲ **Honesty:** People trust salespeople who tell the truth.

▲ **Competence:** People trust salespeople who know what they are talking about.

▲ **Dependability:** People trust salespeople who follow through on their promises.

▲ **Customer orientation:** People trust salespeople who put buyers' interests ahead of their own.

▲ **Likeability:** People trust salespeople whom a buyer enjoys knowing.[8]

Figure 4-2

Market Intelligence	Which of the customer's products are most important in terms of revenue and profit contribution? What markets do they serve, and which are the most important? Who are their major competitors?
Financial Intelligence	When does the annual capital budgeting process begin? When does it end? Who initiates capital project requests? What hurdle rate is required to win approval? What is the projected capital spending for the year?
Organizational Intelligence	What reporting relationships in each department influence purchasing decisions? What are the top business objectives each relevant department manager is expected to achieve in the current year?
Operational Intelligence	What are the details of the process used by Operations to produce results (e.g., raw materials coming in, processing equipment, budget to produce finished goods, etc.)? Are there specific measures of performance for your products or services?
Personnel Intelligence	Who are the people having a direct or indirect influence on buying decisions for your products? What are their formal responsibilities? How often have you met with them in the past year? What is your relationship with each person? Who are their friends and enemies with the account?
Competitive Intelligence	Which of your competitors have an installed base position in the account? What is the account share for each competitor? Which ones are likely to gain share?

Account intelligence.

Studies of buyers' perceptions of salespeople's trustworthiness also indicate that the importance of each attribute to buyers' overall feelings of trust varies according to the stage of the purchasing relationship. Early in a relationship, the company's and salesperson's reputations for competence are dominant. As the buyer gains experience with the seller and the particular salesperson, dependability becomes more important. In a fully committed stage of the relationship, customer orientation is most important to the feelings of buyer trust. Honesty and likeability are important during all phases of the purchasing relationship.[9]

Trust building is not entirely a matter of being liked, however. There is also evidence that people place greater trust in those whom they feel have good listening skills. These three relationship binders—creating value, meeting expectations, and building trust—are needed to build lasting relationships with customers. How these relationship binders are achieved, the activities involved, and the skills needed to enhance them differ, depending on the account relationship strategy involved.

4.7.3 Relating Skills

In most social situations, both of the people meeting for the first time experience a degree of tension. Salespeople have long recognized **call reluctance**—that is, the fear of making contact with a customer—as a problem. It is estimated that call reluctance reaches intense levels for up to 40 percent of salespeople at some point in their careers.[10] Customers are also likely to feel a form of anxiety referred to as **relationship anxiety** when meeting a salesperson. This anxiety arises because people don't like to be sold; they like to buy.

In one sense, the role of the salesperson is to help the customer buy wisely. This calls for well-developed **relating skills**—that is, the ability to put the other person at ease in a potentially tense situation. The first few moments of a selling encounter are important because people formulate initial impressions at this time. Impressions of competence, honesty, and likeability all have important impacts on the ultimate outcome of a sales encounter.

To help establish rapport, salespeople should be forthcoming about the purpose of a sales call. Many experts, for example, admonish salespeople to avoid asking "How are you?" because this question is meaningless and contrary to what the salesperson should be, which is genuinely helpful and direct. Given the time pressures everyone is under today, it is a good idea to first say "Thank you for your time" and then to hand the prospect a business card and introduce yourself. If you do this, the prospect can both see and hear your name.

FOR EXAMPLE

Introducing Yourself

Take a look at the introduction one salespeople uses: "Hello, Mr. Smith, I am Mary Johnson of the Hamilton Company. Thank you for seeing me. I am here today to see if we can help you save money on your duplicating budget." Mary identifies herself as well as the purpose of the visit and signals that she plans to focus on a possible customer benefit (lower costs). She follows the introduction quickly by laying out an agenda for the meeting, which relieves the client's anxiety about time.

Figure 4-3

Propriety	Show buyer respect; dress appropriately.
Competence	Know your product/service; third-party references.
Commonality	Have common interests, views, acquaintances.
Intent	Reveal purpose of call, process, and payoff to the buyer.

Means of reducing relationship anxiety.

It's important to quickly and smoothly proceed to questions to uncover needs. Continuing with our previous example, in her introduction, Mary might say something like, "My experience has shown me that I can do a better job of meeting your needs if I know what's important about these issues and the role your copier plays. So, Mr. Smith, help me understand: What's important to you about the copy machines you are considering purchasing?"

In many customer interactions, non-business topics are often discussed initially in the selling process. We'll discuss the importance of building rapport in Chapter 7.

Much more is involved in demonstrating relating skills than simply getting a dialogue started between you and the other person. Figure 4-3 discusses four strategies salespeople can use to reduce relationship tension. It is critical that salespeople utilize each of these means to reduce tension when meeting with a prospect. With established customers, a relationship already exists. Many of the rules of the relationship, therefore, are already set. However, salespeople should constantly try to reinforce these impressions.

SELF-CHECK

1. Outline and describe the five stages of relationship evolution.
2. Describe the three relationship binders.
3. Define **relationship anxiety, call reluctance,** and **relating skills.** How would you use relating skills to reduce relationship anxiety?

SUMMARY

Good communication leads to good relationships, and good relationships are the goal of every successful salesperson. Increasingly, a company's profitability and growth depend on establishing good relationships with the right customers and managing each relationship so as to deliver value to the customer. In this chapter, you've learned about the communication skills and concepts involved in the successful management of account relationships.

KEY TERMS

Analyzers	A type of buyers who study every detail and want an organized salesperson.
Believers	A type of buyers who are easygoing, believe in the salesperson and company, and remain loyal customers.
Call reluctance	The fear of making contact with a customer.
Cynics	A type of buyers who fight change, are suspicious, and question everything.
Complainers	A type of buyers who focus on negatives.
Decision maker	The person who has the ability or power to make decisions about the products or services you sell.
Disorganized and controlling buyers	A type of buyers who are self-proclaimed experts but poor at delegating authority.
Evaders	A type of buyers who refuse to return a salesperson's calls and are difficult to reach.
Expectations	Rules or norms, with respect to acceptable conduct and performance.
No-nonsense buyers	A type of buyers who are distant and want an all-business relationship.
Personal space	The distance between people during a conversation.
Power-seekers	A type of buyers who want to advance in their company and tend to trust salespeople who have done extensive research to uncover the customer's needs.
Relating skills	The ability to put the other person at ease in a potentially tense situation.
Relationship anxiety	A fear that a customer has in meeting a salesperson.

Relationship evolution   A five-stage process in which a relationship progresses.

Trust   The belief that an individual's word or promise can be believed and that the long-term interests of the customer will be served.

Value   The perception that the rewards exceed the costs associated with establishing and/or expanding a relationship.

Wheeler-dealers   A type of buyers who like to bargain and gain an advantage over the salesperson.

ASSESS YOUR UNDERSTANDING

Go to www.wiley.com/college/hopkins to evaluate your knowledge of communication skills.
Measure your learning by comparing pre-test and post-test results.

Summary Questions

1. Great salespeople are also:
   (a) great explorers.
   (b) great neighbors.
   (c) great communicators.
   (d) great risk takers.

2. You can use one presentation style for all your communication needs. True or false?

3. The type of buyer who tends to be distant and matter-of-fact and to carry a high level of responsibility is:
   (a) an evader.
   (b) a wheeler-dealer.
   (c) distant and controlling.
   (d) no-nonsense.

4. If you're a salesperson, a good rule of thumb is to talk about your product twice as much as you listen to your client's explanation of his or her needs. True or false?

5. A salesperson should usually try to avoid all the jargon associated with the client's industry when the client is from another culture. True or false?

6. The most important necessity for communicating the benefits of your product or service is having a sincere belief in it. True or false?

7. Which of the following is *not* a positive nonverbal gesture?
   (a) smiling
   (b) open-handed gestures
   (c) folded arms
   (d) nodding

8. Which of the following is *not* a means to ensure error-free communication?
   (a) Write everything down.
   (b) Keep your eyes focused on your writing.
   (c) Listen intently to the speaker.
   (d) Repeat the message to the speaker.

9. Feng shui is an important consideration in dealing with a customer from China. True or false?

10. You should always keep at least an arm's distance between you and your client. True or false?

11. Each stage of relationship evolution occurs in order. True or false?

12. Which of the following is *not* an important factor in relationship binders?
    (a) meeting expectations
    (b) building trust
    (c) asking any and all questions that come to mind
    (d) creating value

13. Trust in salespeople and their companies is essential to the buyers' evaluation of the quality of a relationship and to establishing working partnerships. True or false?

14. The ability to put the other person at ease in a potentially tense situation is referred to as:
    (a) relating problems.
    (b) relating aspects.
    (c) relating talent.
    (d) relating skills.

Applying This Chapter

1. Describe how you would uncover the true decision maker for buying your product. What are some of the obstacles you might face in determining who this decision maker is?

2. This chapter describes a number of buyer personalities. Explain how each of the following examples best suits one of the personality types. Given the person's personality types and other factors of the example, how might you deal with each of these people?
    (a) George has just been promoted but still has to handle many of the responsibilities of his previous position until a replacement can be found.
    (b) Maria is vivacious and talkative. You learn that she was born in a culture in which bargaining is part of the sales experience.
    (c) Ian rarely smiles and tries to avoid any nonessential conversation. You notice that he keeps a very clean desk and almost no memorabilia in his office.
    (d) Jenny is new to the company but worked in a similar position for another company. She wants to learn all she can about her new employer and is taking the time to do so.

3. Visualize yourself as a salesperson who has to travel to India. What are some of the cultural differences you need to learn about in order to communicate effectively? You might want to do a web search using the term "cultural etiquette" or "cultural protocol."

4. Think of an experience you had in which miscommunication caused you to make an error, such as missing an appointment or a movie time. How much did listening play a part in this miscommunication? How could you have ensured that you heard the information correctly?

5. Think of a close friendship. Using the five stages of relationship evolution, describe how this friendship has evolved.

YOU TRY IT

Speaking Your Customer's Language

China has one of the fastest-growing economies in the world. As a result, the country needs to improve its highway system for an increasingly mobile population. You work in sales for a major U.S. contractor specializing in building roads. Your company wants to be involved in building roads in China. Develop the first steps in building a communication plan with your Chinese prospects. What might you do to relieve any anxiety they have?

5
PROSPECTING
Finding the Buyers

Starting Point

Go to www.wiley.com/college/hopkins to assess your knowledge of prospecting in sales.
Determine where you need to concentrate your effort.

What You'll Learn in This Chapter

▲ The importance of prospecting
▲ Where to find prospects
▲ The importance of qualifying prospects
▲ Organizing your prospect information
▲ Developing a prospecting and sales forecasting plan

After Studying This Chapter, You'll Be Able To

▲ Identify and evaluate appropriate prospects for your sales effort
▲ Analyze the appropriate avenues for finding prospects
▲ Identify and evaluate ways to organize prospect information
▲ Understand the elements needed for a prospecting and sales forecasting plan

INTRODUCTION

Prospecting is the most important area for a new sales professional to develop. Without adequate knowledge of and skills in prospecting, a salesperson is treading in deep water without first learning to swim. The sources for prospecting are virtually everywhere. Knowing how to find the prospects that are right for you, however, is key to your success. The next step is knowing how to qualify a prospect to find out if that person truly needs your product or service. Rounding up the final phase in prospecting is developing a system that keeps all the information about prospects organized. During your career, you may be asked to develop a prospecting and sales forecasting plan. This chapter examines important elements necessary for devising this plan.

5.1 Prospecting: An Introduction

In this book, you've read about developing a sales strategy and the first step in the selling cycle, which is called **prospecting**. This is, essentially, searching for people who will buy your products or services. Obviously, a new salesperson needs prospects in order to start selling. Many times, experienced salespeople must also continue the search for prospects. In fact, many companies rely on their salespeople to find new customers to achieve growth objectives. No matter how strong their products, how great their customer service, or how aggressive their sales forces, businesses lose customers every year.

Few companies can afford to neglect new business development. Indeed, firms that have developed effective prospecting skills are more profitable than those lacking such skills. These findings underscore the importance of prospecting for a salesperson. Remember that your prospecting efforts must concentrate on getting to the decision maker. If you never get the opportunity to get in front of the right people, all the selling techniques you've learned are wasted.

FOR EXAMPLE

Getting to the Right Person

Elizabeth, the sales representative for a woman-owned graphics design firm, knew that the employee communications department of the major employer in her town worked with outside design firms. She contacted an acquaintance in the employee communications department and asked for the name and number of the person in that department who works with graphic design. She then contacted the referral, mentioned her connection in the department, and set up an appointment. Elizabeth had reached the right decision maker and had a new prospect.

When you're just starting, your time should be split between learning about your product, honing your skills, and finding people who need your product. Yet the key to success in a people business such as selling lies in how many people you can see in the time you have. New salespeople should place their primary focus on prospecting. In the beginning of your sales career, you should invest about 75 percent of your time in prospecting. The other 25 percent of your time should go toward developing your product knowledge and presentation skills. Initially, you'll probably find yourself working very hard just to find a few prospects. But with every experience, you'll discover a little more and refine your strategies and techniques, and you'll eventually find yourself working smarter.

Be sure to have plenty of business cards and be generous in handing them out. By hand-writing thank-you across the top of your card, you present a unique opening for talking to a prospect. The idea is to appeal to the prospect's curiosity, causing them to wonder how you might serve them in the future. Plus, it's a way to make the prospect feel a little more important and build rapport.

SELF-CHECK

1. Define **prospecting** and its importance to a sales professional.
2. Describe how new salespeople should allocate their time.

5.2 Where to Find Prospects

You've developed your sales strategy. Now you need to begin finding prospects. Many successful sales veterans can tell you how important prospecting is, even after they have built a large customer base. They want to reach the top of their profession and stay there. Therefore, prospecting is a part of their everyday selling strategy. They understand that achieving success doesn't mean they can stop looking for new business opportunities. Successful sales professionals explore every avenue in search of new customers, no matter how long they've been in the business.

The following are some suggestions to explore in prospecting.

5.2.1 Current Customers

The best place to start prospecting is with people who have already paid money for products and services similar to yours. They may already be customers of your company, or they may be patronizing a competitor. You know the items in your portfolio will be very appropriate to these customers.

If you're selling exercise equipment, for example, you could begin with people who jog, belong to health clubs, or join local recreational sports teams. Why? You know they're already health conscious. The convenience of being able to exercise at home may be just what they're looking for. If you're selling graphic design, you might start with the people who are responsible for advertising in local companies. If you've already worked for people in a certain type of business, such as gift shops, you might want to concentrate on other gift shops in the area.

To some degree at least, where you find your prospects depends on what you represent. If you sell products or services for a company, you probably found out during your product-knowledge training about the most likely places to find your products or services in use. Those places are, obviously, the best places to begin prospecting.

When you work for someone else's firm, the company usually handles the details of advertising and marketing to generate leads for you and the other salespeople. But in order to become a great salesperson, you should always be prospecting on your own, too. That way, if the company-led program hits a lull, you'll be prepared. A slow period isn't the time to begin developing your prospecting skills. If you're prospecting all along and encounter a minor setback, you'll barely break stride in your business activity level.

You may be in a position to help answer questions that are e-mailed to your company by customers or prospective clients. If that's the case, you shouldn't just reply but make the inquirer curious for more information. You need to do your best to capture more than the person's return e-mail address: Get the person's name, street address, and phone number if at all possible. You can add that information to your contact list and follow up with the person to ensure that he or she is satisfied with your reply. You can offer to provide the prospect with additional service as well. This strategy is just one way to increase your list of prospective clients.

Finally, it's often a good idea to contact past customers. Nearly every tangible product has a limited life span. A past customer may be ready to buy a new, improved version of whatever you sell. You should know your product's life span and then review past customer files to find people who purchased at the beginning of this life span. You might even call some customers and ask when they think they might like to make another purchase. An established company probably has a customer list. Managers don't always take the time to complete the basic task of transferring clients to new salespeople when the former salespeople move on, so it's a good idea to ask your manager for names. If those customers weren't reassigned to another salesperson, you might want to ask to be given the authority to contact those clients yourself. If nothing else comes of your contacts, you'll leave a positive impression of the type of follow-up your company provides.

5.2.2 Chambers of Commerce and Public Libraries

Your local chamber of commerce and public library have many kinds of listings available, including local businesses, national business directories, international directories, and toll-free directories for businesses. Many libraries also provide free Internet access for patrons.

You should take advantage of any functions that a chamber of commerce sponsors. These are usually great opportunities for networking.

5.2.3 The Internet

You can conduct online searches for businesses of the type that would use your product or service. For example, you might search for all manufacturers of computer software if your product applies to that field. All you need to do to narrow your list of potential prospects to the right ones to begin contacting is ask the right questions. You can post bulletins on message boards related to your product or service; this way, you can provide valuable information in addition to selling your product or service.

Another tactic is to visit the Web sites of companies where your business contacts work. You should look for the names of other businesses affiliated with these companies so you know before contacting them whether they may have further good contacts for you. If the affiliates posted on their Web sites aren't good candidates for your product or service, or if they could be considered part of your competition, you shouldn't waste their time or yours in asking for these particular contacts.

Not everything you find on the Internet is 100 percent accurate. However, information posted by large, respectable corporations generally provides source listings. You should verify information that appears without source listings through a reputable source before relying on it yourself or passing it on to your clients.

5.2.4 List Brokers

If you have some money to invest in lists, you might want to contact a **list broker.** This is an individual or a company that has many lists available and can review your particular demographic needs with you to give you the best list of potential customers to contact.

If you prefer to market via e-mail (which is a very economical method), you should ask your list broker for an **opt-in e-mail list,** which is a list of people who have agreed to have information sent to them via e-mail. Opt-in e-mail lists receive a response rate ranging from 5 to 15 percent. This is a huge increase over traditional direct mail response rates. Using opt-in e-mail lists can also help you avoid e-mailing unwanted information to people and making a negative impression on them.

5.2.5 Your Current Contacts

Perhaps the most straightforward place to start prospecting is with the people you already know. Talking with these people first will help you find easy leads and give you an opportunity to practice your prospecting presentation. Your friends and family members like and trust you, and they want to see you succeed. That means they're almost always willing to help. They may even need your product or service.

You should start by contacting your friends and family members and telling them that you're in a new business or career and that you want to share the news with them. This interested audience gives you the perfect opportunity to test your presentation skills.

A key statement you can use in this situation is "Because I value your judgment, I was hoping you'd give me your opinion." This statement is bound to make them feel important and be even more willing to help you.

After you've contacted all your family members and close friends, you can move on to acquaintances. Here's a list to get you started:

▲ Your parents.
▲ Your grandparents.
▲ Your siblings.
▲ Your aunts, uncles, and cousins.
▲ Your coworkers.
▲ Members of your sports team.
▲ Fellow churchgoers.
▲ Parents of your children's friends.
▲ Your neighbors.
▲ Your hairstylist.
▲ Your friends.
▲ Members of business or civic groups you belong to.
▲ Your mechanic.
▲ Grocery store cashiers.
▲ Your drycleaner.
▲ Your pest-control person.
▲ Your pet's veterinarian.
▲ Your doctor.
▲ Your dentist.
▲ Your lawyer.
▲ Your accountant.
▲ Your kids' teachers.
▲ Your teachers.
▲ Your kids' coaches.
▲ People you used to date.
▲ Tellers at your bank.
▲ Fraternity or sorority friends.
▲ Your kids' babysitters.
▲ Your spouse's friends.

If approached properly, most people are willing to give you advice or opinions. If your friends and relatives are not good candidates for your offering, contact them anyway. In prospecting, you should never assume that someone can't help you build your business. They may not be prospects themselves, but they may know others who are. Don't ever be afraid to ask for a referral. If you ask the right questions, people can advise you into a great connection with a big client.

Don't forget about your current business contacts. Whether or not you're new to selling, you've probably been involved in some sort of business. Even if you're just out of school, you've probably held part-time jobs throughout your school career. Business contacts can be easier to talk with than some social contacts because business contacts prospect all the time, too.

Pay attention to the e-mails you get from your business associates. You may have received their e-mail as part of a group of recipients, and one of those people may be a prospective client for you. Getting a new lead may be as simple as having the person who sent you the message give you those other people's phone numbers so you can contact them. When you receive a group e-mail from a business contact, you may be able to see the e-mail addresses of all the recipients. If you want to try prospecting with them, you should call the person who sent the e-mail and see whether the people you want to contact would mind if you contacted them. Without permission, you may make both parties irate.

To avoid showing all your recipients each others' e-mail addresses, you should put all the recipients' e-mail addresses in the blind carbon copy (BCC) field instead of the To or CC field. This prevents recipients from seeing the other addresses.

5.2.6 The Yellow Pages and Toll-Free Directories

If you sell a product or service that is appropriate for businesses, you can look through your local Yellow Pages. Businesses invest their money in listings because they're serious about being in business. Their listings also tells you that they're serious about staying in business. If your product or service can bring in more business or efficiency, those companies may be interested.

To broaden your field of prospects, you can check out a toll-free directory. These directories list businesses by company, number, and type of industry, regardless of long-distance carrier.

5.2.7 Your Colleagues and Other Professionals

Getting advice from veterans in your field is a wise move—no matter how extensive your experience. You should look for a **mentor**—someone who has more experience than you, an interest in what you're doing, and a willingness to guide your actions. A mentor can help you overcome obstacles he or she faced and let you learn from his or her experience.

If you're new to sales, your company may partner you up with one of its veteran salespeople as a mentor for a brief training period. You can learn from the successes and failures of experienced professionals. At the same time, a mentoring program gives recognition to these veterans for their knowledge and expertise. If your company doesn't have an organized mentoring program, you might want to talk to your manager to see if you can be paired with someone. Your interest in learning and becoming the best salesperson you can be will most certainly be looked upon favorably.

Another source to contact is the Service Corps of Retired Executives (SCORE). SCORE has an excellent reputation for matching people new in a field with retired or semi-retired professionals from similar fields. SCORE is a U.S. government program that has contact offices in most major metropolitan areas. The experience that the helpful people of SCORE can provide is exceptional, but you must be open to discovery. Although some of their experiences may not apply to your current marketplace, the information available through SCORE can be like a life jacket thrown to you as you flounder in the middle of the ocean. If SCORE doesn't have an office in your area, keep an eye out for a mentor in your community who can offer similar assistance.

You can hire an advertising agency and a public relations firm to handle much of your market awareness and prospecting for you. Agency assistance varies: An agency can take on everything for your business, or it can help you with occasional, one-shot promotional ideas. The fees agencies charge for their assistance differ around the country, so be sure to do your homework when researching agencies. You need to ask the agencies to send you information on what they've done for other businesses, and you should always check out the people who give testimonials and references for a business.

You can also get involved in clubs or organizations for business professionals and prospects. You can find excellent opportunities in sales and marketing clubs and at functions held by chambers of commerce.

Another source is other salespeople. Talking to salespeople you buy from is one of the most overlooked prospecting strategies. Other companies send you highly knowledgeable, professional salespeople who know many people. Because they're in noncompeting businesses, you should talk to them about leads. At the very least, you should ask them to keep you in mind the next time they call on their customers. Any extra sets of eyes that are out there looking for prospects on your behalf are of tremendous value, especially when your only investment is likely to be returning the favor sometime down the road.

Writing a thank-you note to another company for its excellent service is another prospecting method. Many businesspeople publish or display these letters in their places of business or on their marketing literature. Another purchasing agent or department might notice the letter and remember your name when they need the services you offer.

5.2.8 The Newspaper

One of the greatest prospecting tools around can be delivered to your doorstep for under a dollar a day in most areas: the newspaper. You can also access most newspapers online.

Unless you do business internationally, you'll probably want to stick to the local news, business, and announcements sections. For most salespeople, the most beneficial portion of the paper is the parts written about average citizens. Learning how to read a newspaper for leads takes only a few days of practice. When you get started, you'll be amazed at the number of leads you used to glance over. Be open to the possibilities. Here are two ideas of how to find prospects through the newspaper:

▲ Review the birth section to find new mothers and fathers. People having babies need more insurance, bigger homes, minivans, delivery services, and diapers.

▲ Check out the real estate section for people selling their homes. Families who are moving into new homes may need garage door openers, security systems, ceiling fans, homeowner's insurance, and landscaping.

SELF-CHECK

1. Outline the sources for prospecting and describe how you could use each one.

5.3 Qualifying a Prospect

At the qualification stage in the selling cycle, you've found your prospect, made an initial contact, and gotten an appointment. The prospect has shown a certain level of interest in your product, service, or offering. You may have also found the decision maker for the purchase. Now you need to determine whether your prospect needs your product and confirm that the client has the power to make the decision to buy. Both of those factors must be present in order for you to consider this person a qualified buyer. If they are not, you need to politely withdraw and move on to another potential client.

If you present to and trying to close an unqualified buyer, you're wasting the client's time and allowing your confidence to take a hit, although you are getting in a little practice with your presentation. This step in the selling cycle is particularly important in situations such as these:

▲ When you don't have a relationship with your prospect to know whether he or she needs your product or service.

▲ When the person needs to make a financial or personal commitment in order to proceed.

What circumstances would keep someone from being able to make a commitment? For a financial commitment, the prospect needs to have the money or some credit to draw on. If it's a personal commitment, the client may need to check with someone else, such as a spouse. You need to know your prospect's circumstances before you go into a full-fledged presentation and closing.

Using the qualifying step in the selling sequence is the single greatest factor separating those who win most often in their selling presentations from those who don't. Statistics from surveys of more than 250,000 sales professionals show that the biggest gap between six-figure-income earners and those averaging around $25,000 per year is their skill in qualifying.[1] All it takes is asking the right questions.

5.3.1 Following the NEADS Formula

Before we examine how to form and ask the right questions, let's take a look at a simple formula for qualifying prospective clients. **NEADS** is an acronym for now, enjoy, alter, decision, and solutions. Each of the letters represents an aspect of a prospect's needs. Let's examine each area:

▲ **Now:** Generally, average consumers don't make drastic changes in their buying habits. Most people are creatures of habit. If you know what your prospect has now, you have an understanding of that person and that person's desires and needs in the future. Because past experiences often dictate future decisions, you need to explore your customers' past experiences. You need to know what customers have now in order to determine future buying decisions.

▲ **Enjoy:** You need to know what your customers enjoy about what they have now. What were their major motivations for getting involved with a specific product or service? To discover what your customer enjoys, you need to structure your questions so you can discover the customer's past. The answer is probably what the customer wants again.

▲ **Alter:** Although most people are creatures of habit, they always strive to achieve more benefit, more satisfaction, and more comfort. A customer's normal urge to improve his or her present condition is why you want to develop questions to find out what the customer would like to change. What would your customer like to alter or improve about what he or she has now? When you know a customer's answer to that question, you can structure your presentations to show how your company can provide the desired changes.

▲ **Decision:** Specifically, you need to know who will be making the final decision on the sale. You should never assume anything about your customers. A customer may be scouting or researching and planning to consult another person when it's time to make the final decision. So you need to ask qualifying questions to discover whether the prospect is the decision maker. You need to be equally enthusiastic to everyone you meet. A person who is not the decision maker can be an influencer or a champion of your cause.

▲ **Solutions:** As a salesperson, you're in the business of creating solutions. You find out what your prospects need, and then you develop a solution. In most cases, the solution is that your customer owns the benefits of your products or services. You serve customers by finding out what they need and then creating the right solutions. When you do this, you create a win–win relationship where people want to do business with your company and they get the products or services they need. They give you business and, in turn, you both grow and prosper.

5.3.2 Questioning Your Way to Success

Discovering a customer's needs naturally involves asking questions and actively listening to the customer's responses. In Chapter 4, you learned tips on listening. Now let's take a look at how to phrase the right questions.

Asking questions is not as easy as it may first appear. You want to know perceived needs, and you also want to obtain the information in a way that does not irritate or alienate the other person and helps that person better understand his or her own needs. Research indicates that obtaining information through questioning is most important in complex sales situations, such as in consultative and relationships.[2]

Questions may be classified as closed ended or open ended. **Closed-ended** questions, also known as alternate-of-choice questions, can be answered with a simple "yes" or "no" or by selecting from a list of responses. This strategy involves giving a prospect two acceptable suggestions from which to choose. It's most often used for calendar events, such as appointments and delivery dates. Here are some simple examples:

▲ "I can arrange my schedule so we can visit on Thursday at 3:00 p.m., or would Friday at 11:00 a.m. be better?" Either answer confirms that you have an appointment.

▲ "This product comes in 55-gallon containers and 35-gallon containers. Which would you prefer?" No matter which container your prospect chooses, a choice is made to take one.

▲ "We'll have our delivery truck at your home on Monday at 9:00 a.m. sharp. Or would 2:00 p.m. be more convenient?" Whichever option your prospect chooses, you've nailed down the delivery.

You can also use closed-ended questions when you want to focus or limit the conversation to certain points. These questions are particularly effective in surveys: The market researchers are seeking particular information, not general answers, so they build the questions such that prospects are limited in their responses.

Open-ended questions can be answered with a simple "yes" or "no" and used to identify a topic. Here's an example: "How are the new tax laws affecting your decision regarding the purchase of fleet cars for your salespeople?" You're most likely to ask these questions when discovering information about an opportunity.

Several additional types of questions may be used in the discovery process:

▲ **Permission questions:** This closed-ended questioning technique involves asking the other person's permission to ask questions or to probe further into a subject (e.g., "May I ask you a few questions about your current shipping process?"). It is designed to put the other person at ease and to observe social courtesies.

▲ **Fact-finding questions:** These questions focus on factual information about the business, the person, and the current situation. Factual information might include a question such as: "Who is your current supplier of sutures?" A follow-up question about the client's current situation might be "Do you have a just-in-time arrangement with Ethicon in supplying sutures?"

▲ **Feeling-finding questions:** These are open-ended questions that try to uncover the client's feelings about a situation and the potential consequences of the situation. These inquiries help determine the importance of the client's need. Two examples are "How do you feel about your current inventory levels in sutures?" and "What effect does this level of inventory have on your operating costs?"

▲ **Checking questions:** At this point, the salesperson is checking to see if he or she understands exactly what the client has said and to get the client's agreement concerning the statement. An example is "If I understand you correctly, you have said that you are happy with the quality of your current supplier but feel that you may be able to get the same quality of service at a lower price from another supplier. Is that accurate?"

Discovering a customer's needs usually requires asking a series of questions. This process generally begins with a permission question and open-ended questions, followed by fact-finding and feeling-finding questions and checking questions. The prospect needs to share certain information in order for you to know what to tell the person about your product. Your goal in qualifying is to involve the prospect in an educational experience in which learning occurs through the use of questions. Each question builds on the answers to the previous ones.

Part of qualifying prospects includes knowing the right questions to ask. But questioning is a technique you use throughout the selling cycle. You shouldn't be afraid to use these strategies when you're presenting, addressing customer concerns, and closing as well.

You can use questions to acknowledge or confirm a statement your prospect made that is important to your final request and the decision you want your listener to make. For instance, a prospect may tell you that gasoline mileage is an important consideration in buying a new car. When you're getting ready to ask the prospect for a final decision, you could include a similar question to this: "Didn't you say that fuel economy was your primary concern?" Such a question starts the prospect thinking "yes," which is the momentum you need to encourage a final decision. This "yes" momentum is a good step in the decision of a sale. The idea is to keep the prospect agreeing to aspects favorable for the sale. The process is like a flowchart, with the prospect following where you want to lead. In addition, the prospect will have enough information at the end to make an informed decision.

One of the most popular questioning techniques is called the **tie-down technique.** This technique involves making a statement and then asking for agreement by adding a question to the end of it. Here are some of the most effective tie-downs:

- ▲ **Isn't it?** For example, "It's a great day for golf, isn't it?"
- ▲ **Doesn't it?** For example, "Jet-skiing at the lake this weekend sounds like fun, doesn't it?"
- ▲ **Hasn't he (hasn't she or haven't they)?** For example, "The previous homeowner has done a great job with the landscaping, hasn't she?"
- ▲ **Don't you?** For example, "Cleaning up the area where our children play is important, don't you think?"
- ▲ **Didn't you?** For example, "You had a great time the last time we went hiking, didn't you?"
- ▲ **Shouldn't we?** For example, "We should come here for dinner more often, shouldn't we, honey?"
- ▲ **Couldn't we?** For example, "We could let the children organize the games for the neighborhood picnic, couldn't we?"

Remember that the goal of using tie-downs is to get your prospect thinking in the affirmative about the subject you've just tied down. While the prospect is agreeing with you, you can confidently bring up the subject for commitment.

Before you ask any question, you need to keep in mind that in order to sell or persuade, you need to make the other person feel important and knowledgeable.

You should never ask a question your listener cannot answer. If you tell your prospects specifically the information you need, they can give it to you. But if you assume that they know the information, and they don't, you embarrass them.

You should also use the following important questioning techniques:

▲ Take notes and refer to this information repeatedly. This helps direct future efforts.

▲ Make comments on the facts and figures provided by your customers. Compliment them on their knowledge.

▲ Wait to discuss prices until you believe you have satisfied the client's needs and concerns.

▲ Heed both verbal and nonverbal responses. Be aware of a customer's posture, dress, and surroundings.

▲ Build on the answers. Don't assume anything.

▲ Relieve any tension that your questions create. If you notice tension, get the prospect thinking about something else. A common way is to appear ready to leave if a potential client has not gone ahead with a purchase. This usually causes a prospect to relax and start thinking about what he or she will do after your leave.

▲ Use nonthreatening language and a sympathetic tone. Use lay terms or define any lingo necessary to use in your presentation.

▲ Let your prospects know you'll follow up. Leave the door open for further discussion.

SELF-CHECK

1. Explain the NEADS formula and how to use it in qualifying a prospect.
2. Discuss the importance of asking questions and describe how to use them effectively.

5.4 Organizing Your Prospect Information

You've examined how to research for sales calls as well as sources for finding prospects. When you have the information, how do you organize it? This section provides some suggestions for organizing your prospect information.

5.4.1 An Organized Workspace

One of the main causes of wasted time and lost income is disorganized office space. Having a clear working environment clears your mind—you can focus on one task at a time—and enables you to be an effective salesperson. So where do you start? Try these tips:

▲ **Clear everything off your desk:** Then either file or discard paperwork.

▲ **Keep everything except your most pressing tasks out of sight:** Keep everything you need to accomplish the immediate tasks somewhere nearby (in a place you'll remember). This way, you don't waste time searching for the information.

▲ **Designate a specific place for every item you use regularly:** Then make sure you always use that place.

▲ **If you suffer innumerable interruptions, close your door:** If you don't have a door, try earplugs or a headset attached to an MP3 player to isolate yourself.

▲ **Develop your ability to focus on your work:** Let your coworkers or family members know that sometimes they simply cannot interrupt you.

▲ **Don't answer your telephone if you need uninterrupted time:** Let voice mail be your receptionist for a while.

▲ **Make yourself less accessible:** If needed, set up a specific time of day for your associates to freely walk into your office. Make all other times off-limits.

5.4.2 Technological Tools

Some people may still find their giant old wheels of names and addresses useful and convenient. If you're just starting out in developing an organization system, however, you might prefer the advantages of technological tools. You might need to spend some time upfront learning how to use these tools, but the end result may be worthwhile for you. If you can think of a task that needs to be handled, there is likely a device that has been invented to handle it.

Here are some tools that can help organize information. As you read about these tools, remember to be careful about trying to use too many technological gadgets. You want to simplify your organization, not add additional work to manage your equipment.

Address Book and Contact Management Software

Your business needs may be simple: You might just need to maintain only name, address, and telephone contact information on each client. If so, you can get by with nearly any simple address book, such as the ones found in Microsoft Outlook or Lotus Notes. But if you need to track each contact with your clients and have those contacts coordinate with your calendar, using **contact management software** makes more sense. Contact management software works with a database of information about your present and future clients. You can include any information you think is relevant, including

▲ Names (make sure to get the spelling correct).

▲ Company names.

▲ Addresses.

▲ Various phone numbers.

▲ E-mail addresses.

▲ Assistants' or secretaries' names.

▲ Best times of day to reach each client.

▲ Dates, locations, and times of appointments.

▲ Notes on each conversation with a client.

▲ Descriptions of correspondences sent.

▲ Products or services ordered.

▲ Delivery dates.

▲ Challenges that have arisen and how you've overcome them.

▲ Future growth plans for the company or division.

▲ Birth dates.

▲ How long clients have been with their companies.

▲ Hobbies (to establish common ground).

▲ Where clients took their last vacations.

With contact management software, the information is quickly and easily accessible or alterable as your relationship with each client evolves. Some contact management programs also allow you to link to word processing systems and generate letters or process orders for clients. The name and address information for clients can be automatically placed in the letter.

Company Software

Your company may want you to use a certain software program that's being used by the whole sales team. Many such programs provide reporting information or sales analysis information for management so they can analyze efficiency. You may want or even be required to use this type of program. If that's the case, you should take advantage of whatever training on the software is available.

Personal Digital Assistants

A personal digital assistant (PDA) is almost as small as a mobile phone and works like a computer. (We can expect PDAs to continue decreasing in size.) It has a screen display and works on a touchpad system. Price ranges from about $130 up to around $600, depending on the PDA's functionality.

PDAs are useful for maintaining contact lists, merging personal and business calendars into one organized program, and getting connected to the Internet for current information. Most PDAs are compatible with many software programs.

You can even check your e-mail, download calendar changes from the PDA to your computer, and download music from the Internet.

The downside of PDAs is that you primarily enter data by using a stylus, which means you hunt and peck on a keyboard display. However, some PDAs can be plugged into a standard keyboard for easy data entry.

Mobile Phones and Smart Phones

Mobile phones allow you to be virtually anywhere and still make necessary phone calls. Many also allow you to receive e-mail and access the Internet for information. These services are available for a fee, and the cost can vary widely, depending on the types of service you need.

Business Card Scanners

If you're like most other salespeople, you collect a lot of business cards. Then you have to manually enter each card's information into some sort of program in order to keep the information accessible. A business card scanner can handle that step of organizing your information. It allows you to insert a business card and have the information transferred into your software program.

5.4.3 Organization in Contacting Prospects

Chapter 1 discusses the five major ways to contact your prospects: by the person-to-person approach, telemarketing, direct mail, or e-mail and the Internet. Most professional salespeople integrate all five methods into an effective prospecting strategy. For some people, some methods work better than others. However, different situations call for different strategies, so you need to be well versed in how to handle each. As you gain experience in prospecting, you'll figure out which methods work best for you and at which times. Let's look at these approaches and how to manage them.

Person-to-Person Sales

The face-to-face approach to sales is almost always the best method, but it's also the most time intensive. It can be physically exhausting as well. You should therefore make the most of your travels and get vital information from any available source.

Your first contact may be a receptionist. These people can be powerhouses who help you either eliminate a company as a prospect or advance your chances of obtaining an appointment for making your presentation with the decision maker. It's important to treat receptionists and secretaries with the respect they deserve. Their time is valuable.

When you engage in face-to-face prospecting with decision makers, you need to make the time count. You are taking valuable time out of the busy schedules of important people. This is your opportunity to show them how they can benefit from your product or service. You need to be prepared and get to the point. This is also an important aspect in building clients' trust in your professionalism.

Telemarketing

You may feel like telemarketing calls are intrusions or interruptions in your daily life. The common reaction to a telemarketing call is to say, "No, thanks" and then quickly hang up. So if that's your response to most telemarketers, you probably wonder why businesses keep using telemarketing. The reason is that telemarketers can reach more potential users of a company's product or service in one hour than most salespeople working face-to-face can meet in a week. Plus, telemarketers don't have to travel from one location to the next; they just dial the next few digits.

Salespeople who use telemarketing must be emotionally able to face frequent rejection. One successful method telemarketers use is the **survey approach,** which is a way to establish rapport and qualify a prospect. By using a survey approach, you ask questions to get the person you called to talk to you instead of just trying to set appointments right away. A certain amount of rapport building needs to take place with every new contact. When you show concern for the person's time, his needs, and his situation, the prospect feels important. People want to be involved in the phone calls they receive. That's why you need to script your call so that it's courteous and filled with brief questions that your prospect can answer easily. People have to decide whether they like you before they'll consider doing business with you. The survey method is a simple, nonthreatening way of doing exactly that.

When you're using the survey method in your telemarketing calls, you need to create a brief but effective survey. The survey needs to provide you information about whether to pursue a contact as a customer. It also needs to pique a prospect's curiosity about your product or service. Your goal is to get the person talking. The more the person talks, the more information you'll gather that may point you toward or away from future contact with him.

You should stick with five or fewer questions. And you should always tell the person you're talking to that the firm you represent has asked you to conduct a quick survey and tell him that you need his help. If he says it's a bad time for him, acknowledge the bad timing, apologize, and try to get an appointment for a better time to call. Unless the person appears very interested in what you're saying, the call should take no more than two minutes.

Your questions should generate answers that tell you whether the person you've called may potentially qualify as a good client.

Direct Mail

If you use mail as your primary method of prospecting, you need to choose your mailing list carefully. Mailing is a great way to prospect, but mail sent to the

> ## FOR EXAMPLE
>
> ### Asking the Right Questions
>
> Sarah operates a diaper service, and her responsibilities include sales. She discovered that a new housing development was quickly filling with new homeowners. Sarah was able to obtain the telephone numbers for the households. During a quick phone call to each home, she asked only a few questions. Her purpose was to determine whether the family had babies in diapers. If the answer was yes, she followed up with information on her diaper service. If no, she asked for a referral. She was able to obtain several new customers this way.
>
> Remember that you have two possible goals for a telemarketing call:
>
> ▲ To arrange a time for a face-to-face meeting.
> ▲ To get permission to send information via mail or e-mail and make another brief follow-up call.

wrong list of people is a tremendous waste of your time, money, and effort. It's easy to get rid of a piece of paper that arrives amid a stack of other papers.

Instead of sending a piece of mail that describes your product or service, you can mail a single-page introductory letter, indicating that you'll be calling on a certain date and time. You may want to include your photograph on the letterhead or on a magnet or other enclosed novelty item.

Whatever you send in the mail, you need to be certain that it includes your Web site address and your e-mail address. Today, most people are likely to check you out by visiting your Web site to determine if it's worth their time to talk with you in person. Or, if the purpose of the mailing is to generate sales, you should let the recipients know whether they can order online at any time.

E-mail and Internet

You can handle e-mail prospecting in two ways. One is to purchase an **opt-in e-mail list** from a list broker (see Section 5.2.4) and send an e-mail message to people who express interest in your type of product or service. The other way is to search for the e-mail address of a consumer or purchasing agent through an online directory or corporate Web site and mail a very specific, customized e-mail message. In either case, you want to use your e-mail message like the introductory letter: Introduce yourself, your company, and the benefits your product provides to the recipient. With an opt-in list, you might wrap up your letter with a call to action, such as "Reply to this e-mail within 24 hours, and we'll have a specific proposal to you by Friday of this week." Or, in a custom e-mail, you could use the survey approach and tell the recipient that you'll call within 48 hours to ask two quick questions.

Sending an e-mail that looks like an advertisement is not as effective as sending a letter. Your goal with e-mail is to make a personal connection, pique the recipient's interest, and explain how to learn more.

SELF-CHECK

1. Discuss the importance of organizing prospect information.
2. Describe the tools that are useful in organizing prospect information.
3. Describe the organization aspects of the four approaches in contacting prospects.

5.5 Developing a Prospecting and Sales Forecasting Plan

You've read about the importance of knowing how and where to find customers. This section examines key elements in predicting how much they will buy. Developing a prospecting and sales forecasting plan is particularly useful. A key to a successful plan, however, is being as accurate as possible. Inaccurate demand predictions can have disastrous effects on profitability.

It is incredibly important to be able to measure the size of market opportunities. Your research to find this measurement may or may not be extensive, depending on the audience you want to reach, but you still need an understanding of key elements.

FOR EXAMPLE

Losing Big

Hewlett-Packard was unable to predict the proper mix of products demanded by its customers for two quarters in a row. Demand for low-end printers and workstations was high, and demand for commercial computers was low. As a result, earnings were 14 percent lower than analysts expected. The stock market was dismayed with Hewlett-Packard's forecasting problems and knocked the company's stock down 5 percent in one day.

Sales forecasting and forecasting for prospects are concerned with predicting future levels of demand. These projections are vital for budgeting and planning purposes. For new products, you can use a few simple routines. In the absence of past sales, you have to be more creative in coming up with predictions of the future.

5.5.1 Qualitative Methods

Sales forecasts for new products are often based on executive judgments, sales force projections, surveys, and market tests. These **qualitative methods** are based on interpretations of business conditions by executives and salespeople.

A favorite forecasting technique for new and existing products is the **sales force composite method.** With this procedure, salespeople project volume for their customers. These projections are combined and reviewed at higher management levels. A territory estimate is often derived based on demand estimates for each of the largest customers. Estimates are also compiled for the remainder of the customers as a group and then for new prospects. This technique is favored by industrial concerns because they have a limited number of customers, and salespeople are in a good position to assess customers' needs.

The **jury of executive opinion** technique involves soliciting the judgment of a group of experienced managers to give sales estimates for proposed and current products. This method has two main advantages:

▲ It is fast.
▲ It allows the inclusion of many subjective factors, such as competition, economic climate, weather, and union activity.

The continued popularity of the jury of executive opinion method shows that most managers prefer their own judgment to other less well-known statistical forecasting procedures. However, available evidence does not suggest that the jury of executive opinion method leads to more accurate forecasting. Perhaps the main problem with this method is that it is based on experience, and it is difficult to teach someone how to use this method for forecasting.

5.5.2 Data Needed in Order to Use Qualitative Methods

If you are asked to contribute to a prospecting and sales forecasting plan, you first need to examine your market potential—an estimate of maximum demand in a time period, based on the number of potential users and their purchase rate. Consider, for instance, the U.S. market potential for DVD players. The potential could be defined as the total number of households with television sets, based on typical purchases of one unit per family. The market reflects a potential more than actual sales for two reasons:

▲ It takes time to convince the people targeted to buy discretionary items such as DVD players.

▲ Some of these people just can't afford to buy these items.

Next, you need to examine the company sales potential. This is a portion of total industry demand and the maximum amount a firm can sell in a time period, under ideal conditions. The ratio of company sales to industry sales is a measure of the market share of the organization. You or your management might be asked to estimate current values for market and company potential for products assigned to your care. Completing this assignment can be tricky because the number of users and the purchase rate change over time. In addition, price declines, industry promotions, and changing economic conditions can also influence the size of the market. Besides measuring current levels of demand, you have to forecast into the future.

All estimates of potential are based on two key components:

▲ The number of possible users of the product.

▲ The maximum expected purchase rate.

Sometimes you can get estimates of these numbers from trade associations or commercial research associations, but you have to come up with your own potential figures. You may even have to break down these figures by geographical area, industry, and customer type.

One way to estimate the number of buyers is to rely on secondary sources. A wide variety of commercial data are available that provide the potential number of buyers, size of firms, age of consumers, income levels, and locations. Dun's Marketing Services and *Sales & Marketing Management* magazine sell these types of data in electronic form, for use with personal computers. You can also access potential data banks through computer networks for a fee. Large firms often have their own data banks that can be mined for potential information.

You can usually derive purchase rates from trade organizations or government publications. For existing products, you can use the ratio of current sales to the number of households or sales per person. You can obtain these ratios from trade publications such as those from The Conference Board, or you can calculate them from published data. For example, you could derive average demand per household by dividing total industry sales for an area by the number of households. In the case of new products, you might estimate conversion rates from experience with other items. For example, if a similar product was sold to 4 percent of U.S. households during the first year, you could apply that rate to obtain demand estimates for your new product.

Market potentials for consumer goods are usually estimated by constructing indexes from basic economic data. One of the most popular multifactor indexes of area demand is the **Buying Power Index (BPI)**, published each year by *Sales*

Figure 5-1

Data Used to Calculate Buying Power Index

	2004 Effective Buying Income		2004 Total Retail Sales		2004 Estimated Total Population		Buying Power Index
	Amount ($000,000)	Percentage of United States	Amount ($000,000)	Percentage of United States	Amount ($000,000)	Percentage of United States	
Total U.S.	$5,466,880	100.0%	$3,906,482	100.0%	$292,936	100.0%	100.0
Atlanta Metro	$99,691	1.824%	$69,071	1.768%	$4,704	1.606%	1.7636

CBSAs.

& Marketing Management magazine. This index combines estimates of population, income, and retail sales to give a composite indicator of consumer demand in 922 geographic areas known as **core-based statistical areas (CBSAs).** CBSAs are subdivided into either metropolitan or micropolitan statistical areas. See Figure 5-1 for an example.

Business market potential can be built up from data made available through the U.S. Census of Manufacturers. The Census of Manufacturers, which is available every five years, combines businesses into **North American Industry Classification System (NAICS)** codes according to products produced or operations performed. The first step in estimating potentials from census data is to identify all the NAICS codes that make use of a particular product or service. This is usually accomplished by doing the following:

▲ Selecting industries that are likely customers.
▲ Using judgment to pick codes from the NAICS manual.
▲ Running surveys of different types of firms to see where products are employed.

Next, it's important to select an appropriate database for estimating the amount of the product that will be used by each NAICS code.

Where sales are influenced by basic changes in the economy, **leading indicators** can be useful guides in preparing sales forecasts. The idea is to find a factor series:

▲ That is closely related to company sales.
▲ For which statistics are available several months in advance.

Changes in the factor can then be used to predict sales directly, or the factor can be combined with other variables in a forecasting model. For example, General

FOR EXAMPLE

Calculating Company Potential

The sales team for a food machinery manufacturer reviewed past sales data to determine the relationship between the number of its machines in use and the number of production workers in a particular industry. The team found that

▲ 24 machines were used for every 1,000 grain-milling employees.

▲ 15 machines were used for every 1,000 bakery workers.

▲ 3 machines were used for every 1,000 beverage workers.

The team then enlisted data from the current Census of Manufacturers, showing that North Carolina actually had 811 grain-milling workers. The team calculated that if 24 machines were used per 1,000 workers, the market potential would be 19.5 machines. Similar calculations for other codes yielded a total market potential of about 165 machines for the state of North Carolina. The potential built up for North Carolina was then added to estimates derived for other states to yield national figures.

These figures were converted into annual measures of market potential by adjusting for the average life of the machines. If the machines lasted an average of 10 years, then approximately 10 percent of the North Carolina potential of 165 units, or 16 machines, would be replaced each year. The team multiplied annual demand potential by the firm's current market share to derive estimates of company potential. See Figure 5-2.

Figure 5-2

Estimating the Market Potential for Food Machinery in North Carolina

NAIC Code	Industry	(1) Production Employees[a]	(2) Number of Machines Used per 1000 Workers[b]	Market Potential (1 × 2)/1000
3112	Grain milling	811	24	19.5
312	Tobacco mfg.	9,328	15	139.9
3121	Beverages	1,757	3	5.3
				164.7

[a]The production employee data are from the *1997 Economic Census of Manufacturing, Geographic Area Series, North Carolina*, p. NC8. The codes are the new NAIC codes.
[b]Estimated by manufacturer from past sales data.

Electric has found that sales of dishwashers are closely related to the number of housing starts several months earlier. Therefore, if GE observes a 4 percent increase in housing starts in California, it can expect demand for dishwashers to increase by about 4 percent two months later.

Obviously, the key issue is finding indicators that have forecasting value for your products. Some of the most useful leading indicators include prices of common stocks, new orders for durable goods, new building permits, contracts and orders for plant and equipment, and changes in consumer installment debt.

Perhaps the greatest contribution of leading indicators is their ability to predict turns in sales trends. If sales have been increasing, for example, leading indicators may indicate a leveling off of sales or a decline. Leading indicators are sensitive to changes in the business environment, and they often signal turns in the economy months before those turns actually occur.

5.5.2 Quantitative Techniques

Quantitative techniques are procedures based on the use of historical data.

Before reviewing data-based forecasting techniques, it's important to understand how seasonal factors influence predictions of the future. Sales forecasts are often prepared monthly or quarterly, and seasonal factors are frequently responsible for many short-run changes in volume. What appears to be a good forecast, therefore, may turn out to be a poor one because of the failure to consider seasonal factors. When historical sales figures are used in forecasting, the accuracy of predictions can often be improved by making adjustments to eliminate seasonal effects.

The first step in seasonally adjusting a time series is to collect sales figures for the past several years. Next, sales for months or quarters are averaged across years to build a seasonal index. For example, four years of quarterly sales could be averaged to give a rough indication of seasonal effects. The quarterly averages are then divided by sales for all quarters to give seasonal index numbers.

You need to keep in mind two facts about seasonal adjustments:

▲ Seasonal adjustments are widely used in business.
▲ Seasonal adjustments reduce forecasting errors.

Most initial sales forecasts today are prepared with computer programs. A recent survey of 207 firms revealed that 76 percent of the companies allowed managers to make adjustments to computer-generated forecasts by using judgmental procedures.[3] Perhaps a major reason for using the "judgmental procedures" is that most quantitative forecasting does a very poor job of telling managers when sales are going to change direction. In any case, firms using quantitative methods usually rely on commercial software packages. Such a program must work for the time series you plan to predict. You should look for a program that can do the following:

▲ Plot data.
▲ Seasonally adjust data.
▲ Measure the percentage of forecasting errors.

Using any search engine on the Internet can lead you to plenty of forecasting software alternatives. Many are offered online with no software installation required.

When you have selected a forecasting program, you need to remember that simple procedures often have lower forecasting errors compared with more complex methods. This suggests that you should start with the basic procedures and move on to more complex models only when you need them. It is rare that one technique is best in all situations, so you might want to base your predictions on the average of several methods to help reduce forecasting error.

Finally, you must select techniques that you can sell to management. If managers cannot understand how forecasts are prepared, they are likely to reject the techniques in favor of their own judgmental forecasting methods.

SELF-CHECK

1. Discuss why developing a prospecting and sales forecasting plan is important.
2. Describe the tools you could use in developing this plan.

SUMMARY

Prospecting is the first step in the sales cycle, and it is particularly important for new sales professionals. The sources for finding prospects are numerous, and you need to learn which are the most effective to use for selling your product or service. To uncover a prospect's needs for your product or service, you need to develop skills in qualifying the prospect. This might involve extensive research or merely posing a simple question to the prospect. This chapter examines suggestions for posing the right questions and ways to organize the information you obtain. It also reviews key aspects in developing a prospecting and sales forecasting plan.

KEY TERMS

Alternate of choice questioning	A strategy used to involve prospects by presenting two acceptable suggestions for the client's choice.
Buying Power Index (BPI)	The multifactor index of area demand, which is published each year by *Sales & Marketing Management* magazine.
Closed-ended questions	Questions to be answered with a simple "yes" or "no" response or by selecting from a list of responses. Also known as alternate-of-choice questions.
Contact management software	Software that works with a database of information to organize information about present and future clients.
Core Based Statistical Areas (CBSAs)	922 geographic areas used by *Sales & Marketing Management* magazine in its Buying Power Index
Jury of executive opinion technique	A forecasting technique that involves soliciting the judgment of a group of experienced managers to give sales estimates for proposed and current products.
Leading indicators	A tool used in forecasting that is particularly useful in predicting changes in sales trends. Examples of leading indicators include prices of common stocks, new orders for durable goods, new building permits, contracts and orders for plant and equipment, and changes in consumer installment debt.
List broker	An individual or a company that sorts through lists, sometimes separating them into demographic needs, and offers these lists for sale.
Mentor	A person who has experience in a specific field of endeavor who serves as a guide for a less experienced person.
NEADS	An acronym for now, enjoy, alter, decision, and solutions, with each letter representing an aspect of a prospect's needs.
North American Industry Classification System (NAICS)	Codes used by the Census of Manufacturers to combine businesses according to products produced to operations performed

Open-ended questions   Questions to be answered with a simple "yes" or "no" response that are used to identify a topic.

Opt-in e-mail lists   Lists of people who have agreed to have information about certain things they're interested in sent to them via e-mail

Prospecting   The search for people who will buy products or services.

Qualitative methods   Forecasting techniques focused on subjective methods that are based on interpretations of business conditions by executives and salespeople.

Quantitative techniques   Forecasting procedures that are based on the use of historical data.

Sales force composite method   A forecasting procedure in which salespeople project volume for their customers.

Sales forecasting   The predication of future levels of demand for a product.

Survey approach   A telemarketing method you can use to establish rapport and qualify a prospect.

Tie-down technique   A technique that involves making a statement and then asking for agreement by adding a question to the end.

ASSESS YOUR UNDERSTANDING

Go to www.wiley.com/college/hopkins to evaluate your knowledge of prospecting. *Measure your learning by comparing pre-test and post-test results.*

Summary Questions

1. The first step in the selling cycle is called prospecting. True or false?
2. New salespeople should devote 25 percent of their time to prospecting. True or false?
3. Which of the following is a source for prospecting?
   (a) a chamber of commerce
   (b) your current customers
   (c) the newspaper
   (d) all of the above
4. You should give your sales presentation to anyone who will listen. True or false?
5. Part of qualifying prospects includes knowing the right questions to ask. True or false?
6. One of the main causes of wasted time and lost income is disorganization of office space. True or false?
7. The survey approach in telemarketing is a way to establish rapport and quickly qualify a prospect. True or false?
8. In developing a prospecting and sales forecasting plan, you should think big and include as many prospects and sales as you can. True or false?
9. Procedures used in sales forecasting that are based on use of historical data are referred to as:
   (a) qualitative methods.
   (b) quantitative techniques.
   (c) leading indicators.
   (d) company sales potential.

Applying This Chapter

1. Define **prospecting** and discuss its importance to a salesperson.
2. Think of five of your current contacts. How could they help you in developing your prospect list? Does each bring a unique perspective? What type of questions could you ask these contacts to help them think of prospects for you?

3. Discuss the importance of mentoring. Do you know someone who would be a good mentor to you and who might be interested in mentoring you?

4. Imagine that your best friend's new job requires that the friend give presentations occasionally. That friend's greatest fear is public speaking. What are some questions you could ask in order to sell that friend on learning how to conquer that fear?

5. Take a look at your current workspace. What could you do to better organize your assignments and other important documents?

6. Visualize yourself as a sales representative for a wholesale tire center that sells to retail outlets. Your territory consists of the state in which you live. What information do you need to find in order to develop a prospecting and sales forecasting plan?

Developing a Plan of Action

You've accepted a job as a sales representative for a catering firm in your area. Your primary target audience is wedding planners and special event coordinators. Your boss wants to know your plan of action for finding new customers. Your boss also asks about your sales expectations. Outline your ideas for finding new customers and the information you need to know for developing a simple forecasting plan.

6

PLANNING A SALES CALL
Education Beforehand Pays Off

Starting Point

Go to www.wiley.com/college/hopkins to assess your knowledge of planning a sales call.
Determine where you need to concentrate your effort.

What You'll Learn in This Chapter

▲ Sources for obtaining information on your product, customers, sales organization, competition, and environment
▲ Specific areas of a marketing strategy
▲ Objectives for sales presentations
▲ The importance of advocating skills

After Studying This Chapter, You'll Be Able To

▲ Analyze needed sources of information
▲ Establish objectives for a sales meeting
▲ Establish planning skills in preparation for a sales presentation

INTRODUCTION

In most business-to-business sales that occur today, a salesperson needs a deep understanding of the customer's problems and challenges to drive the sale. That understanding is also becoming more important in sales to individuals and families. To gain this insight, you need to have the skills and resources to obtain appropriate knowledge about your product, the customer, your competition, and your industry's environment. This chapter focuses on the skills and resources to obtain that knowledge. It also describes considerations in establishing your sales presentation objectives.

6.1 Obtaining Knowledge

One of the best advantages of a career in selling is that good sales skills are portable. When you master the skills, you have the education you need to sell almost any product that interests you. First, you need the skills that help you obtain the necessary knowledge to accommodate your customer's needs. When you have obtained this fundamental knowledge, you go through three phases:

1. **Pre-interaction:** The actions that are initiated prior to interaction with key decision makers, requiring skills in pre-call planning.
2. **Interaction:** The actions initiated while interacting with decision makers, calling on such skills as relating and needs discovery.
3. **Post-interaction:** The activities following a transaction involving supporting skills.

Figure 6-1 provides more details on these three phases.

The pre-interaction phase, in which you gather the knowledge you need before making your sales call, is the primary focus of this section. The three sides

Figure 6-1

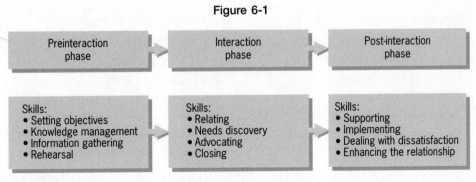

Phases and steps of the selling process.

of the selling triangle (refer to Chapter 1) are equally important to success in sales:

▲ Product knowledge.
▲ Selling tactics and strategies.
▲ Attitude and goal setting.

Somewhere in the midst of the triangle, you also need to develop in-depth knowledge about the following:

▲ Your customers.
▲ Your sales organization.
▲ The competition.
▲ The environment.

You can use a number of sources to obtain information in these areas. You've already learned about many of those sources, such as company records, other salespeople, published information, and your own observation. In fact, by observing a prospect's retail operations, for instance, a veteran consumer goods salesperson can tell a lot about a client's pricing strategy, merchandising strategy, and vendor preferences. To illustrate the importance of this, Figure 6-2 shows the results of a study comparing the customer interaction techniques of very successful with less successful salespeople in the life insurance industry. One of the biggest differences between the two groups was that the more successful salespeople devoted more attention to conducting background research on a prospect before contacting the prospect. But equally important is knowing all you can about your product.

Figure 6-2

Successful Salespeople	Less Successful Salespeople
Research prospect background	Do little background research
Use referrals for prospecting	Use company generated prospect lists
Open by asking questions	Open with a product statement
Use needs-satisfaction type presentation	Use standard presentations
Focus on customer needs	Focus on product benefits
Let prospect make purchase decision	Close by focusing on the most important customer objection

Successful vs. less successful salespeople.

6.1.1 The Product

It's important that you know the following about your product:

▲ **The product's name, number, and function:** You need to know the specific product name and model, as well as the product/part number. If your customers refer to it by a number, you need to know exactly what they're talking about. You also need to have a clear understanding of the product's function.

▲ **The company's latest model:** Many of your potential clients will want the latest version of your product.

▲ **Improvements over the last model:** You need to be able to list the new features or options and their benefits.

▲ **The product's speed, accuracy, and power:** You should be able to offer a comparison of the product to its competition, preferably by an independent study group. If there's not an independent study available, you can at least have your satisfied clients who are already using the product give you testimonials.

▲ **Operation:** You don't want to be in a situation of trying to demonstrate a product to a prospective customer without knowing how to make it do what the customer has asked. You need to be able to operate the product as well as you operate the car you drive every day.

▲ **The product's colors and other variations:** Being able to tell your customers immediately whether you have a specific color available will come in handy when they want to know whether it meets their needs. The same goes for other variations in the product.

▲ **Delivery dates:** Your client may have seen a review of your product in a magazine, even though it's not due out for two more months. You need to inform the customer of delivery delays and determine needs during the interim. If the product is currently in production but on back-order, you can brag about its popularity and tell the customer the projected delivery dates.

▲ **The customer's investment in the product:** You need to phrase the price of the product in terms of an investment as opposed to a cost. You should also be prepared to reduce that amount to a monthly amount if your product is something that requires financing. Many purchasing agents consider how much something will add to monthly overhead and how soon they can recover their investment.

▲ **Terms and financing:** If your company offers financing, you should consider that another product. You need to know how your company's financing works as well as you know the product itself. You don't want to risk losing a sale when you've reached the financing stage.

▲ **Distribution:** If you work for a manufacturer, there may be distributors that offer your product for less. You need to know these distributors and their prices of the product.

Even companies with the most basic product training should cover these topics with new salespeople before sending them out to talk with customers. Unfortunately, some companies provide only the bare minimum of information. In such a case, you have to develop the rest on your own.

If you can provide the answers listed here, you should be prepared. You may, however, encounter a potential client who asks an odd question—something out of the ordinary that you don't currently know. In this type of situation, you shouldn't make up an answer. Instead, you should tell the person that you'll research the information and quickly find an answer. Then you should do it before the prospect can consider the competition's product over yours. You may have to do a lot of additional information gathering in the course of researching the answers to your customers' questions. Keep in mind that if a potential client ever comes to you with valid information about your product or service that surprises you, your credibility with that client will be damaged. You're supposed to be the expert.

How can you be sure you're armed with the knowledge you need before you head out to make a sale? You should take advantage of as many different resources as you can. If your company offers training sessions on the product, attend. If the manufacturer hands out brochures and pamphlets, know them backward and forward. Talk with your customers about the product so you know what questions they have and discuss the product with your fellow salespeople to get suggestions.

Another good idea is to try sending your questions to your customer support department online to see how long it takes them to provide an answer and how detailed the answer is. What you receive from the department is what a customer would likely receive when using that service after a sale. If the return time is unacceptable for the type of question you asked, you should see if you can do anything within the company to help speed things up. Or, if you know the response time is slow, you may recommend, during your presentation, that your clients contact you directly with questions. This strategy shows that you provide added services and that you're knowledgeable about the product. However, taking care of customer support questions and concerns shouldn't take up so much of your time that it interferes with your selling time. You're paid primarily to find and serve new customers for your business, in addition to keeping those you've already gained.

6.1.2 Your Customers

Pre-interaction planning is the time to review individual, company, and industry information about clients and their companies. For an individual, you should

> **FOR EXAMPLE**
>
> ### Pitching for Fun and Profit
>
> Steve is a medical equipment salesperson who is finding it very difficult to persuade doctors at the hospital to allow him to make a presentation. The doctors are usually pressured for time while at the hospital and are concerned about their immediate patients. He found out that many of the doctors belong to a health club near the hospital. In this environment, they were more relaxed and willing to listen to his sales pitch.

know such basic information as the exact spelling and pronunciation of name, title, age, residence, education, buying authority, clubs and memberships, hobbies, and idiosyncrasies.

Not only is personal information important, but you should also review what you know or do not know about the client's organization. Apparently, there is a lot of room for improvement in this area, even in today's competitive selling environment. According to a recent survey conducted by PepperCom, a consulting firm in New York, 47 percent of salespeople admitted to not having a clue about their customers' biggest concerns.[1]

The importance of knowing your customers and uncovering their needs and wants are topics covered throughout this book, which underscores just how important it is. You've studied how to uncover the needs of your prospects. Plus, you've touched on how to research your clients through observation, the internet, and information published by the client.

You should also be aware of any **customer relationship management (CRM) software**, which can also play an important role in this phase of the process. The purpose of CRM software is to ensure that every person from a supplier's organization who comes into contact with a customer has access to all the latest information on the customer. The information is supposed to be relevant, accurate, and up-to-date. CRM software enables people to share information easily. For example, it can provide salespeople with accurate and timely leads from telemarketing.

Finally, you need to get as much feedback as you can from people who already use and benefit from what you sell. You should ask what their experiences have been with your product. Your surveys can be printed pieces mailed to your clients or, for even better response, e-mails or internet surveys they can quickly complete with a few clicks. If you prefer the personal touch and feel the time would be well spent doing so, you can handle those surveys in personal phone calls. The advantage of talking to people personally is that you can get the client talking and, hopefully, discover something new that will help you serve all your clients better.

FOR EXAMPLE

Developing a New Mind-set for Scott's Salespeople

Scott Paper Company felt the threat of major competition from larger companies, such as Procter & Gamble, as well as demanding retailers and mature markets. Scott's management knew it had to make major changes. It therefore switched its mission from gaining volume at any cost to profitability. This meant changing the mind-set of Scott's 500 salespeople in terms of the retail trade. They no longer took just a volume or promotional approach to gaining their customers' business. "It's more about understanding brands and how the consumer's response to various actions on our part is timed so we can eliminate waste and improve profit," explained one Scott marketer. The company wanted its salespeople to gain a better understanding of the needs of its consumers and retailers to enhance its bottom line.

6.1.3 Your Organization

Being surprised by a customer who has information about your company that you don't know hurts your credibility. You need to know your own company. Most large companies have some type of employee communication outlet, either a printed or electronic newsletter. You need to read it or at least keep yourself updated by asking questions of your superiors.

Your company or the manufacturer of the products you represent may hold regularly scheduled training sessions about the products. If they do, you should definitely go to those training sessions. You should always attend these sessions with a list of questions and a notepad for writing down the answers. If the speaker doesn't answer your questions during the presentation, you need to find a way to ask your questions before this knowledgeable person gets away.

In between training sessions, it's a good idea to watch for e-mail or Web updates of product information from the company as well. You should visit your own company's Web site every morning and look for a product revision date, if those are posted on the site. If something has changed in the past 24 hours, you need to read it and be familiar with it as soon as possible. After all, your best new prospect may have read that information already, and you want to be able to show that your information is current.

6.1.4 The Competition

It's important that you know your competition's product so you can tell your customers how your product measures up. Most companies designate a person or department to gather information on the competition and to prepare analyses of that information for the sales staff. If your company doesn't provide this service, you need to take it on yourself. You should take advantage, at least once a week, of online searches that seek out any information for you, based on keywords you specify, such as your competitor's company or product name. This information should include the competition's latest news releases and products.

You shouldn't rely on just one source for information. If you're in business on your own, you might want to enlist a family member to help you by finding juicy tidbits of information on competitors' products.

If you call on customers who've had past experiences with your competitors, you should ask them if they would mind sharing with you their thoughts on their product and service. What did they like about a competitor's product and its particular features and benefits? How were their contacts with customer service handled? What would they like to see improved upon? Asking in a sincere, caring manner sends the message that you want to do better, be better, and help the customer have a better experience than ever before. When they tell their tales, take good notes and keep them handy for future reference. If a new customer has just switched from the competition to your product, you need to find out exactly what the deciding factor was and work it into any presentations you make in the future where circumstances are similar. Of course, you need to be certain that feature is remaining in the product if an upgrade is planned.

6.1.5 The Environment

In order to fully understand your product, customer, and competition, you need to know about your industry's environment. You therefore need to do the following:

▲ **Keep up-to-date on the latest news:** If you get information from online news sites, take advantage of the customizing features at those sites. Many news sites let you tell them which industry or company news you need. Then, when you visit your customized homepage on the site, links to that information will show up automatically.

▲ **Attend conferences and workshops about your field of endeavor:** Not only does this help keep you up to date on the latest news, it might help you meet some prospective clients.

▲ **Remember that your current customers are also a source:** You should talk to your current customers about current events and ask their opinions. Not only does it show that you value their opinion, but it also helps you learn more about their interests and concerns.

▲ **Consult your colleagues:** Veteran and top salespeople have all kinds of information about products that have never documented. You should talk with them as much as you can in order to put their knowledge to work for you. You should also ask them to give you their research Web site addresses. It's important to keep meetings with other salespeople focused

FOR EXAMPLE

Purchasers Discuss Salespeople's Mistakes

A panel of purchasing executives was asked to comment on some of the typical gaffes they had seen salespeople commit. The following are some excerpts from their responses.

"The first rule of selling is to know how your product or service impacts or adds value to your client," said a purchasing agent at A. T. Kearney. "If you don't know anything about your client and have no conception of how your offering can be employed by him or her, you have no right to be there."

"There are times when salespeople just won't let their clients talk," noted the president of Multimedia Marketing, Inc. "The salesperson thinks it's more important for him or her to be heard. They don't realize how important listening is in determining the needs of their customer. Consequently, they wind up talking themselves out of a sale."

"I've seen many salespeople who over-promise the delivery of their product and simply don't follow up enough," said a purchasing manager at John H. Harland Company. "To avoid this, I suggest they develop a contact sheet of all their accounts in order to make sure they call each one periodically and see them as often as possible."

on product knowledge and information. Otherwise, your time will not be well spent. When two or more salespeople get together, it's easy to get off the subject at hand and descend into old war stories or other unrelated matters.

Remember that you cannot know too much. You can find the information you need in scores of places—not just your product's manual. In seeking out as much information as possible, you earn and keep your expert status, and more people will want to take your advice. Customers want to believe in your competency

Perhaps one of the best ways to learn the importance of adequate planning, along with other sales skills, is from the experience of others.

HU

SELF-CHECK

1. Describe how you would find information about your product, customers, organization, competition, and environment.

6.2 Developing a Marketing Strategy

When you have an idea of some of basics of your market, you need a more in-depth **marketing strategy**—a set of integrated decisions and actions a business undertakes to achieve its marketing objectives by addressing the value requirements of its customers. Your marketing strategy could be an intricate system of decisions made by your company managers or a simplified version for a one-person organization. Because marketing programs must have a customer focus in order to be effective, companies segment the market and select target markets on which to concentrate their marketing efforts.

Your marketing strategy should be concerned with decisions related to three steps:

1. Market segmentation.
2. Target marketing.
3. A positioning strategy.

Your marketing strategy may or may not be formed for you by your company. If it is, the company has saved you some time. Otherwise, you need to put some effort into developing at least some basics.

6.2.1 Market Segmentation

Market segmentation involves aggregating customers into groups that

▲ Have one or more common characteristics.
▲ Have similar needs.
▲ Respond similarly to a marketing program.

Because segments are identified in developing an overall marketing strategy, there is a fundamental relationship between a firm's overall marketing strategy and its **go-to-market strategy**—that is, who will perform activities and for which customers. The process for determining a go-to-market strategy consists of answering the four major questions shown in Figure 6-3.

Customer segments and go-to-market strategies vary, depending on the product sold. Adult diapers and baby diapers are very similar in how they are manufactured, but they have very different go-to-market strategies. Most adult diapers are sold in bulk to nursing homes via distributors, and with very little advertising. Most baby diapers are sold at retail, with massive advertising support.

Figure 6-3

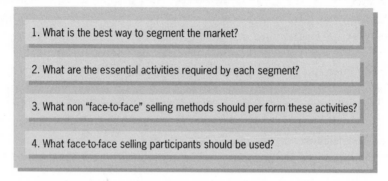

1. What is the best way to segment the market?

2. What are the essential activities required by each segment?

3. What non "face-to-face" selling methods should per form these activities?

4. What face-to-face selling participants should be used?

Steps in developing a go-to-market strategy.

Customer characteristics commonly used to segment a market for purposes of developing a go-to-market strategy include, but are not limited to, the following:

▲ **Industry:** What business is the customer in?
▲ **Size:** What is the revenue size of the customer? How many employees does the customer have? What is the sales potential?
▲ **Geography:** Where is the customer located? Does the customer have global operations?
▲ **Behavior:** Who are the key decision makers? What are their adoption tendencies? Does the customer currently use our product? a competitor's product? Does the customer buy centrally for all its plant locations?

Perhaps the best approach to segmenting a market is one that generates groups of customers whose members require similar customer attraction and retention activities. For example, some segments may require significant prospecting and attraction activities because the customer is still learning about the offering, and other segments may require significant servicing activities because they are already current customers.

When the market segmentation is complete, company management makes decisions regarding sales process activities and go-to-market participants.

Sales process activities consist of all the activities needed to serve a customer properly. Essential sales process activities can be divided into four groups:

▲ Interest creation.
▲ Pre-purchase.
▲ Purchase.
▲ Post-purchase.

FOR EXAMPLE

New Avenues for IBM

IBM once sold all its computers through the company's 5,000-person sales force. When low-cost computers hit the market, IBM reacted by expanding into new channels. Now the company sells through dealers, resellers, catalog operations, direct mail, telemarketing, and the Internet. In total, IBM added over 18 new channels in addition to its own sales force to communicate with customers.

These activities recycle because good post-purchase activities and support can lead to interest creation, building a continuing relationship with the customer.

Go-to-market participants are the avenues used to access customers, including the internet, telemarketing, advertising, direct mail, and person-to-person selling. Companies today are using multiple methods so they can reach different target markets.

6.2.2 Target Marketing

Target marketing refers to the selection and prioritization of segments to which the company will market.

FOR EXAMPLE

Target Marketing in the Insurance Industry

The Graham Company, a Philadelphia-based commercial insurance broker, provides a good example of how important target marketing is to a company and the job of the sales force. Graham is the 51st-largest insurance broker in the United States, with an annual premium volume of more than $200 million, yet its sales force represents less than 10 percent of its 170 employees. It generates premiums from only 200 clients, while its nearest competitors in size have 2,000 to 3,000 clients. It typically contacts only 350 prospective clients per year, seeks relationships with only 35 of those prospects, and earns the business of 28. In pursuing clients, Graham invests substantial resources in diagnosing each customer's situation.

The broker sends a sales team that may include, in addition to an account manager, attorneys, risk managers, engineers, certified public accountants (CPAs), and experts in the customer's business to evaluate the prospect's insurance issues and exposures. How well does such a selling strategy work? Graham enjoys a 75 percent conversion rate in an industry with a 15 percent average and maintains a 98 percent customer retention rate.[2]

6.2.3 Positioning Strategy

After you have settled on specific marketing goals and identified the target market(s), the next step in the planning process is to develop and implement a positioning strategy, based on product, price, distribution, and promotion decisions. **Positioning** occurs in the mind of the consumer and refers to how the consumer perceives your product, your brand, competitors, and your company.

The following are some of the fundamental questions that customers ask about brands:

▲ Who are you? (This speaks to **brand identity.**)
▲ What are you? (This speaks to **brand meaning.**)
▲ What do I think or feel about you? (This speaks to **brand responses.**)
▲ What kind of association and how much of a connection would I like to have with you? (This speaks to **brand relationships.**)

You achieve a clear and strong position in the customer's mind by designing the proper **marketing mix**—the blending of considerations regarding price, product, promotion, and channels. A significant change in any of these elements usually has ramifications for the sales force program. For instance, when a company chooses to introduce a new product, the most likely sales program changes affect sales quotas, the compensation plan, and the sales support material the sales force has at its disposal.

In some cases, repositioning involves helping your channel partners reposition themselves as well. For instance, Cisco found it necessary to reposition itself to provide network-related solutions for leveraging voice-, video-, and data-based applications. To accomplish this repositioning, Cisco needed to help its more than 36,000 resellers redefine their businesses as providers of value-added network-based solutions. Cisco now helps each reseller partner select appropriate target markets, and then it provides the reseller with the appropriate training, tools, and support to succeed in those market segments.[3]

Your company's upper-level management may undertake a more in-depth look at strategic implementation decisions that create customer value and achieve competitive advantage. Although these decisions may play an important role in how you conduct your sales, an in-the-field salesperson usually isn't responsible for their development. However, you feel the effects, so let's take a brief look at some of the usual questions discussed:

▲ How will customers be accessed?
▲ How will new offerings be developed and existing products be improved?
▲ How will physical products be created and delivered to the customer?
▲ How will customer relationships be enhanced and leveraged?

The company's choices in answering these questions have an important influence on the activities required of the sales force and around which the sales program is built. They also play an important role in how a salesperson identifies a prospect, as discussed in previous chapters.

6.2.4 Understanding the Purchasing Process

To better understand how the sales force can create customer value, let's look at the different points in the purchasing process where a sales force can potentially add value. The typical sequence of steps that purchasers go through in business-to-business acquisitions includes the four steps shown in Figure 6-4.

A key determinant of the nature of the purchasing process is the buying situation a customer faces. Three different types of situations are possible, each of which influences the nature of the four steps in the purchasing process and the opportunity for the seller to provide value to the customer in completing the purchasing process:

▲ **Straight rebuy:** In a straight rebuy, the product has been previously purchased and there is no change desired in the product or offering; this often involves replenishing inventories of products. In such a situation, the seller can add value for the customer by making the purchase easy, convenient, and as hassle-free as possible. The purchasing department is likely to be responsible for the entire purchasing process in this situation.

▲ **Modified rebuy:** A modified rebuy occurs when some changes are anticipated in a product that the buyer has previously been purchasing. As a result, the first step of the process—evaluation of options—is much more extensive than usual, and it is here that the seller can add the most

Figure 6-4

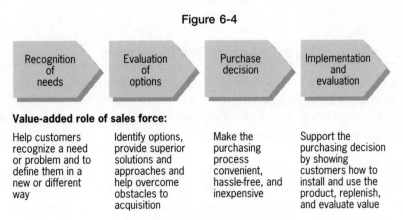

Value-added role of sales force:

Recognition of needs	Evaluation of options	Purchase decision	Implementation and evaluation
Help customers recognize a need or problem and to define them in a new or different way	Identify options, provide superior solutions and approaches and help overcome obstacles to acquisition	Make the purchasing process convenient, hassle-free, and inexpensive	Support the purchasing decision by showing customers how to install and use the product, replenish, and evaluate value

The typical purchasing process.

value. A group of people from various functional areas of the purchasing organization is usually involved in the purchasing process.

▲ **New buy:** In a new buy, the seller has the opportunity to add value for the buyer during the interaction phase of the purchase. The actual purchase decision itself follows naturally though the whole purchasing process and may take some time to complete.

The primary point to remember is that the purchasing process does not end with the purchase. During the immediate post-purchase phase, the seller's obligation is to ensure that all promises are fulfilled and customer expectations are met or exceeded. This includes making sure the product has no defects and arrives on time as promised and at the right place and ensuring that warranties are honored, repairs or exchanges are handled quickly and smoothly, needed information is provided, and adequate e-training is provided.

After the immediate post-purchase activities are performed, the seller's focus should shift to customer retention and growth. Activities focus on nurturing a continuing business relationship with the customer. This may include performing customer market analysis, developing joint customer marketing programs, monitoring inventory, providing customer service, providing ongoing training, and handling complaints.

SELF-CHECK

1. Define **marketing strategy**.
2. Describe the three primary areas of concern in developing a marketing strategy.

6.3 Establishing Sales Presentation Objectives

Many sales experts have stated simply that salespeople should not make a call unless they can specify an action that they want the client or prospect to take. The objective should not be vague, such as "to collect information" or "to build a good relationship." Here are some examples of good objectives:

▲ The client agrees to supply information on historical inventory levels.
▲ The client tells you who will be involved in the purchase decision.
▲ The client arranges for a meeting with the chief design engineer.
▲ The client agrees to a trial run on the system.

Note that each of these examples calls for the customer to take a specific action. Objectives should be stated in terms of client actions so that the salesperson knows whether the objectives have been met. Also, as you can see in the first two objectives listed here, some objectives involve gathering information.

In complex selling situations involving multiple calls over a period of time, a customer-action objective may be subtle. For example, it may take a number of calls to understand a customer's needs, identify the key decision influencers, and fully educate a client on the benefits of the product. Or, you may be calling to ensure that the customer is satisfied after the sale or to handle a specific customer complaint.

Considerations for establishing your sales presentation objectives are similar to those in goal setting. You've learned that one of the characteristics of a successful salesperson is focusing on goals. Professional persuaders have set their goals and put them in writing. They know exactly what they're striving for and when they expect to accomplish it. This applies to their sales presentation as well.

All salespeople should have at least some idea

▲ How they will initially start an interaction.
▲ What questions they will ask.
▲ What benefits they plan to present.

Salespeople should anticipate concerns a customer is likely to raise and should prepare strategies for addressing these concerns.

When preparing to call on clients, it is helpful to put yourself in their position. What would you want to know about your company and its products if you were the customer? If you are prepared to address such questions, you are probably ready for the interaction and have a much better chance of success. Successful salespeople tend to use questions focused on the other person when beginning their interactions. Although these questions may be in the client's mind, they are often not asked because they expect a good salesperson to address these questions without requiring them to be asked by the customer. Therefore, not addressing these questions may prevent a sale.

One other suggestion for preparing your presentation is to visualize a successful sales encounter. This technique simply means creating a mental picture of the sequence of events that will lead to accomplishing your interaction objective. With practice, this exercise should help you reduce your anxieties and increase your confidence.

You should never dismiss or underestimate a prospect. In doing so, you show a lack of respect toward your client, which will eventually become clear. You also shouldn't take shortcuts. Your primary objective is to show decision makers that you're sincere about their needs and their importance to you.

SELF-CHECK

1. Discuss the importance of establishing objectives for sales presentations.
2. What are some considerations in establishing objectives for sales presentations?

6.4 Advocating Skills

After you've discovered the customer's needs, you should clearly and fully present a solution that customers can see helps address their needs. Achieving this objective requires **advocating skills.** Although the ultimate goal may be to address the customer's needs, advocating is also an opportunity to demonstrate your knowledge of the customer and product and your ability to provide solutions that fit the customer's needs. Research has found that successfully demonstrating these qualities is associated with greater customer satisfaction.[4]

Advocating has two primary aspects:

▲ Presenting a specific solution to a problem.
▲ Addressing customer concerns regarding the solution being proposed.

Both of these aspects are covered in Section 8.3. At this point, just be aware that you need to plan ahead for these areas.

SELF-CHECK

1. Define **advocating skills.**

SUMMARY

A wide range of knowledge is necessary for a successful career in sales. Before any initial sales call, you should know as much as you can about your product, customers, company, competition, and environment. Many research avenues are available to you, and you should find the ones that work for you. This research is also valuable for you or other people developing your company's marketing strategy. With this arsenal of information, you're ready to plan your sales presentation objectives.

KEY TERMS

Advocating skills	The ability to clearly and fully present a solution that customers can see helps address their needs.
Brand identity	The consumer's perception of who you and your company are.
Brand meaning	The consumer's perception of what you are.
Brand relationships	Consumers' preferences for associating with you.
Brand responses	Consumers' answers about how they think or feel about you.
Customer relationship management software	Software designed to ensure that every person from a supplier's organization who comes into contact with a customer has access to all the latest information on the customer.
Go-to-market participants	Avenues used to access customers, such as the internet, telemarketing, advertising, direct mail, and person-to-person selling.
Go-to-market strategy	Identification of who will perform sales activities and for which customers.
Interaction	Actions initiated while interacting with decision makers, calling on such skills as relating and needs discovery.
Market segmentation	The part of a marketing strategy that involves aggregating customers into groups that have one or more common characteristics, have similar needs, and will respond similarly to a marketing program.
Marketing mix	Marketing considerations regarding the blending of price, product, promotion, and channels.
Marketing strategy	The set of integrated decisions and actions a business undertakes to achieve its marketing objectives by addressing the value requirements of its customers.
Post-interaction	The activities following a transaction involving supporting skills.
Positioning	The consumer's perception of your product, brand, company, and competition.

Pre-interaction   The actions initiated prior to interaction with
                                     key decision makers, requiring skills in pre-call
                                     planning.

Sales process activities   The activities needed to serve a customer properly.

Target marketing   The part of a marketing strategy that refers to
                                     the selection and prioritization of segments to
                                     which the company will market.

ASSESS YOUR UNDERSTANDING

Go to www.wiley.com/college/hopkins to evaluate your knowledge of planning a sales call.

Measure your learning by comparing pre-test and post-test results.

Summary Questions

1. The actions that require skills in planning for a sales call fall into the category known as:
   (a) pre-interaction.
   (b) interaction.
   (c) post-interaction.
   (d) none of the above.
2. Doing background research on a prospect is less important than focusing on a customer's needs. True or false?
3. CRM software is a compilation of the knowledge of all salespeople in one company regarding a specific client. True or false?
4. Which of the following is *not* an area that needs to be developed for a marketing strategy?
   (a) positioning
   (b) target marketing
   (c) advocating skills
   (d) market segmentation
5. A good sales presentation objective calls for the customer to take a specific action. True or false?
6. In addition to addressing the customer's needs, advocating is an opportunity to show your knowledge and gain the customer's respect. True or false?

Applying This Chapter

1. Visualize yourself as a sales representative who is responsible for selling corporate suites at a major sports venue. Your primary clients are major corporations in your community. Develop a set of questions you need to answer regarding a prospect's company in order to sell your product.
2. As the sales representative for a major sports venue described in Question 1, who do you think is your competition? What do you need to know about this competition?

3. As the sales representative for a major sports venue described in Question 1, what information do you need to know regarding your environment?

4. Visualize yourself working for a small company that employs only three sales representatives. How would answering questions regarding market segmentation benefit this small company?

5. Imagine that you want to establish a consultative relationship with a new prospect that wants to renovate an existing factory. You know the decision maker and have made an initial contact, during which you piqued the person's interest. You still need to convince this person to use your company's services for the renovation instead of using the competition. List three sales presentation objectives you want to achieve during your next meeting.

Selling to the Community—Part I

You work as a sales representative for an architectural firm, which has been commissioned by your community to build a new arts center supported by an increase in residents' taxes. One faction in the community opposes the project. Your supervisor wants you to work with the lead architect on a presentation to this faction. Your goal is to convince your audience of the benefits of the new center. You need to obtain knowledge in order to start planning your presentation.

1. Describe the type of knowledge you need to obtain to plan this presentation.
2. List some sources where you will obtain this information.
3. Develop sales presentation objectives.
4. Visualize at least three benefits that the arts center would give to the community.

7

MAKING A SALES CALL
Approaching the Decision Maker

Starting Point

Go to www.wiley.com/college/hopkins to assess your knowledge of making a sale call.
Determine where you need to concentrate your effort.

What You'll Learn in This Chapter

▲ Ways to get an appointment with a prospect
▲ The importance of a first impression
▲ How to approach a customer
▲ How to overcome barriers to the first contact with a customer
▲ The importance of building rapport before opening your presentation
▲ How to use attention-getters
▲ The common sales mistakes you should try to avoid

After Studying This Chapter, You'll Be Able To

▲ Plan an effective approach to contacting and meeting prospects

INTRODUCTION

At this point, you're ready to learn about actual contact with a prospect. This chapter explores how to get an appointment and handle the first few important moments before you make your sales presentation.

7.1 Getting an Appointment

In most sales situations, you want to meet your prospect face to face. (In telephone sales, of course, you want to speak with someone directly.) You want to have personal contact with a prospect in order to discover his or her needs so that you can satisfy them.

How do you get directly involved with the people you want to persuade? In order to meet in person, you first must sell someone on scheduling an appointment with you or, at the very least, agreeing to allow you to pop by and visit. You must schedule an appointment before you can persuade a prospect to own your product, start using your service, or consider your idea.

First, you have to find the right people to contact in the prospecting stage, which you've already studied. You also have to be firmly convinced that what you have to offer is right for the prospect. If you're not convinced of that, you won't deliver your presentation with enough conviction to persuade a prospect to give you his or her time.

While contacting your prospective clients, you need to keep three things at the forefront: your belief in what you're offering, the happiness of your current clients, and your desire to serve others.

Your first line of approach when contacting a prospective client may depend on how you received the person's contact information. This section looks at some of the various approaches.

7.1.1 Telephone Calls

You can think of your initial phone call as a six-step process:

1. Offer a greeting.
2. Introduce yourself and your business.
3. Express your gratitude for the person's willingness to talk with you.
4. State the purpose of your call.
5. Get an appointment to talk with the person face to face.
6. Thank the person while you're on the phone.

Step 1: Offer a Greeting

When you call a prospective client for the first time, you should begin by using the most important thing for anyone to hear: the client's name. Using a formal

> ### FOR EXAMPLE
>
> #### Cleaning Up in Sales
>
> Janet is a sales representative for a commercial carpet cleaning service. Competition in her area is intense, and Janet knows she has to grab a prospect's attention quickly, in the first seconds of her phone call, to arrange an initial sales appointment. She doesn't merely say that she is in the business of cleaning carpets. Instead, her opening introduction includes this: "We're a local business that helps companies like yours enhance their image with customers and reduce employee sick time." In that one sentence, she is saying that clean carpets give a good impression and dirty carpets harbor germs. Janet's description keeps most of her prospects on the line, waiting for her to describe how she plans to accomplish her stated goal.

approach, such as "Good morning, Ms. James" or "Good morning. I'm calling for Ms. James," is best because it conveys respect. Too often, people are tempted to use a person's first name over the phone. The use of first name doesn't bother some people, but it does bother others, so you should wait for the prospect to suggest that you use a more familiar name.

Step 2: Introduce Yourself and Your Business

After offering your greeting, you need to introduce yourself and give your company name. You should also mention briefly the function of your business. You should come up with a succinct and creative line for describing your business before your call. You should paint a tantalizing picture with the words you use, but you should also keep it simple. You have only seconds to get the prospect to give you anything with which you can extend the conversation.

Step 3: Express Your Gratitude

After you introduce yourself and your business, you need to acknowledge that your prospect's time is valuable and thank that person for taking your call. This shows that you consider the prospect to be an important person. Here are two short examples:

> *I appreciate your giving me a moment of your valuable time.*
>
> *Thank you for talking with me. I'll only be a moment and then let you get back to the important work you do.*

You don't need to gush, but you should be professional and businesslike in your manner.

Step 4: State the Purpose of Your Call

After you thank the prospect, you need to get down to business and express your purpose with a question, such as:

> *If I can show you how to reduce employee sick time while improving the image your company presents to its customers, would you be interested?*

If the answer is "yes," you should obtain permission to ask the prospect a few brief questions. After permission is granted, you can proceed with your questions. If the answer is "no," you need to be prepared with one more question that may pique interest, such as:

> *Do you believe an improvement in the image of your business would have the effect of increasing sales?*

If you get another "no," you might want to be more direct in asking a question that pertains to your product or service, such as one relating to the age of the product or service currently used. For example, Janet might want to ask about the date of the prospect's last carpet cleaning.

Many sales representatives have benefited from the survey approach. Using this approach, you ask the prospect to answer a couple questions for you. When you ask for the prospect's help and show that you value the person's opinion, the prospect is likely to comply. You're also likely to gain the prospect's empathy and cooperation.

Remember that the purpose of conducting this brief survey is to get the person on the other end of the line talking. Hopefully, what the prospect tells you will give you the information you need to build enough curiosity to commit to that vital face-to-face visit.

Step 5: Get an Appointment to Talk with the Person Face-to-Face

You need to be prepared to set a time limit on the appointment, keeping this initial contact as short as possible. Most prospects balk at giving you an hour or even 30 minutes of their time. For most people, 20 minutes or less seems to be an acceptable time commitment. After a prospect agrees to give you the 20 minutes you need, you should present options for appointment times. Committing to an appointment is your goal.

It's a good idea to schedule an appointment for an off time such as 2:10 p.m. instead of 2 p.m. Using off times differentiates you from all the other salespeople who call. It also shows that you must know the importance of punctuality if you can keep a schedule using such precise times. If your visit will last only 20 minutes, this method also lets your prospect schedule other appointments around you in the more standard time slots.

Step 6: Thank the Person

After you've secured an appointment, you move on to thanking your prospect again, reiterating the time that has been agreed to and verifying the location of the meeting. You don't want to show up late because you got lost. If the location is difficult to get to, now is the time to ask for explicit directions. You may even want to drive to the office the day before and get familiar with the area. You should know at least one alternate route in case traffic or road construction presents a problem. It's important to never be late.

You should also keep this six-step procedure in mind when you use the other means of contact described in this section.

7.1.2 In-Person Calls

Dropping in to a prospect's office or home to set an appointment is as effective as a phone call. In this situation, you should still use the six-step procedure described in Section 7.1.1. The disadvantage of this method, however, is that it is the most time-consuming method possible. You want to use this method only if you are already traveling in the same neighborhood as the prospect resides or works.

7.1.3 Letters

Mailing a request for an appointment has two advantages:

▲ You can reach hundreds of prospects within a short period of time.
▲ You can send essential information that the prospect needs to know ahead of your initial meeting.

The disadvantage of sending letters is that you don't know if the recipient even opens the mail. You need to follow up with a phone call to ensure that the prospect has received your letter.

If your goal is to reach a select few prospects, there are better uses for writing than to find prospects. For example, you can send thank-you notes. If your appointment is more than two days from when you call, you can immediately send your prospect a thank-you note (either by regular mail or e-mail), confirming the details of when you spoke and what you agreed to. A professional-looking piece of correspondence can solidify any doubts the person may have about this commitment. Including your picture on your letterhead or on your enclosed business card can be helpful. Knowing what you look like increases the prospect's comfort level in meeting you.

In many business situations, e-mail is the preferred means of correspondence. Therefore, you should be sure to obtain an e-mail address as well as a mailing address for each prospect. If prospects leave their names and e-mail addresses on your Web site, they would probably prefer to be contacted first by e-mail and maybe later by phone. (Many Web sites ask in their visitor registration area how the client would prefer to be contacted. If your Web site doesn't have that option, you should have it added. It's a simple yet powerful courtesy that can open the door to further business, if used correctly.)

7.1.4 Third-Party Introductions

If you got a person's name from a referral, you should ask the person doing the referring to introduce you to the new prospect. Or you can call the prospect to inform that person of your initial contact. Then you can decide whether an introductory letter or a phone call would be better. The means of contact generally depends on the formality of the situation.

Remember that your goal when you contact a prospective client (whether by phone, mail, or e-mail) is to get in direct, live contact with the prospect. You need to approach the sale of the appointment very carefully. You first have to sell a prospect on the fact that meeting face to face is beneficial to that person, so you have to offer some benefits in your first contact.

SELF-CHECK

1. Outline the methods you can use to contact your clients. Discuss the advantages and disadvantages of each.

2. Discuss the six-step process for telephoning a prospect. How do these steps apply to other tools?

7.2 Making a First Impression

Your prospective clients make many decisions about you in the first 10 seconds after they meet you. You need to help the people who meet you for the first time see that they made a good choice in agreeing to see you. Your clients must immediately see some benefit in investing their time with you. Knowing how to maximize those first 10 seconds allows you to make a good first impression so that you can comfortably move forward in your selling.

If you're new to the sales profession, you need to be careful not to cram everything you know (or think you know) into the first 10 seconds. Instead, that time needs to be natural and comfortable, to help your prospective client relax, which always makes a good impression. Here are some tips:

▲ Before you arrive for your appointment or visit with a potential client, consider the way you dress. Your goal is to ensure that your prospects like you and see that you're like them, so you should dress like your clients. Or, even better, you should dress like the people they turn to for business advice. Know your clients, and you'll know what to wear. If you're new in sales or new to a particular group of clients, pay attention to what the other successful salespeople at your company wear, and then dress like they do. If your company has a dress code, there's probably a good reason for it: The firm has probably done some research and determined that clothes in line with the dress code are what customers expect to see. You should be sure to abide by it.

▲ Pay attention to your body language. In addition to the message you communicate to your clients with what you wear, the body language you use also expresses something. Your carriage, your facial expression, the placement of your hands, the amount of bass in your voice, the frequency with which you have to pry your tongue from the roof of your mouth as you talk—all these factors and more govern first impressions. Being aware of your body language may require some time in front of a mirror or video camera. You might need the advice of a trusted colleague. If your normal body language doesn't present an image of success and confidence, you should watch and emulate someone whose does. Generally, you want to walk with your shoulders comfortably back, not slouching. Your arms should be at your side, and you should not have your hands in your pockets.

If you doubt the power of projecting positive body language, think again. In a study of 10,000 people conducted by UCLA, each person was asked for his or her initial impressions of a person who sold or persuaded the person on something. Seven percent said the person had good knowledge of the topic, product, or service. Thirty-eight percent said the person had good voice quality and sounded confident and intelligent. Fifty-five percent said the person walked with an air of confidence and self-assurance.[1]

▲ Make good eye contact with the people you meet. Don't stare them down or eye them as if you're assessing their clothing.

▲ Smile warmly with both your mouth and your eyes.

▲ Keep your tone of voice confident.

If you're sincere about your pleasure in meeting people, this behavior will be automatic.

SELF-CHECK

1. Describe the importance of a first impression.
2. Describe some ways to help ensure that you make a good first impression.

7.3 Approaching a Customer

Your goal is to meet with the decision maker. Unfortunately, in addition to facing the challenge of that initial phone call with a prospect, you may find yourself unable to get through to the person you want to reach. In fact, your prospect may have established a hierarchy of people who screen calls. This section reviews some tips for getting around these people and getting to the decision maker.

You may have to begin with the receptionist who answers the phone when you call. The **receptionist** is the person who has to know what each employee's area of responsibility is in order to direct calls properly. If at all possible, you should get the name of the decision maker on your first contact by telling the receptionist that you need help and asking for the executive's name. Then, whenever you make follow-up calls, you should use the decision maker's name. You should be sure to ask for the correct pronunciation and spelling of any names the receptionist gives you. It never hurts to get the receptionist's name as well.

If the receptionist is especially helpful to you, you should take a moment to send a thank-you note along with your business card. This little bit of recognition now can prove valuable later on.

The decision maker may have an assistant, who might be your first contact. You should treat this person with the same respect and courtesy you would use with the decision maker. The assistant can make or break your chances of ever getting an appointment with the decision maker, so you want to ask for the assistant's help as well. You can accomplish a great deal of research with the assistant's help, and you may even be able to prequalify the decision maker through the assistant. As you talk with the assistant, you should simply ask how to get an appointment with the decision maker. Many businesses have established procedures for setting up appointments with their executives. By asking what that procedure is, you show that you're not trying to beat the system; you just want to find out what it is so that you can work with it. When you show respect for the system that's in place, you move up a notch on the respect scale.

Whatever method you choose for getting in touch with the decision maker, it's important to consider how the other person will receive it. Your goal is to find a creative method for getting people's attention, but your method has to be inoffensive, too. You don't want to risk alienating anyone. Again, this is where receptionists, secretaries, and assistants can come to your rescue.

Another creative way to make a good impression on a decision maker is to ask the receptionist or assistant who the executive respects and listens to in his or her field. Our planet of billions of people really is a small world when it comes to making contacts. If you find out that your prospect is a member of the Rotary Club, think about who else you know who's a member. You can try to network your way into an appointment that way.

If the decision maker's schedule really is strict and all else fails, you can try to arrange for a telephone meeting instead of a face-to-face one. You'll have to adjust your presentation to give it impact over the telephone, but it may be a method worth trying.

When you reach the decision maker, you need to be knowledgeable about your product and the client and be ready with your questions to uncover the prospect's needs.

> ### FOR EXAMPLE
>
> **Using Ice-Breakers Creatively**
>
> Brenda is a sales representative for a catering company. She has tried repeat-edly to reach one executive who uses catering services for the seminars he conducts. She has decided that she wants to add this person to her client list. Brenda attended a reception following one of his seminars and knows that he sometimes has an open bar for attendees. After a short brainstorm-ing session with her colleagues, she decides to send a loaf of bread and a bottle of wine in a basket to this hard-to-reach decision maker. She includes a note that said, "I hate to w(h)ine, but I know I can save you a lot of dough if you'll just meet me for 10 minutes." It broke through the barrier in a cre-ative way, and Brenda got a confirmed appointment.

7.3.1 Managing Sales Call Anxiety and Motivation

From your list of prospective clients, you may have to contact many people to find one who wants or needs your product. So you need to stay focused on your ultimate goal and not let a little bit of rejection send you away. If you're truly nervous when meeting new people, you should take a few slow, deep breaths to calm yourself before entering the room.

Probably the best way to minimize your anxiety is to maintain enthusiasm for your job by thinking about what motivates you. **Motivators** are the factors that allow salespeople to move forward in their careers.

Some motivators include the following:

▲ **Making money:** The paycheck can be one of your motivators, or even your primary motivator, but it shouldn't be the only one. Many top pro-ducers look at the amount of money they make as a reflection of the excellent service and high sales standards they develop over the years in their industries. When champion salespeople notice a decline in income, they look to improve service and product knowledge.

▲ **Achievement:** Each individual defines achievement differently, but basi-cally, it is achieving a goal that you set for yourself. You can measure achievement by the influence and power you wield or by the humanitar-ian efforts you give to those in need.

▲ **Recognition:** Most people have a need for some kind of recognition. A pat on the back for a job well done suffices for some. Others need to win awards and accolades.

▲ **Acceptance from others:** If acceptance from others motivates you, you should try to surround yourself with positive people who support you in

your effort toward a successful career. You should stay away from negative people.

▲ **Self-acceptance:** Usually, self-acceptance is or has been tied to other
motivators. When you achieve self-acceptance, you've earned a certain
freedom from needing other motivators.

At the same time you examine your motivators, you should think about the
de-motivators that could prevent your advancement. The following are some
examples:

▲ **Self-doubts:** To overcome self-doubts, you need to confront them. You must
decide how to conquer them and develop strong habits to replace them.

▲ **Fear of failure:** Most people have some anxiety in trying something
new. If fear of failure is a major de-motivator for you, remember that each
attempt gives you practice. The process gets easier each time you make
yourself do the thing you fear. You can think of failure as a learning experience. It may be a cliché, but it's a good way to defeat this de-motivator.

▲ **Change:** Change is a fierce opponent of progress. If resisting change is
one of your traits, you need to find a way around. Every time you meet
a new prospect, you encounter some type of change in your life.

7.3.2 Courtesy and Common Sense

Although the following instructions are simple, they are important and often
overlooked.

▲ **Always be courteous:** Say "please" and "thank you." Refer to the person
as Mr. or Ms., with the person's last name. Don't be too quick to use first
names.

▲ **Give the prospect as much convenience as possible:** If your prospect
is many miles away, you should be the one doing the traveling.

▲ **Pique the person's interest right away:** Tell prospects about a benefit
they would be likely to enjoy by buying from you, such as saving money,
making money, or improving their lifestyles.

▲ **Confirm all the details about the time and place of the meeting:** Verbal confirmation is a must. Written confirmation is even better. You can
include in your confirmation note that you'll invest plenty of time in
researching just the right information for the meeting.

If you do your best to be courteous, secure an appointment no matter how
busy the prospect is, and confirm the details of when you will meet, you're well
on your way to a great appointment.

7.3.3 Being Observant

After the introductions and the first 10 seconds of a meeting with a prospect, you need to establish common ground with your prospect. By allowing your prospects to first see the human side of you rather than the sales professional side, you can help them break through the natural wall of fear that descends around them when typical salespeople walk through their door. How do you do that? By being observant. The power of observation is vital in your overall selling skills.

If you notice that the prospect has photos of family members or trophies along the wall, you should make a casual comment about the items. You should allow the prospect to direct the conversation from there. Or, if you were referred to the prospect, you can mention the mutual acquaintance, and that's usually a great starting point. Remember that you want to stay away from controversial subjects.

A sales professional working in retail might notice a customer who doesn't look around but remains by one item for a while. The salesperson could walk up to the prospect and ask an involvement question. This is a way to get the prospect to provide more than "yes" or "no" for an answer. Plus, the salesperson might discover something that will help keep the conversation going.

Generally, in a business that has a display area or showroom, you need to let your customers look around before you approach them. This is much less threatening and far more professional than immediately pouncing on a potential prospect. However, some businesses are so large that customers need a guide. If you work in such a setting, you have to take your customers to the type of product they want. It's important that you step away from them when you get them where they want to be and let them relax. When they're ready to talk with you, they can still find you quickly, but you haven't invaded their space and taken control of their shopping experience.

Whatever the setting, it's important that you search for clues to build rapport with your prospects.

SELF-CHECK

1. Discuss some of the obstacles you may face in approaching the decision maker and how to overcome them.
2. Describe elements that help in managing your sales call anxiety and motivation.
3. Discuss the proper way to treat a prospect.
4. Explain how looking for clues is important to making a first impression and building rapport.

7.4 Before Opening the Presentation

Before you open a presentation, you should try to build rapport. If all else fails, you can bring up something from the local news—as long as it's a noncontroversial subject. You should try your best not to bring up the weather. If you start off talking about how hot or cold it is today, your prospect will know you're struggling for something to talk about or that you're nervous.

Another good tactic is to give your prospect a sincere compliment. Blatant, insincere flattery gets you nowhere.

To keep the conversation moving forward, you could try an approach called **piggybacking**. In this technique, you simply ask a question. When your prospect gives you an answer, you acknowledge it either verbally or nonverbally and then ask another question, based on the prospect's response.

When you piggyback, you don't ask further questions unless you think the other person is agreeable to answering more.

It's important to always avoid controversy. You should never let a prospect tempt you into a conversation about a controversial subject. Some people do that just to test you. Specifically, you should avoid discussing politics and religion at all costs.

In any business contact, you should never use any profanity or slang. It doesn't matter if such language is widely used on today's most popular television programs; it has no place in the business world. You never know the values of the person you're talking with, and you don't want to risk offending a prospect. The same goes for off-color, political, ethnic, or sexist jokes. You need to be sensitive to the values, beliefs, and morals of the person sitting or standing across from you.

Remember to keep pace with your prospect. Taking time to become aware of your normal speed of talking is extremely valuable, as is noticing the rate of talking of everyone you encounter. You should try to time your rate of talking

---

FOR EXAMPLE

Piggybacking Toward a Sale

Here's a conversation starter that Robert, a sales representative for a chemical supply company, had with one prospect:

Robert: *Good afternoon, Ms. Thompson. I appreciate your time. How long has the company been in this location? I know I've seen your sign on the building for many years.*

Ms. Thompson: *We've been here 25 years.*

Robert: *That's great. And how long have you been with the company?*

Ms. Thompson: *I started 10 years ago, in the area of inventory control. For the past 5 years, I've handled all the purchasing.*

to your prospect's rate of talking. If the person you're trying to persuade talks faster than you do, you need to increase your rate of talking in order to keep the prospect's attention. If the person speaks much more slowly than you do, you should slow down or pause more often on your side of the conversation. Any distortion in your rate of speaking can be deadly.

SELF-CHECK

1. Discuss the importance of building rapport before opening a presentation.
2. Outline ways to build rapport with a prospect.

7.5 Using Attention-Getters

Attention-getters are verbal and nonverbal messages that can project a positive or negative image. The process of achieving this image starts the second you meet your prospect. You want to leave your prospect with a positive impression. There are many aspects to accomplishing this goal. We've discussed many of them in previous chapters, from using body language to project confidence to handing out business cards showcasing creative slogans.

You can hand out items to prospects and clients as attention-getters. Many salespeople like to leave some type of physical reminder. A magnet with a photo of the salesperson is a popular item. Pencils and pens with the company's name are also common. Or, you could get much more creative.

FOR EXAMPLE

Pointing in the Right Direction

Malcolm, a sales representative for a consulting company, worked with a five-member team at a client's company that directed his efforts in formulating a new marketing campaign. He wanted to commemorate the job with something unusual. Malcolm decided on a desktop pencil sharpener for each member, with a bronze plate stating, "Thanks for pointing me in the right direction." The team members not only appreciated their gifts, they also remembered who gave the sharpeners to them each time they sharpened their pencils.

SELF-CHECK

1. Describe the value of an attention-getter.

7.6 The Biggest Sales Mistakes

As discussed in previous chapters, examining the mistakes of others can be a valuable learning aid. Based on experience and conversations with other salespeople, the following are the 10 biggest sales mistakes:

1. **Not understanding selling:** Selling is done through the gathering and sharing of information via professional skills. Those skills help a prospective client make decisions that move the person to making the final ownership decision. Any sales trainer who teaches persuaders to become pushy and aggressive is incompetent. Professional salespeople or persuaders are low key and service oriented, and they're relationship builders. Sales skills are not a gift of birth. They are learned skills that anyone can master with a little study and work.

2. **Expecting things to improve by themselves:** If you aren't satisfied with your personal rate of persuasion or volume of sales, you should take steps to improve. You need to learn the skill of persuading, just as you must learn the ins and outs of your product or service in order to succeed.

3. **Talking too much and not listening enough:** A typically good talker tries to tell the customer enough about the product to influence the sale. A good salesperson, however, is like a great detective: The salesperson asks questions, takes notes, and listens intently to the customer.

4. **Using words that kill sales:** In any presentation you make, your words paint a picture. A few wrong word pictures can ruin the entire image you are tying to make. By using the wrong words, salespeople create negative pictures in the minds of the people they strive to serve. (Sales vocabulary is discussed in Section 8.2.6.)

5. **Not knowing when to close the sale:** You should ask for your prospect's decision when you recognize his or her buying signs.

6. **Not knowing how to close the sale:** In many cases, all you have to do to close the sale is ask for the order.

7. **Lacking sincerity:** A great salesperson keeps the discussion focused on the customer's benefit. Honesty and integrity are the key elements in every successful selling career.

8. **Not paying enough attention to details:** Lost or misplaced orders, letters with typographical errors, and missed appointments or delivery dates all ruin your credibility.

9. **Letting yourself slump:** Most people have patterns to their selling cycles and efforts. If you watch your cycles carefully, you'll see a slump coming long before it hits. You'll be able to correct the errors of your ways to even out your successes.

10. **Not keeping in touch:** People who switch from your products have likely done so if you haven't paid enough attention to them. Someone else may have kept in contact on a regular basis and made them feel important.

SELF-CHECK

1. List the 10 biggest sales mistakes.

SUMMARY

Making your first few sales calls can be both exhilarating and frightening. Managing your anxiety and keeping yourself motivated in making these calls are vital in building a successful career. This chapter examines the motivators and de-motivators that a salesperson should consider. It also provides tips on how to approach the customer, make a good first impression in entering a prospect's office or home, and leave a positive memory in exiting. Finally, it covers some common sales mistakes you should strive to avoid.

KEY TERMS

Attention-getters	Verbal and nonverbal messages that can project a positive or negative image.
De-motivators	Factors that keep salespeople from advancing in their careers.
Motivators	Factors that keep salespeople moving forward in their careers.
Piggybacking	A rapport-building technique in which a question is asked, the answer is acknowledged, and another question is asked, based on the response.
Receptionist	A person who knows what each employee's area of responsibility is in order to direct calls properly.

ASSESS YOUR UNDERSTANDING

Go to www.wiley.com/college/hopkins to evaluate your knowledge of the elements necessary for making a sales call.

Measure your learning by comparing pre-test and post-test results.

Summary Questions

1. An important aspect in calling a prospect for the first time is grabbing the client's curiosity regarding the benefits of your product or service. True or false?

2. The primary goal of any salesperson is getting a third-party introduction to a prospect. True or false?

3. Which of the following is a consideration in making a good first impression?

    (a) body language that expresses confidence

    (b) a warm smile

    (c) the way you dress

    (d) all of the above

4. The receptionist or assistant of a decision maker is not an important consideration in approaching the customer. True or false?

5. A motivator that can help salespeople move forward in their careers is:

    (a) fear of rejection.

    (b) a pat on the back.

    (c) resistance to change.

    (d) the inability to overcome self-doubt.

6. Building rapport before you open your sales presentation is important for any salesperson/client relationship. True or false?

7. Attention-getters refer to both verbal and nonverbal messages. True or false?

8. Which of the following is *not* one of the 10 biggest sales mistakes?

    (a) letting yourself slump

    (b) lack of sincerity

    (c) using words that kill sales

    (d) buying great gifts

Applying This Chapter

1. Imagine that you are a sales agent for an insurance company. Develop a short script for contacting prospects.

2. Outline how and when you would use the following approaches for contacting prospects:

   (a) telephone calls

   (b) in-person calls

   (c) letters

   (d) third-party introductions

3. Think of a recent experience with a salesperson. Describe your first impression of that salesperson. How did this impression affect your sales experience?

4. Visualize yourself standing in front of the receptionist of a decision maker you hope will become a client. The receptionist's instructions are to keep salespeople away. What would you do?

5. Discuss how your motivators could overcome any sales anxiety you might face. How do you plan to overcome any de-motivators?

6. Think about a recent encounter in which you met someone for the first time. Were you able to establish some kind of rapport? If so, how did you accomplish it? If not, what could you have done differently?

7. Imagine that you sell light bulbs. Develop a slogan or describe an item that would serve as an attention-getter for your business.

Fuel for Thought

Corporations in the United States are increasingly looking at revamping their fleets of cars to run on ethanol-based fuel. Visualize yourself as a sales representative for a manufacturer of ethanol fuel. You know that a large company in your area is considering switching to ethanol for its fleet, and you know the person who will make the final decision for the switch. You see a great opportunity to supply this company with its fuel.

You've made several telephone calls, asking to speak to this decision maker, but you can never get past the receptionist. Devise a plan that will help you make contact with the prospect and build rapport.

8

ELEMENTS OF A GREAT SALES PRESENTATION
Getting a Prospect's Full Attention

Starting Point

Go to www.wiley.com/college/hopkins to assess your knowledge of developing a sales presentation.
Determine where you need to concentrate your effort.

What You'll Learn in This Chapter

▲ The importance of a sales presentation
▲ Components of a successful presentation
▲ The structure and effect of a solution presentation
▲ Adjuncts to a presentation
▲ Proof devices to use in a presentation

After Studying This Chapter, You'll Be Able To

▲ Incorporate the elements of a successful sales presentation into your own

INTRODUCTION

It's show time. The sales presentation is your chance to show the benefits of your product. How you present your show depends on the product or service you represent and the potential investment of the prospect. A presentation can be as simple as giving out a brochure along with a quick explanation or as complex as you want to make it. Major companies prepare for the presentation stage by investing hundreds of thousands of dollars and a great deal of time in creating graphics, models, and samples. The blending of these devices is designed to fully involve the prospect and keep the audience's attention on the message. These are some of the elements discussed in this chapter.

8.1 The Importance of the Sales Presentation

You established rapport with the key players in the preliminary stages. Now it's time to prove yourself to the potential buyer by giving a great presentation. Having an appointment to give a presentation, however, doesn't automatically grant you favored status or guarantee you a warm welcome. It doesn't mean that you'll become the prospect's favorite supplier.

In fact, your contact person may not even be the decision maker. You may have to present to someone designated to narrow the field to two or three potential suppliers for the real decision maker to meet. Many times, a purchasing agent brings in several competing companies to give presentations to a committee. If you've done your homework well, you know exactly who will be present and why each one of them is to be there. You need to identify the players and what's in it for each of them. This way, should you decide to accept your mission, you know who needs to be persuaded and how to go about doing that. Understanding the perspective of your contact person is vital.

SELF-CHECK

1. Why is a sales presentation important?
2. What is your first objective in a presentation?

8.2 Components of a Successful Presentation

You've probably heard or read about the general guidelines for telling a good story:

▲ Tell them what you're going to tell them.
▲ Tell them.
▲ Finish by telling them what you've told them.

This method serves the same purpose in oral and written presentations. It helps the person on the receiving end understand and remember the message. You should apply this method when you're selling to make it a memorable occasion for the decision maker.

This section reviews some of the basics of presentations. Master these, and you're on your way to earning favored status in the mind of every prospect who hears your presentation.

8.2.1 Finding the Power Players

When you begin an in-person presentation, you need to thank and acknowledge the person who invited you. Then you should make eye contact with each person in the room and see if you can tell which member of your audience is the power player. There's one in every group, and that person may or may not be the one who has directed your conversation. Workplace behavior isn't much different from what you see in a documentary about the social habits of wolves. Just as in wolf packs, in most workplaces, the subordinates usually defer to the power players when important issues arise.

Knowing the power players becomes important as you gauge reaction to your presentation by assessing interest levels and interpreting body language. Watching how the members of the group treat each other should give you some clues. Another hint for identifying the top dogs in a workplace is that they often take the best seat in the house during presentations. The best seat is usually at the head of the table or at the 12 o'clock position at a round table, with you at the 6 o'clock position. Or, the power player may sit closest to the door, in anticipation of an interruption for a vital call or message. Some power players don't play the game the way you'd expect and may sit unobtrusively in the back of the room. By watching everyone else's body language, though, you should still be able to recognize that person.

You may not be able to make a perfect call every time, but as you hone your skills at the people game, you'll get to the point where you can pick out the power players in minutes.

8.2.2 Keeping the Presentation as Brief as Possible

In today's world of the 10-second TV commercial, few people bother to develop their ability to concentrate. In fact, the average person has a short attention span, which means you must compress the heart of your presentation down to a matter of only a few minutes. After those few minutes, you can spend the rest of your time involving your prospects directly in the presentation, through questions, visual aids, or a hands-on demonstration.

To help a prospect focus on your presentation and to keep yourself on track, you should state your objectives prior to beginning your presentation. It's important to limit your objectives to three, such as the following:

++ 167

▲ To better understand your business.

▲ To demonstrate a product that would be beneficial to your company.

▲ To obtain action steps that will help you obtain this benefit.

Experts suggest that a presentation should last about 17 minutes. Go past 17 minutes, and your prospect's mind wanders. Besides helping to keep your prospect awake, brevity and conciseness demonstrate concern for the client's valuable time. This concern will make a difference to the prospect at some conscious or unconscious level.

The magic 17 minutes do not begin the moment you enter the room or while you're building rapport. This period begins when you get down to business and begin to cover the finer points of your product's features and how those features can benefit your client.

The 17-minute time constraint may challenge you if your product is a complicated system. If that's the case, you might want to plan for a short break, a summary, or a question-and-answer period after the first 17 minutes. Letting your prospect relax for a few moments will increase the person's level of concentration.

8.2.3 Handling Breaks

If you choose to schedule a break during your presentation, or even if an unplanned break occurs, you should do a brief recap before starting back into your presentation after the break. A **brief recap** is a restatement of the major points that you've covered so far, a quick way to bring everyone back to where you were before the break.

Any break in the action allows your listener's mind to wander. Your prospect may start thinking about lunch or the next appointment. The client may even leave the room to make a call. If that happens, the prospect's mind focuses on the person on the other end of the call, not on your presentation. After a break and before you move on with your presentation, you must take a moment or two to bring the focus back to your presentation. After an interruption, it typically takes 10 minutes to get back to the same level of concentration and emotional involvement as before the interruption.

8.2.4 Preparing Beforehand

You've done your research. You've established rapport. You've completed all the presentation materials, and you know all the important details about your product and client. You're ready—or so you think. Do you know the location of the meeting? Is your equipment working properly? Is the seating adequate to handle all attendees? Dozens of details can prove devastating to a successful presentation. This advice may seem simple, but it's sound: You have to prepare for all situations beforehand.

FOR EXAMPLE

Even the Best Slip Up

Jim is a manufacturer's representative for a line of products sold to automotive service shops. Once or twice a year, Jim coordinates large-scale presentations of the latest innovations in equipment from his company. Jim puts weeks of work into each presentation, including building models, coordinating slides, conducting interviews with end users, and doing whatever else it takes for his presentation to succeed.

At one of Jim's last presentations, however, he stayed at a new hotel. The hotel's alarm clock failed, and he overslept on the morning of his presentation. He had only 10 minutes to shower, dress, and dash to the meeting room. He was able to start on time. However, about 10 minutes into his well-planned presentation, the newly placed light bulb in his slide projector burned out. He didn't count on a new bulb being bad. It took him half of a very embarrassing hour to find the correct staff people to locate a replacement bulb so he could move on with his presentation.

Luckily for Jim, his rapport with these long-time clients was established and his credibility didn't suffer much. He did learn, however, to have at least two extra light bulbs, know the name of the audiovisual person who can help in case of an emergency, and carry a backup alarm clock.

Here's a checklist of some of the items that commonly cause problems for salespeople trying to make presentations:

▲ **Electrical outlets:** If your demonstration requires the use of electrical power, find out in advance exactly where the available electrical outlets are and how you can plug into them. If you're relying on your computer battery to show slides, check and double-check that it's fully charged prior to your presentation. In addition, bring a spare, fully charged battery, just in case.

▲ **Power cords:** Is an outlet close enough to accommodate your power cord? In case it's not, be sure to bring an extension cord.

▲ **Visual aids:** Review each and every piece of equipment or presentation material. Be sure that everything is in order. Also, check your materials after someone else has been through them. Misplacement is rarely intentional, but it does happen.

▲ **Equipment:** Always arrive early to test your equipment on-site. Test it early enough that you can replace it if a problem occurs.

++169

▲ **A protective pad:** If you're scheduled to make a presentation in someone else's office, don't take a chance that any of your equipment will mar the furniture. Bring a protective pad with you.

5

8.2.5 Customizing Your Materials

By making the extra effort to customize your materials for a prospect as much as possible, you will appear competent and knowledgeable about your customer's specific needs. That's just the kind of person the client wants.

As you customize a presentation, you should not skip over materials in your generic, full-blown presentation. People will feel slighted by the absence of this information. Instead, you should remove pages or slides you don't need. You can page past graphics on your computer screen that are unnecessary. If you can't skip them, you should go ahead and show them. Just make sure you offer a brief explanation that you know those particular graphics don't apply to your present audience's needs and that you won't waste their valuable time going over them in detail.

8.2.6 Developing Your Selling Vocabulary

Words are readily available to anyone who wants to use them. Everyone has access to the same dictionary, and everyone has the same opportunity to choose the words that can make a speech outstanding and memorable. Every time you need to convey a concept to someone, you can choose from among thousands of words to establish your meaning. Developing your **selling vocabulary** involves taking the time to make a list of powerful but easy-to-understand words and phrases that are specific to your product or service. Then you can test those words on a friend or relative—someone who is not a qualified prospect. If your test person doesn't have a clear understanding of the terms and they are vital to the transaction or if the terms will recur frequently in your discussion, you need to prepare brief definitions of those terms in **lay language**—language that most people understand. The first time you use the terms with new or prospective clients, you should be prepared to give them the definition in lay terms.

You need to strike a balance between speaking the language of your clients and educating them about the terms they need to know if they're going to use your product or service. You should not make any assumptions about the terminology with which your clients are familiar, and you need to be ready to explain any terms they don't know.

This example shows a winner, who radiates calm enthusiasm and a thoughtful manner. But the turning point in Sue's interview is her choice of the phrase *I will* instead of an indefinite phrase such as *I guess*. This difference is subtle but very effective. Sue also creates positive word pictures with her words.

FOR EXAMPLE

Speaking Up

Hilary, the sales manager for a line of hair care products, has been courting an account with a major chain of salons owned by Mr. Dunn. These salons now carry the products of one of Hilary's competitors, but Mr. Dunn has agreed to hear a presentation delivered by someone from Hilary's staff. Hilary needs to choose the salesperson who can consummate all her hard work and land the account. She calls a meeting with each salesperson she is considering. The one who succeeds in representing the company can receive a sizable increase in earnings. Here's a look at the conversation with the winner, Sue:

Hilary: *Now that you understand what will be expected of you, how will you handle this presentation?*

Sue: *I believe the first step would be to contact Mr. Dunn and request a meeting at his convenience. Then, with your approval, I would examine your files on the salon, so I'm prepared for the presentation.*

Hilary: *What's your next step?*

Sue: *I will ask Mr. Dunn to show me his salons. I will familiarize myself with Mr. Dunn's needs, his stylists' needs, and the needs of the salon's clientele. Then I will offer Mr. Dunn the opportunity to use our products and ask his permission to present the products to his stylists.*

Hilary: *I'm interested in hearing how you would do this, Sue.*

Sue: *Although considering his financial benefits is important, I will encourage Mr. Dunn to examine the improved condition of hair that has been treated with our products. Making hair more beautiful will give Mr. Dunn happier customers as well as increased profits. Would it be possible to take a few company models with me on the presentation?*

It's important to think about the word pictures you paint. Just a few careless words can destroy hours of hard work. Words create images, which in turn evoke emotions, so you need to pay careful attention not only to your prospects but also to the effects your words have on them.

Many words common to sales and selling situations can generate fearful or negative images in clients' minds. Replacing such words with more positive, pacifying words and phrases is crucial. Take a look at Table 8-1 for some examples.

The first terms you should remove from your vocabulary for your presentation are *sell* and *sold*. The words remind people of high-pressure sales tactics,

5

Table 8-1: Words to Eliminate from Your Sales Vocabulary

Instead of . . .	Use . . .
Sell	Get them involved or help them acquire
Contract	Paperwork, agreement, or form
Cost or price	Investment or amount
Down payment	Initial investment or initial amount
Monthly payment	Monthly investment or monthly amount
Buy	Own
Deal	Opportunity or transaction
Objection	Area of concern
Problem	Challenge
Pitch	Present or demonstrate
Commission	Fee for service
Appointment	Visit (as in "pop by and visit")
Sign	Approve, authorize, endorse, or okay

?   # 171

which no one likes. Replace *sell* or *sold* with *helped them acquire* or *got them involved*—phrases that create softer images of a helpful salesperson and a receptive customer becoming involved together in a process.

Another commonly used word in sales is *contract*. For most people, *contract* evokes negative images. Contracts involve fine print, legalities, and being locked into something. Unless your particular line of business requires the use of the term *contract*, use *paperwork, agreement,* or *form*. These are much less threatening than the images the word *contract* evokes.

It's a good practice to substitute the word *investment* or *amount* for *cost* or *price*. When most people hear the word *investment*, they envision the positive image of getting a return on their money. For products for which the word *investment* just doesn't fit, you can use the word *amount*, which is less threatening to most consumers than *cost* or *price*.

The same idea applies to the terms *down payment* and *monthly payment*. Most people envision down payments as large deposits that lock them into many smaller monthly payments for at least a few years. They see themselves receiving bills and writing checks every month. So you should replace those phrases with these: *initial investment* or *initial amount* and *monthly investment* or *monthly amount*. These terms are called **money terms**, and anyone who wants to persuade someone to part with money needs to use these terms well.

Instead of *buy*, you should use the term *own*. *Own* conjures images of what someone will get for the money. Salespeople tend to overuse the term *deal*. This word brings to mind something people have always wanted but never found. Top salespeople never give their clients *deals*. They offer *opportunities* or get them involved in a *transaction*.

Similarly, you should not say that customers raise *objections* about your products or services. Instead, you should say that they express areas of *concern*. And you don't want to say that you earn *commissions*; clients respond better to the term *fee for service*. If a client ever asks you about your commission on a sale, you can elevate your conversation to a more appropriate level with language such as this: "I'm fortunate that my company has included a fee for service in every transaction. In that way, they compensate me for the high level of service I give to each and every client, and that's what you really want, isn't it?"

Another word that can potentially raise concerns in the mind of a consumer is *appointment*. Now, in the business-to-business world, this may not be as much of a problem. However, consumers view an appointment as interfering with their regular schedule, even if the schedule shows that time as free time. You might consider using the term *opportunity* instead.

It's been drilled into people from early childhood never to *sign* anything without careful consideration. Your objective is to get your client happily involved with your product. Instead of asking your clients to *sign*, you should ask them to *approve, authorize, endorse,* or *okay* your *paperwork, agreement,* or *form*. Any of those word pictures carries the positive associations that you want to inspire in your clients.

The words you use are not minor details. They are strong tools in a salesperson's arsenal. They are at the very center of your profession. So, when you write down and practice your sales presentation, you should go through it and make sure your words stress comfort, convenience, and ownership from your prospects' perspective.

It's important to speak as though your prospect already owns what you're selling. Giving your prospect the ownership of your idea, product, or service helps move the person closer to making a decision. This is called **assumptive selling**. There is a difference between assumptive selling and **suggestive selling**. With suggestive selling, you offer something the prospect hasn't yet asked for or about. With assumptive selling, you know the client has made the decision to own a product or service you have. Take a look at the following examples:

▲ **Assumptive selling:** "When we meet, you'll enjoy the value of participating in our neighborhood safety awareness group."

▲ **Suggestive selling:** "Would you like to join our neighborhood safety awareness group to meet other like-minded neighbors?"

Finally, you need to be careful about how you use your industry's **jargon**—the words and phrases particular to a given field of work. If you sell medical supplies to doctors, for example, you need to know the jargon that medical professionals speak and use it yourself, liberally. But if you sell medical supplies to the general public, you should limit your use of technical terms to the bare minimum until you determine your client's level of knowledge about the product. You don't want to alienate your customers by using acronyms or words they don't know. Remember that your goal is to make your customers feel important, which is tough if they don't feel very smart.

The human mind can assimilate information rapidly only if it understands what is being said. Many people don't stop to ask you for explanations because they're afraid of showing their lack of knowledge and being embarrassed in the process. Others may get the gist of your message but struggle to keep up. While they're trying to keep up, they miss the next few valuable points you relay to them. In other words, you've lost them.

If your subject sounds more complicated than your customer can comprehend, you risk squelching the person's desire to ever own or use your product or service and you risk losing the sale. You're likely to lose such customers to a salesperson who uses lay terms and simple definitions.

8.2.7 Deciphering Body Language

Body language has been studied for a long time. Most people are aware of body language but don't consciously read it and benefit from it. The following are a few examples of the kinds of messages your body language communicates to those around you:

▲ **Leaning forward:** Leaning forward when you're talking to someone shows that you're interested and paying attention. When you recognize that positive sign in other people, you should keep moving forward, too. In fact, you may be able to pick up the pace of your presentation a bit if your audience is leaning forward.

▲ **Leaning back or glancing away:** When you lean back or glance away from someone who's talking, you're showing that you're losing interest in what's being said. What do you do if you recognize this body language in your audience? You pause if you're in the middle of a long monologue, summarize the last couple points, and ask the client a question to bring the person back. If it's a group presentation and you see several people displaying this body language, you might suggest a short break or a question-and-answer period.

▲ **Crossed arms:** Crossing your arms when you're listening to someone indicates that you doubt what the other person is saying. When you receive this sign from your audience, you should move to a point-proving demonstration, chart, graph, or diagram.

You should practice positive body language cues as a part of your presentation. They can be as critical as the words you say. If you want to successfully persuade your prospects, you need to be able to give positive, warm, honesty-projecting gestures, such as the following:

▲ **Sit beside, instead of opposite, the person you're trying to persuade:** You want to convey the message that you're not on an opposing side, but you're on your prospect's side.

▲ **Use a pen or pointer to draw attention, at the appropriate times, to your visual aids:** Some people hesitate when they use a pen or pointer, and that hesitation says they are uncomfortable. (You want to avoid any suggestion of discomfort during demonstrations.)

▲ **Use open-hand gestures and eye contact:** Open-hand gestures and lots of eye contact say that you have nothing to hide. Don't use the palm out (or pushing) gesture unless you're trying to eliminate a prospect's negative concern. Even then, you should push to the side, not toward the prospect.

These are the basics of body language, but the field of study on body language can help you so much more. When you begin paying attention, many other body language cues will become obvious to you.

8.2.8 Being Comfortable with Long-Distance Presentations

Sometimes you may have to conduct a presentation by telephone or through a videoconference. In this situation, you can apply certain strategies.

First, you may not be able to see your clients, so you might have trouble knowing whether they're being distracted or interrupted. Even though you can't read body language over the phone, you can definitely listen to a person's vocal inflections. You can tell fairly easily whether a person is paying attention by counting the length of pauses between their comments. If you doubt whether your prospects are on the same page with you, you can ask a question of them. You might ask how something you just covered relates to their business or what they think of it. You should restate that point or benefit clearly so they're not embarrassed if they really weren't paying attention.

Another strategy to use when you're giving presentations from a distance is to pause to recapture their attention. If you briefly pause during your presentation, your prospects will wonder what happened and pay attention to what you say next.

It's important to send any visual aids, particularly a sample of your product, if appropriate, beforehand.

If you are working with videoconferencing equipment, you need to be aware of what else is in the picture with you. For example, you should make sure your camera doesn't allow your next potential major client to see a torn poster hanging on the wall behind you, or a neglected plant. You need to have an attractive background, even if you have to borrow something to put up behind you. In addition, you should try to maintain eye contact with the camera and smile into it.

If an online presentation requires you to show slides or other visuals, you should maintain as much control of the flow goes as you can. For example, you can control a PowerPoint presentation from your computer while it's being viewed online from someone else's computer.

8.2.9 Establishing Trust

You've studied about building rapport prior to a presentation. Now you have the opportunity to continue establishing the prospect's trust in you, your product, and your company.

You need to know enough about your prospect going into the presentation that you can talk with the person at his or her level. What does it mean to talk on someone else's level? Consider an example. Suppose you're in your 30s, and you're trying to sell a refrigerator to an older couple who want to replace a 20-year-old appliance. What would you say to them? With these prospects, you'd probably talk about dependability and the new features that your product displays. You'd also point out the benefits that would accrue to a couple who owned those features. The benefits would be lower utility bills with the increased efficiency of new appliances, longer food storage time (which means less waste and greater convenience), whether it has an outside beverage door, and so on.

Now suppose you're trying to sell the same refrigerator to a young, newly married couple for their first home. Would you talk to them the same way you did to the older couple replacing an old appliance? No. With the younger couple, you would accent the features and benefits that apply to their situation and satisfy their present needs. The features are the same, but the benefits are seen in a different light when viewed from their perspective. They may want something less expensive because that's all they can afford. But if you could show them the overall savings of getting a bigger or better fridge now, as opposed to the replacement costs down the road, you'd be farther ahead because they'd be more comfortable making the investment with the decision rationalized for them.

When you give a presentation to a prospect, you need to be sensitive enough to adopt the proper demeanor with each client. This part of your presentation is similar to what stage actors and actresses do: They play off the attitude and enthusiasm of the audience. If you're too energetic for your audience and speak at too fast a rate, they'll be turned off. Then again, if you're too mild mannered for them and speak too slowly, you may lose them. The ideal approach is to pay attention to the rate and pitch of your prospect's speech and then closely match it. On some subconscious level, this helps to establish commonalities between the prospect and you. Plus, the customer will understand you better.

4

SELF-CHECK

1. Outline the components of a successful presentation.
2. Describe how each component adds to a presentation.

8.3 Solution Presentations

Perhaps the most effective structure to adopt for a presentation is that of a solution presentation. The objective of a **solution presentation** is to convince customers that the goods and services offered match their requirements and satisfy their needs. It is very important to remember, however, that the purpose of a solution presentation isn't just for the other person to understand what you are selling. A solution presentation should help that person visualize the end result benefits—how your product or service will satisfy his or her task and personal needs.

A solution presentation is primarily a discussion of a series of tangible or intangible features of a product or service that are connected with benefits the client has already indicated are important. This type of presentation also provides evidence that the benefits will in fact be delivered. For example, a feature of a long-distance telephone service might be that billings are based on one-tenth of a minute rather than the usual full-minute increments. This feature might be emphasized because this person's task motive is cost savings. Therefore, the salesperson might state the benefit of this billing feature in the following terms: "What this means is that on a call of 2 minutes and 6 seconds, you will be billed for only 2.1 minutes. Other companies would bill you for 3 minutes. This will provide you with a significant cost savings on those high monthly telephone bills that are contributing to your operating budget overruns."

Notice that the feature (one-tenth-of-a-minute billings) is connected directly with a stated benefit (billed for 2.1 versus 3 minutes). Also notice that although the feature is product or service centered, the benefit focuses on the client and is related to a task motive (cost savings, in this case). The benefit, not the feature, is being sold. Benefit statements are most powerful when connected to an explicit need expressed by the customer.

Finally, you need to offer some evidence to support your claim, such as presenting the product or a model of the product, showing test results, sharing testimonials from satisfied customers, or allowing trial periods. For example, in the case of one-tenth-of-a minute billing the salesperson might show savings by using testimonials from satisfied customers as well as actual savings from other installations or test results.

Perhaps the most widely used means of providing evidence to prove problem-solving claims is the use of demonstrations. Demonstrations encourage participation and often allow the client to experience the product benefits firsthand. Involving more of the senses than just hearing improves communication. A good demonstration should impress a client in order to stimulate interaction. The objective is to get the prospect to ask questions and to become more involved in the selling process. Demonstrations shift the focus from selling to showing how the client's needs would be fulfilled.

SELF-CHECK

1. What is a solution presentation, and why is it an effective structure?

8.4 Adjuncts to a Presentation

In addition to giving a presentation, you may have additional work to do to illustrate your product's features. For example, you might have to prepare product specifications and written proposals.

8.4.1 Product Specifications

Product specifications are precise statements of the requirements and tolerances of a product. The exact specifications are usually dictated by the anticipated demand for the organization's products and by the technological requirements of its operations. This stage is often critical for potential suppliers because final specifications dictate the cost to produce the product and can favor one supplier's product over another. Getting involved in this phase is therefore often critical.

In most transactional relationships, customers have developed their own product specifications before a supplier gets involved in the process. In consultative relationships, however, customers and suppliers generally work together to jointly develop product specifications. In advanced buyer/seller relationships, the supplier is often chosen prior to completion of detailed technical specifications, which may be jointly developed by the supplier and customer.

8.4.2 Written Proposals

In today's competitive world, most prospects want to "see it in writing." There is simply too much at stake to make uninformed decisions. This is especially

---

FOR EXAMPLE

Working Together on Specifications

Johnson Controls, Inc., was chosen to supply seats for one of Daimler-Chrysler's models. Johnson was able to meet the customer's cost target but fell far short on safety, weight, and comfort. Therefore, 10 Chrysler engineers met with 10 Johnson counterparts. Together, they agreed on weight, cost, and performance targets and subsequently helped Johnson meet these targets.[1]

---

true with complex sales. As an adjunct to your sales presentation, therefore, you might have to provide a written sales proposal.

A **sales proposal** is a written offer by a seller to provide a product or service to a purchasing organization. The proposal may represent the culmination of sales activities spanning several months and involving extensive client analysis. On the other hand, a proposal may result from receiving a **request for proposal (RFP)** from a buyer. An RFP is a notice that a customer sends out to qualified suppliers, asking them to bid on a project that has a certain set of specifications. Regardless of how the process was initiated, it is important that the proposal development process be integrated into the selling process. In purchasing materials and equipment, for example, building contractors may consider service, quality of product, supplier support, low price, and/or reputation for fair dealing among their most important purchasing criteria when choosing suppliers.

Although a proposal may be organized in various ways, it should convey the following five quality dimensions:

- ▲ **Reliability:** It should identify solutions and strategies to achieve the prospect's needs and wants.
- ▲ **Assurance:** It should build trust and confidence in your ability to deliver, implement, and produce benefits.
- ▲ **Tangibles:** It should enhance and support your message and invite readership.
- ▲ **Empathy:** It should confirm your understanding of the prospect's business and needs.
- ▲ **Responsiveness:** It should be developed in a timely manner.

Formal sales proposals are advantageous because they put everything in writing, which means there is less room for misunderstanding. Written proposals also improve communication when purchase decisions are made at buying or executive committee meetings that are off limits to salespeople. Sales proposals have a durability that allows them to be read and evaluated over a period of time. However, written sales proposals take time and money to prepare, and they may not be cost-effective in all selling situations. In addition, formal sales proposals must be constructed carefully because they are binding contracts.

SELF-CHECK

1. Define **product specification** and **sales proposal**.
2. When would you develop specifications or a written proposal?

8.5 Proof Devices for Effective Sales Presentations

To fully obtain a prospect's attention, most sales professionals need more than a well-developed speech. That's why most salespeople incorporate other devices into their presentations. This section examines the use of a product, visual aids, and demonstrations in a great sales presentation.

8.5.1 The Product

The star of your presentation is your product. You're basically the host who introduces the key players (your product and your prospect) to each other and then fades into the background to let them get acquainted. You should think of that object in terms of the future primary relationship between the product and its new owner. Then you need to let the possibilities for that relationship develop.

Even though the product must be the star, you should not forget that your prospective client needs to always remain the focus of your presentation. You should never give so much attention to the product and what it can do that you ignore what it will do for the person sitting there with you—your prospective client.

If your demonstration involves the use of equipment, you shouldn't let your prospective client come in and begin punching buttons or demanding answers to a lot of questions—all of which take control of the presentation away from you. Keeping control can become a challenge when you have several things to display. If your demonstration falls into this category, you should bring something (such as a cloth) to cover your display items, uncovering only the items you're prepared to discuss. If you're using a video or computer screen, you should be sure to have an attractive screensaver that you can go to when you need your prospect's attention focused back on your planned presentation. Otherwise, your prospect may try to read ahead on the screen instead of listening to what you're saying.

8.5.2 Visual Aids

Most people learn and understand best when they involve as many of their senses as possible. However, each person usually has one dominant sense. Some people learn best by closing their eyes and listening. Others have a strong need to touch and feel things. Most people, however, gain the best understanding by seeing things. That's why you should incorporate visual aids into your presentation.

Visual aids should show three things to new clients:

▲ **Who you (and your company) are:** Visual aids should identify your company and the industry to which it belongs. If you are worldwide suppliers of your particular type of product, you should put that information in your visual aids. The story of your company builds credibility.

▲ **What you've done:** You should illustrate some of the primary accomplishments your company has achieved. But you should be careful not to belabor the point. There's a difference between being proud and being an obnoxious braggart.

▲ **What you do for your clients:** This is the most interesting part for your prospective client, who is thinking, "What's in it for me?"

The best visual aids include all three of these key points. If yours don't, you need to try to verbally incorporate these points into your presentation.

Your company may have slick, high-quality sheets with graphs, charts, diagrams, and photos that you can use as visual aids. These sheets often contain quotes from various well-thought-of authorities about your product or service.

For organizing and storing printed visual aids, you can use an attractive binder that also stands up like a miniature easel. You can also show computer-generated graphics on a projection screen, using a program such as Microsoft PowerPoint. This software program, which is often bundled together with other Microsoft programs, allows you to create simple or intricate slideshow presentations, using your computer. PowerPoint provides ready-made templates for creating charts, graphs, and text at your fingertips—you just follow the instructions and fill in the information. When you're ready to give a presentation, you can use the PowerPoint slides you've created in a couple different ways:

▲ Print the slides and give them to your audience as handouts.

▲ Use a projector to display the slides on a wall or screen.

You can also customize a PowerPoint slide presentation for each prospect in much less time than it would take if you were doing it all by hand. Plus, you can include audio files in your presentation, time music to go along with the messages, or add photos or diagrams to better make your points.

For these computerized presentations, you'll most likely have a laptop computer and multimedia projector. When you prepare for one of these high-tech presentations, you need to be sure your prospective client has a whiteboard or screen to project your images on.

You may also find yourself working with videotapes in your presentations. Videos often include recorded testimonials from actual customers your prospect can relate to.

Whatever your specific visual aids depict and whatever form they take, your company invested in the creation of its visual aids for a reason—probably because experience has proven that visual aids are very effective when used properly.

So what's the best way to use visual aids? Most likely, it's the way your company recommends. Typically, companies rely on a task force that includes top salespeople, manufacturing people, and marketing people for suggestions on presentation.

If you don't like or have trouble using your company's visual aids, you should talk with the people who trained you on their use. Or you can confer with a top salesperson who uses them effectively and observe that salesperson's presentation.

Perhaps your company doesn't provide visual aids. In this case, you have to develop them yourself. As you do so, it's important to remember to involve the prospect's senses. For example, say you want to sell your family on vacationing in the woods when you know they'd rather go to the beach. You may want to rent a video on all the outdoor adventures available to them in the woods. Many vacation spots now offer free videos as promotional items in information packages. Or you could get a video on nature in general, with flowing waterfalls, gentle breezes blowing in the trees, canoeing, horseback riding, whatever might appeal to your audience (in this case, your family). Such a video would involve two senses: sight and hearing. If possible, you might even want to have a little campfire going in the yard to evoke the smell of wood burning. Or prepare some hot dogs and s'mores ahead of time to tie their sense of taste in to the joy of that vacation in the woods. You could show your family hiking boots, lightweight canvas backpacks, or canteens filled with spring water to get the sense of touch involved. All these things—the video, the campfire, the food, the equipment—are sensory aids that are vital to your presentation and can help you get full involvement.

The same strategy applies to formal business sales presentations as to the vacation example: The more senses you can involve, the better. If your aids limit you to sight and sound, you should find ways to get additional sensual involvement. You can involve your prospects' sense of touch just by handing them things. Involving smell and taste may be difficult, depending on the product. If you're selling kitchen products, however, the smell of cooking and the taste of the sample are possibilities.

> ## FOR EXAMPLE
>
> ### Evoking all Five Senses
>
> Becky works as a sales representative for a cleaning service. When she presents to prospects, she tries to awaken her audience's five senses:
>
> ▲ **Sight:** Through visual aids.
>
> ▲ **Hearing:** Through her well-developed, but brief, speech.
>
> ▲ **Touch:** By handing out brochures on her service.
>
> ▲ **Smell:** By talking about the fresh smell of a clean house.
>
> ▲ **Taste:** By giving them a small box of mints as a new-client gift. The gift doesn't directly apply to her service, but it's a gesture that is usually appreciated.

With intangibles, such as a service, you might want to paint visual pictures that bring those senses into play.

8.5.3 Demonstrations

You should think of selling not as a spectator sport but as a sport in which you're fully involved. If you let your prospective clients perform functions related to your product or service, they will feel involved. During your demonstration, your prospects should be able to perform all the functions simply and to find out something about new features that are going to make their job easier.

The best computer salespeople stand or sit at their clients' shoulders and give instructions. They make sure the client's hands are on that keyboard and mouse. That way, the client has a positive experience with the product and builds confidence in the capabilities of the machine. Your goal is to get the prospect comfortable in using whatever product or service you sell.

One of the greatest fears all clients have in selling situations is that they will discover that the product doesn't meet their expectations or needs. Good demonstrations give people the opportunity to prove to themselves that what the salesperson is telling them is true.

SELF-CHECK

1. Discuss the role of the product in a successful sales presentation.
2. Discuss the role of visual aids in a successful sales presentation.
3. Discuss the role of demonstrations in a successful sales presentation.

SUMMARY

While creating your sales presentation, you can think of yourself as the producer of a great show: It's your job to handle all the details to create a showcase for your product and entrance your audience—the prospect. The components of a successful presentation are the focus of this chapter. Now you're ready to learn about another possible element of your presentation—how to respond to objections.

KEY TERMS

Assumptive selling	The process of giving a prospect the ownership of your idea, product, or service to help move that person closer to making a decision.
Brief recap	A restatement of the major points during a presentation.
Jargon	Words and phrases particular to a given field of work.
Lay language	Language, or words, that most people understand.
Money terms	Terms such as *initial investment, initial amount, monthly investment,* and *monthly amount.*
Product specifications	A precise statement of the client's requirements and tolerances.
Request for Proposal (RFP)	A notice that a customer sends out to qualified suppliers, asking them to bid on a project with a certain set of specifications.
Sales proposal	A written offer by a seller to provide a product or service to a purchasing organization.
Selling vocabulary	A list of powerful but easy-to-understand words and phrases that are specific to your product or service.
Solution presentation	A sales presentation structure that is used to convince customers that the goods and services offered match their requirements and satisfy their needs.
Suggestive selling	A process in which a salesperson offers something the prospect hasn't yet asked for or about.

ASSESS YOUR UNDERSTANDING

Go to www.wiley.com/college/hopkins to evaluate your knowledge of the components of a great sales presentation.
Measure your learning by comparing pre-test and post-test results.

Summary Questions

1. The importance of a sales presentation is that it gives a salesperson the opportunity to prove the benefits of a product to a prospect. True or false?

2. Preparing a great speech for your presentation is the most important consideration in a successful sales presentation. True or false?

3. Which of the following is *not* a clue to finding the power players in an audience during a sales presentation?
   (a) listening to the person directing your conversation
   (b) the seating arrangement
   (c) watching how the audience members behave toward each other
   (d) assuming that your source for arranging the presentation is the power player

4. The average attention span is:
   (a) 5 minutes.
   (b) 7 minutes.
   (c) 15 minutes.
   (d) 17 minutes.

5. You should never allow a break in your presentation; otherwise, you lose the prospect's focus. True or false?

6. Customizing your presentation means completely revamping your materials. True or false?

7. A selling vocabulary is a list of words specific to your product or service. True or false?

8. In order to impress your prospects, you should show your knowledge and expertise by using complex details and complicated messages. True or false?

9. Part of establishing trust with a prospect is speaking at a rate similar to the customer's. True or false?

10. Most experts recommend a presentation structure known as the:
    (a) trust presentation.
    (b) specifications presentation.

(c) solutions presentation.

(d) precise presentation.

11. The development of a precise statement of a prospect's requirements and tolerances is known as:

(a) a written sales proposal.

(b) the product specifications.

(c) a tangible solution.

(d) the product statement.

12. The star of a presentation is:

(a) you.

(b) your company.

(c) your product.

(d) the power player.

13. Visual aids and demonstrations are useful in evoking all of a prospect's senses. True or false?

Applying This Chapter

1. Visualize yourself as a sales representative for a waste disposal service. In developing a sales presentation, what would you do to present the best image possible for your service?

2. Using the example in Question 1, what kind of visual aids would you use in a presentation?

3. Using the example in Question 1, suppose you wear a suit and a tie to the meeting. Your client wears jeans and a T-shirt. What does this tells you about adjusting your conduct during the presentation? What would you do?

4. What skills do you currently possess that would lead to a successful sales presentation? What skills do you believe you need to work on?

5. Describe an example or an industry in which developing product specifications is an important adjunct to the presentation. What are some items that might be included in product specifications?

YOU TRY IT

Selling to the Community—Part II

You've examined the information you need to help an architect present to local residents plans on a new arts center. You're presenting before a faction of the community that opposes the construction. Describe how you would incorporate the following components into your sales presentation:

1. Your presentation style.
2. Clue-finding techniques.
3. Proof devices.

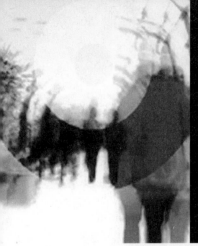

9

RESPONDING TO OBJECTIONS
Addressing Customers' Concerns

Starting Point

Go to www.wiley.com/college/hopkins to assess your knowledge of responding to customers' objections.
Determine where you need to concentrate your effort.

What You'll Learn in This Chapter

▲ How to negotiate customer concerns and problems
▲ Common sources of customer concerns
▲ General strategies for negotiating customer concerns
▲ Specific methods of negotiating customer concerns

After Studying This Chapter, You'll Be Able To

▲ Plan how to handle customer concerns in your area of endeavor

INTRODUCTION

In Section 8.2.6, you learned that your sales vocabulary for a presentation should focus not on *objections* but on *areas of concerns*. It's important to understand what kind of objections or concerns you're likely to encounter. If you sidestep obstacles during your presentation, there's a good chance they'll come back to haunt you after the sale. Unless you expect customer concerns, you won't know how to handle them. By learning how to handle customer concerns, you're taking another step toward reaching a high earning potential in sales. You should go into every presentation anticipating objections. This chapter examines some common objections and how to handle them.

9.1 Negotiating Buyer Concerns and Problems

Customer concerns or questions about a proposed solution to a problem are likely to arise in any sales presentation. Ideally, you want to uncover a customer's most fundamental concerns during the discovery phase, before you recommend a solution. Because customers are not likely to be aware of all their concerns until faced with making a decision, however, customer concerns are probably best considered a natural part of any sales presentation, and you should view them as an opportunity rather than an obstacle.

Xerox research on presentations found that successful interactions have 50 percent more objections than failed ones.[1] When prospects raise concerns, they are actually showing interest and are asking for more information. They may be trying to make a clearer connection between their needs and your offering. Instead of being passive, they are actively involved in the buying process. Xerox also found that failed interactions contain significantly more customer statements of indifference than successful calls. Concerns should be welcomed as a chance to get the prospect involved and to expand the discussion into areas of concern to the client. Most concerns are nothing more than innocent questions and should be viewed as an opportunity for deeper insight into customer needs.

Prospective clients tell you three important things when they voice objections or raise concerns during a presentation:

▲ They are interested, but they don't want to be thought of as an easy sale.
▲ They may be interested, but they aren't clear about what's in it for them.
▲ They may not be interested, but they could be if you educated them properly.

All three situations tell you that the prospect needs more information.

++ 189

If you've properly qualified the prospect, you've uncovered the person's needs. You've also discovered that you're talking to the decision maker for this transaction. If you're armed with that knowledge and you're confident the prospect would benefit from your offering, you know the person is probably interested but doesn't want to be thought of as an easy sale. In that case, you want to slow down the pace, encourage questions, and create a relaxed environment before asking for a decision.

Most persuaders find it difficult to influence people who voice no objections and raise no questions. In other words, the most difficult people to persuade are those who don't respond. In negotiation situations, you carry the presentation forward by directing and redirecting your course of questions and information, based on what your prospect tells you. If the prospect tells you nothing, the communication often stalls. When that happens, you have to guess which direction to follow next. When you guess, you're no longer in control. Guessing is like casting your fishing line without bait on it.

People who don't get verbally involved in your presentation likely have no intention of going ahead with your proposition. Those who do bring up challenges for you to address are, at the very least, interested. If they're really tough to convince, they'll probably become your best customers when you finally do convince them. Getting objections and moving past them are necessary steps in the selling cycle.

SELF-CHECK

4

1. Discuss the underlying meaning of customer concerns in a sales presentation.

2. What are the general guidelines in dealing with customer concerns during a sales presentation?

5

9.2 Common Sources of Buyer Concerns

The most common concern you're likely to encounter in your selling career is this stalling tactic: "I want to think it over." Generally, this means the prospect is interested but still nervous about making a commitment. The customer is thinking of questions such as these:

▲ Will the product or service do what you say it will?

▲ Will you really be able to make the required delivery date?

▲ Have I negotiated the best investment?

▲ Is this a good decision?

▲ Is this product or service something I need right now?

Basically, the prospect is afraid. In all its forms, fear is the greatest enemy you will encounter in persuading clients. The toughest part of your job is helping other people admit and overcome their fears so you can earn the opportunity to do business with them. Fear builds the walls of resistance that salespeople encounter. You need to know how to climb over or break through those walls.

This section discusses eight common fears that you need to help your prospects overcome—fears of salespeople, failure, owing money, deception, embarrassment, the unknown, and repeating past mistakes, as well as fears generated by other people. When you recognize these fears as barriers to your ability to serve your prospects with excellent service, you're ready to discover how to dismantle those walls, one brick at a time, and gain your prospect's confidence and trust.

Remember that your goal is to get your prospects to like you and trust you. They do that when you serve them with warmth and empathy.

9.2.1 Fear of Salespeople

At first, every prospect is afraid of you. The reason is because you, as a salesperson, want something from the prospect. Plus, what you want involves some kind of a change on the prospect's part. Most people are afraid of change, at least to some degree. This is a factor, even if you're selling to someone you already know. When you meet a person in the role of a sales professional, certain fears inevitably arise. The only exception may be selling to your parents or grandparents, simply because they probably believe in you and trust you, no matter what role you play with them. To them, you come across as you'd like to with everyone—with a natural, non-sales personality.

Most people separate themselves from their money only for products and services they believe they need. Your job is to help them recognize the need and to build the value of your product's capability to serve that need. You want any fear they have to be fear of what happens if they don't allow you to help them.

Most people, when you first encounter them, show their fear in their body language. They may cross their arms or lean away from you. In retail settings, they may actually take a small step backward when you approach them on the sales floor. A wise tactic to help overcome this is to warmly invite them to stand or sit beside you while you show them the benefits of your product. You can encourage them to put their hands on the product, push buttons, turn dials, and make things light up or move. When they get involved with the product, their fear of you lessens. They have fun, and you are the one who introduced them to the fun.

9.2.2 Fear of Failure

The fear of failure is one you're likely to encounter in your clients because virtually everyone has this fear to some degree. Everyone has some regrets about past mistakes. Whether that failure was in choosing the wrong hair color or purchasing a vehicle that wasn't right, they know the frustration of making a mistake. Many people remember a mistake as being associated with a salesperson.

No one wants to handle a transaction in which the customer may be dissatisfied with the result. The grief you get from a dissatisfied customer isn't worth the fee you earn on the sale. You must therefore go into every presentation with a sharp interest in the who, what, when, where, and why of the client's needs. It's your duty as the expert to convince the prospect that buying your product or service is in the client's best interest. You need to take the time to talk your prospect through every aspect of that decision very carefully and allow the needed time to make a decision.

Remember that you need to sell to your client's needs, not to your wants.

9.2.3 Fear of Owing Money

Prospects are tremendously afraid of owing too much money to you, your company, or a finance company. Your fee for service is almost always a point of contention with prospective customers. It's not because they're being stubborn but because they're legitimately afraid of owing too much money.

Most people don't attempt to negotiate with a company about its fees, but a client often doesn't see a salesperson as an institution. You're not cold, forbidding concrete walls and walkways. Instead, you're a warm, flesh-and-blood fellow human and because of this, clients are likely to try to negotiate with you. Depending on your clients' negotiation skills, they may do any or all of the following:

▲ Put off making a decision, forcing you to draw them out.
▲ Directly tell you that they're concerned about the cost. In this situation, you need to sell them on the value of the product or service you provide.
▲ Voice their concerns indirectly. For example, a client may say, "Another company I contacted will charge a lot less."

The following example illustrates how to overcome the fear of owing money.

If you have a price-conscious client whose fear of owing money is simply too great, you may have to bow out of the picture. You should do so gracefully and stay in touch with the prospect. The prospect may eventually see the wisdom in spending more for the quality product or service you can provide.

> ## FOR EXAMPLE
>
> ### Overcoming the Price: Sticker Shock, Part I
>
> Dennis is a sales representative at a high-end furniture store. Overcoming the fear of the cost of his furniture is a common practice for him. People think they could save some money for the same look at a discount store. Here's a look at how he usually handles these objections: "You know, I've learned something over the years. People look for three things when they spend money. They look for the finest quality, the best service, and, of course, the lowest investment. I've also found that no company can offer all three. They can't offer the finest quality and the best service for the lowest investment. So, for your long-term happiness, which of the three would you be most willing to give up? fine quality? excellent service? or the lowest fee?" If the customer prefers the lowest fee, then Dennis recommends shopping at the discount store. If not, then he believes that he has the best product for the people wanting quality furniture. His next move is to reiterate every service that his store can provide for its customers.

9.2.4 Fear of Deception

A common fear in buyers is the fear of deception. As a general rule, clients who have this fear doubt everything you say about how much they'll benefit from your product, service, or idea.

When you face a client like this, a strong past track record—on your side or the prospect's—comes into play. Your having a long list of happy clients should help you calm the fear of deception. If you're new and you don't yet have an established track record, you can tell a prospect you made a point of choosing the prospect's company to contact because it has a great track record.

If you're doing something entirely new with a new company, product or service, or concept, you have to build on the personal integrity and credentials of those involved in the project. For some products, the sales process involves a salesperson (you), a technical advisor who reviews technical details of either the manufacture or installation of a product, an installer, and after-market customer services people.

Now is a good place to reemphasize that there is never any reason to lie to a customer. If you're honest with your customers and always share the truth with them, even if it's bad news, they will respect you and give you the benefit of the doubt. Honesty and integrity in every selling situation make you a winner each and every time.

9.2.5 Fear of Embarrassment

Many people fear being embarrassed within their social and business circles. Bad decisions make a person feel insecure and powerless. Because many potential clients fear being embarrassed by making a bad decision, they put off making any decision at all.

If you're selling to more than one decision maker (e.g., a married couple, business partners), odds are that neither person will want to risk being embarrassed in front of the other. Most likely, they've disagreed about something in the past, and they don't want to have that uncomfortable situation arise again.

Knowing that this fear can block your sale, your primary goal when working with clients who are afraid of being embarrassed should be to help them feel secure with you. You need to let them know that they're not relinquishing total power to you—you're merely acting on their behalf, providing a product or service they need.

9.2.6 Fear of the Unknown

Fear of the unknown is a common fear in buyers. A lack of understanding of your product or service, or of its value to the prospect's company, is a reasonable cause for delaying any transaction. National name recognition can dispel some of this fear. But if you work for a local company, you should join forces with the rest of your company's sales staff to earn a great local reputation as a competent business with great products. Over the years, a great reputation saves you a bundle of time in the selling business.

Former teachers (at least the good ones) often make the best salespeople if they switch to careers in sales. This is because selling is all about educating people about the benefits of doing business with you. When you educate them past their fear of the unknown, they feel confident about their decision to do business with you.

You should always spend a little extra time on what your product actually does and the benefits it brings when you're working with a customer who is unaware of your offering—and afraid of the unknown.

9.2.7 Fear of Repeating Past Mistakes

Having a bad past experience generates fear in the hearts of some potential customers. If they've used a product or service like yours before, you should find out what kind of experience it was for them. If they hesitate to tell you, you can probably assume that their past experience was bad and that you have to overcome a lot more fear than if they've never used a product or service like yours before.

To help clients over the fear of repeating past mistakes, you can try offering your product or service on a sample or trial basis. You can also give the prospect the names of satisfied customers who will give unbiased testimony as to the value of your offering. (Of course, you should obtain permission from those past customers first.)

9.2.8 Fear Generated by Others

A prospect's fear may be based on third-party information. Someone may have said something negative about your company, your type of product, or even another representative of your company. That third party can stand between you and your prospect like a brick wall until you convince or persuade the customer that you can help because you are the expert on your product or service. You have to work hard to earn the prospect's trust. You should enlist the aid of some of your past happy clients as references, if necessary.

SELF-CHECK

1. Outline and describe each of the eight fears buyers have.

9.3 General Steps for Negotiating Buyer Concerns

When a prospect raises a concern, it doesn't necessarily mean "no way." It may simply be a way for the prospect to say "not this way." If that's the case, you need to take another path to the same destination. Finding that path has a lot to do with **selling instincts,** which are the messages your brain sends out, telling you what's right and what's not right in a selling situation. Everyone has these instincts, but some people's selling instincts are more developed than others. These instincts can be enhanced through practice and experience.

To start developing and using your selling instincts, you need to carefully listen to your customers' concerns and genuinely put their needs before your own. Then, and only then, can you trust your own instincts. If you can't honestly say that your customers' needs come before your own, then you place your own desires before what you instinctively know is right for the customer. Your self-centeredness will show; your customers will see the dollar signs in your eyes and won't trust you.

The first step in developing selling instincts is to expect a customer to raise concerns. Objections from prospects are just part of the business of selling. It's important that you know how to handle them.

SELF-CHECK

1. Define **selling instincts.**
2. How does relying on your selling instincts help in sales?

9.4 Specific Steps in Negotiating Buyer Concerns

If you get nervous or afraid when you hear a customer's objection and start beating a hasty retreat for the door, you're leaving empty-handed. You may be headed that way anyway if you try to overcome your client's objection and are met with disapproval. So why not experiment with ways to address your client's concerns or handle the person's objections? The worst that can happen is that you won't get what you want, and you'll move on to the next likely candidate. The best that can happen is that your customers will see how competently you handled their concerns and that their concerns weren't strong enough to keep them from going ahead with your offering.

How do you handle real concerns that a customer raises? Wilson Learning Worldwide suggests a method for handling objections that it refers to by the acronym **LSCPA**:

▲ **Listen** to the client's feelings.

▲ **Share** the concerns without judgment.

▲ **Clarify** the real issue by asking questions.

▲ **Problem-solve** by presenting options and solutions.

▲ **Ask** for action to determine commitment.[2]

These steps are recommended because when customers are feeling tense, they are in no mood to listen to a logical clarification or solution. Customer concerns are a signal that the person is feeling discomfort with the sales process. It is a natural part of the process. The listening and sharing steps can reduce tension by helping the customer get objections out in the open and showing that you, the salesperson, care enough to acknowledge and try to understand the customer. This section examines the steps in LSCPA.

9.4.1 Listening to the Client's Feelings

You need to listen actively and encourage the customer to talk. You shouldn't think about how you will respond while listening to the customer. In the sharing stage, you want to demonstrate understanding of the customer's feelings. Listening and sharing take maturity, energy, and patience. The customer is not attacking you personally, so you should concentrate on not being defensive. You need to uncover the client's concerns in order to address them.

You shouldn't quickly address every phrase the prospect utters. Instead, you should allow time for the prospect to complete a thought and encourage the person to tell you the whole story behind that concern. If you don't get the whole story, you don't know what to do or say to change the person's feelings. You shouldn't interrupt, either, or you may jump in and answer the wrong concern.

9.4.2 Share the Concerns Without Judgment

You need to discuss any concerns about fulfilling the needs of the buyer as early in the presentation as is appropriate. You shouldn't let unfulfilled expectations bring your long-term relationship with a potential client to a bitter end. You should cover all concerns and make sure the prospect understands the product.

Dismissing a prospect's concerns as unimportant can cause those objections to be completely blown out of proportion. In many cases, a simple "I see" or "I understand" is acknowledgment enough. In other cases, you may do well to say, "Let me make a note of that so we can discuss it in depth after we cover everything else," and then jot it down. Jotting down the concern validates the concern and shows your professionalism.

To the person you're persuading, every point raised is valid. You need to remember to put yourself in the prospect's situation. How would you react to someone acting as though your concerns were stupid or unimportant? By rephrasing the customer's concerns, in effect, you're asking for even more information and asking for trust. You want to be certain that the prospect has aired all concerns..

9.4.3 Clarifying the Real Issue by Asking Questions

The clarifying step often takes the form of a question, such as "Are you saying . . . ?" At this step, you are likely to uncover misinterpretations. When you do, you need to go back to the beginning of the process in order to listen to and share new understandings with the customer to demonstrate your acceptance and relieve tension. Subtlety and tact are very important during this step.

FOR EXAMPLE

The Subtle Question

Marc is in charge of the neighborhood crime-watch committee. One day, a volunteer objected to wearing a reflective vest while out walking the neighborhood. With experience in sales, Marc knew that asking "What's wrong with it?" would make the volunteer uncomfortable. Instead, Marc asked, "Wearing the vest makes you uncomfortable?" The volunteer said he would feel like a target if he wore the vest. Marc showed the volunteer information, indicating that the vest generates a certain respect from others for the wearer.

9.4.4 Problem-Solving by Presenting Options and Solutions

How the problem-solving stage is handled depends on the customer's concerns and the situation. One strategy is to present a list of the pros and cons for the action requested. Another approach is to admit that the concern is valid but to point out advantages that compensate for the concern. Alternatively, you could present a case history, describing how another prospect purchased the offering and benefited from its use.

This section discusses some basic do's and don'ts of this important step in selling.

If your prospect is asking lots of questions and looks somewhat perplexed or doubtful, the customer is interested but doesn't have a clear picture of the benefits of the purchase. This situation is especially common when the prospect doesn't have previous experience with a similar product and you're educating the person from the beginning. To respond to this kind of prospect, you have to cover the features and benefits in more detail—asking questions along the way to help create the right word pictures in your presentation.

Your questioning client may not have enough information. You may have to first earn the prospect's trust so that he or she gives you the time for education on your product. You also have to build the prospect's curiosity about the product, service, or idea so the person wants to know more. Backing up and clarifying exactly what the prospect is objecting to can help you figure out which direction to take for your next step.

If the client says, "I want to think it over," generally it means the prospect is interested. You need to find out exactly what the person wants to think over. In the majority of the cases, you'll find that money is involved. Everyone wants a bargain. Unless your product or service is severely underpriced, most of your potential clients will want to bargain or will hesitate in order to see if you'll offer an incentive to encourage their purchase.

Your client's hesitation can simply be a sign to slow down the selling process so the prospect can absorb all the information you're giving. When a potential client hesitates or gives you a stall, the person needs time, more information, or clarification.

An important way to address concerns is to get the other person to answer his or her own objections. You're trying to overcome the prospect's natural reservation about being sold anything. Until the prospect realizes that you're acting in his or her best interests, the person will have doubts. Whereas when a salesperson says something, a prospect tends to doubt it, if the prospect says it, he or she tends to think it's true. Prospects are much more likely to believe themselves than to believe you. Therefore, you should provide the information to answer a prospect's concerns and then let the person draw his or her own conclusions. The prospect ends up persuading himself or herself. This technique often works well when you're working with a married couple. When one partner objects to something, you shouldn't respond immediately. Average persuaders are quick to defend their offering. But there's a better way: Learn to sit silently. Many times, one spouse jumps in with the next comment, and there is a good chance that the originally silent spouse will answer the objection for you. The point is that these two people already have a positive relationship and trust each other's judgment. Being quiet while they work it through can cause the objection to evaporate.

During times when you need to exert patience, seconds feel like hours, and you can quickly become very uncomfortable. To keep yourself from jumping in too soon, you can kill that time by silently counting to 30 or reciting a short poem. Whatever method you choose, you need to be careful not to let the prospect see your lips move or look at your watch or a clock. Even a slight glance at a time-piece can distract the prospect because he or she is already looking at you, waiting for your next move. You should practice this until you're comfortable with it.

Although not arguing with a prospect may seem obvious, when you're nego-tiating with someone, emotions can take over, and things can get out of hand. Arguing or fighting over an objection or a concern raises a barrier between you and the person you're trying to persuade. Remember that objections are simply requests for further information.

There is a difference between not being able to afford a product and not want-ing to buy it. For a salesperson, a condition is not an excuse or a stall; it's a valid reason that the prospect cannot agree to what you're proposing. If you're trying to exchange your offering for your potential customer's money, and the customer has no money and no credit, you should move on. With so many potential cus-tomers out there who have no conditions, you have no good reason to beat your head against the wall with those who have valid conditions. It's important to always leave people who voice valid conditions on a positive note, however. You never know how that person's situation may change down the road.

An investment may require the person's time. If you hear "I don't have the time," that's not a valid condition. It's an objection. Everyone has the same 86,400 seconds in every day. How people use them is their choice. If you want someone to invest time with you, you have to show that person enough bene-fits that he or she wants to spend time on your offering.

At times, you might want to bypass an objection and indicate that you'll take note of it and address it at the end of your presentation. The idea is to allow enough information so that the prospect finds a satisfactory answer or sees enough benefit to outweigh the concern. If you're new to persuading, you shouldn't ignore any objection without testing the waters to see how big a concern it truly is. Sometimes just acknowledging a concern is enough. Your prospect may be satis-fied that you're really listening, and then she'll move ahead.

If you raise a concern before your prospect does, you're in control because you bring up the issue when you want to.

One way to handle a concern about money is to build on the credibility you've established, especially with a long-term customer. With this approach, you enhance

---

FOR EXAMPLE

Overcoming the Price: Sticker Shock, Part II

Let's revisit Dennis at the high-end furniture store. He knows his product costs more than others on the market. Generally, his prospects know that fact as well. In his presentations, he often explains up front that his product requires a higher investment than others because it is made with the highest-quality materials. He explains that those high-quality materials maintain their value and look better longer than the competition's. These are the features and benefits of the investment.

---

the credibility you've already established. In effect, you're telling your client that you're not an amateur. You have a concern for your own reputation, and you plan to be in the business a while. You can take advantage of this tactic when the customer voices the objections that are most often heard about your product or service. If people object to the cost, you should have a testimonial at hand from a happy client who had the same objection and now feels her return on investment was well worth it. Many companies post such testimonials on their Web sites. You can easily impress a prospect by calling up the Web site on your computer to address the prospect's concern. Let the prospect read the testimonial. In fact, asking your prospective client to take a look at your company's Web site prior to your presentation is a good idea. You can send the prospect an e-mail with your Web address and a few suggestions of helpful areas within your site.

Sometimes you hear more than one objection or concern from a prospect. If you start running through all steps with each objection you hear, you can spend a lifetime trying to persuade your prospects. Experience helps you tell which concerns you need to address and which you may be able to bypass. If a customer raises a concern or an objection during a group presentation, and you have to do a bit of research to provide an answer, you should be certain you have the contact information (specifically, an e-mail address) for each person in the group. You should never rely on one person to relay vital information in the manner that you know to be best for moving the selling process forward. You should therefore send the same e-mail message to each person and indicate that they're part of a group e-mail. If each person receives it individually, the prospects could all wonder what else you may have shared with the others. You should include a link to your company's Web site in the e-mail. Often in a committee decision-making situation, only one or two members get the whole package of information. They then break it down for the balance of the decision makers. This may be the way the company wants the process handled, but what you want is to equally distribute as much information as possible.

If prospects bombard you with objections, you might want to ask a few questions to get them to express their *real* objections. If people protest too much, they're either not interested and don't have the guts to tell you so, or they're hiding the real reason they aren't going ahead. For some people, liking your offering but being unable to afford it is difficult to admit. So instead of admitting that they're strapped, they come up with dozens of other reasons your product, service, or idea isn't right for them. Eventually, you might need to say something like this: "Mrs. Johnson, obviously, you have quite a few concerns about our product. May I ask, what will you base your final decision on—the overall benefits to your family or the financial aspects of this transaction?"

9.4.5 Asking for Action to Determine Commitment

When you've answered a customer's objection, confirming that the person heard and accepted your answer is important. If you don't complete this step, the prospect is likely to raise that objection again.

You can confirm your answers simply by completing your answer with a statement such as, "That answers your concern, doesn't it?" If the prospect agrees with you that your comment answered his or her concern, you're one step closer to persuading that person. If the prospect isn't satisfied with your answer, now is the time to know instead of later, when you try to get the person's final decision to go ahead.

"By the way" are three very useful words in any attempt to persuade or convince another person. You can use the phrase to change gears and move on to the next topic. When you do, you shouldn't just keep talking. You should take a conscious, purposeful step back into your presentation. If appropriate, you can turn the page in your presentation binder or booklet and point to something other than whatever generated the objection. You should take some sort of action that signals to the other person that you're forging ahead. Now you're ready to close the sale, which is the focus of Chapter 10.

SELF-CHECK

1. Define **LSCPA** and discuss each step associated with LSCPA.
2. Describe how you would respond to each of the following situations:
   (a) Your customer looks perplexed and asks many questions.
   (b) You customer says, "I want to think it over."
   (c) Your client hesitates.
   (d) Your client voices objections.
   (e) Your customer is silent.
   (f) Your client seems to want an argument
   (g) Your prospect can't afford your product.
   (h) You customer says, "I don't have the time to invest."

SUMMARY

Even if you believe you've uncovered your customer's needs in the prospecting and qualifying phases, you should expect to encounter some objections during your presentation and closing. These objections are a natural reaction: Most people have some kind of fear in purchasing an item or service. You need to help a customer overcome this fear and discover the benefits of your product or service. To achieve that goal, you can use the steps in the LSCPA method: listen, share, clarify, problem-solve, and ask for action. These steps, if you practice and apply them properly, can take you a long way toward achieving your goal of selling to others, even when those prospects raise objections or concerns. Using this method, you ask for the real objection to your product or service while still being nice, warm, and friendly. You can't move beyond this step in the selling cycle until you identify and handle any real objections.

KEY TERMS

LSCPA	An acronym that describes the process for responding to customer concerns. Stands for listen, share, clarify, problem-solve, and ask for action.
Selling instincts	Messages your brain sends out, telling you what's right and what's not in a selling situation.

ASSESS YOUR UNDERSTANDING

Go to www.wiley.com/college/hopkins to evaluate your knowledge of responding to customers' objections.

Measure your learning by comparing pre-test and post-test results.

Summary Questions

1. Customer concerns signal that a prospect is:
   (a) not interested in your product or service.
   (b) testing your sales ability.
   (c) uncomfortable with the sales process.
   (d) interested only in being a pest.
2. Research indicates that successful interactions have much fewer objections than failed ones. True or false?
3. The most difficult people to persuade are those who have no objections and raise no questions. True or false?
4. Customer concerns are generated by fear. True or false?
5. Salespeople inspire fear. True or false?
6. The messages your brain transmits, indicating your moves in a selling situation, are referred to as:
   (a) selling skills.
   (b) selling statements.
   (c) selling brainwaves.
   (d) selling instincts.
7. The acronym LSCPA stands for listen, sell, clarify, problem-solve, and ask for action. True or false?
8. An important aspect in the problem-solving step in LSCPA is to get the prospect involved in solving any objections. True or false?

Applying This Chapter

1. Think of a sales experience you have had in which you voiced an area of concern. How did the salesperson react? If you made a purchase, what did the salesperson do to encourage the sale? If you didn't purchase anything, what could the salesperson have done to sway you?
2. Visualize yourself in the market for a used car. Describe any fears you have in making the decision to buy a car.
3. Describe your current ability in handling the LSCPA process. Are there any areas that you think you need to improve?

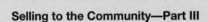

Selling to the Community—Part III

Part of your presentation to the faction of the community opposing the arts center must deal with these residents' objections. You know that most of the people object to the center because the construction would raise their taxes.

1. How would you address this area of concern?
2. What three benefits did you visualize in the Part I assignment (refer to Chapter 6)?
3. What strategies would you use to overcome any obstacles?

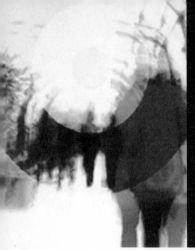

10

CLOSING A SALE
Helping Customers Make a Decision That's Right for Them

Starting Point

Go to www.wiley.com/college/hopkins to assess your knowledge of closing a sale.
Determine where you need to concentrate your effort.

What You'll Learn in This Chapter

▲ Guidelines for closing a sale
▲ Closing techniques
▲ How to deal with stalling

After Studying This Chapter, You'll Be Able To

▲ Recognize the right time to close a sale
▲ Choose the proper techniques for closing a sale

INTRODUCTION *4*

Closing occurs when a salesperson asks a customer for a commitment. Salespeople have differing views on this process. One view is that closing is the most difficult step of the selling process. Many salespeople are reluctant to close, primarily because they fear rejection. They feel that if they do not ask for an order, they cannot be turned down, so they avoid embarrassment or disappointment. Another view is that closing is the fun part of sales—the moment when you unite your client's needs and your product and service. If you adopt this philosophy of selling, you know that, in effect, you start closing the sale from the moment you first contact any prospect.

Regardless of the philosophy salespeople embrace, however, they know that if they want a sale, sooner or later they need to ask for it. The ability to close a sale can separate average salespeople from superstars.

All professional purchasing agents expect a sales representative to attempt to close. It is the job of the salesperson to make the first move. If you have successfully performed the earlier steps in the selling process, the close follows naturally. In this case, closing is simply asking for a decision when you believe a prospect is going to say "yes." This chapter explains the skills and techniques necessary to reach that "yes."

10.1 Guidelines for Closing a Sale *5*

An often-heard suggestion for salespeople is to "close early and close often." This advice is not consistent with efforts to build trusting relationships with customers. By following this philosophy, you're building an adversarial relationship. A client is likely to regard asking for the order before he or she is ready to buy as pushy. You don't want to seem pushy, as though you want the sale too badly, or overly aggressive, or the client is likely to close up and start pushing back. Research supports the idea of not being too pushy when closing a sale.[1] Many successful salespeople tend to simply let the customer make the decision, often through the use of silence.

This doesn't mean that successful salespeople expect to close only once. Often, undiscovered needs still need to be addressed. One of your customer's needs may be to have other people listen. This is one reason that salespeople must be prepared to use multiple closes. It is often said that most acceptances are made on the fifth closing attempt. So you shouldn't give up. A healthy sales quota depends on your ability to close.

If undiscovered needs are likely to exist and multiple closes are often required, how do you avoid being pushy while uncovering hidden needs and making a sale? You can use the techniques described in this section.

10.1.1 Focusing on Buying Motives

Closing a sale starts at the beginning of the transaction, when you first make contact with the prospect. You need to follow all the steps discussed in prior chapters before moving on to the close. You need to primarily focus on the customer's buying motives throughout the process.

You've studied buying motives in previous chapters. If you get to the closing stage and find that you've still not uncovered the buying motives, you might find a technique developed by Benjamin Franklin helpful. This revolutionary inventor, statesman, and philosopher used a decision-making strategy in which he made a list of the positives and negatives surrounding a choice. You can apply this technique by asking a customer to develop his or her own list. Here's how it works:

1. Have your prospect draw a line down a piece of paper. On one side of the page, the prospect writes all the reasons in favor of the decision. On the other, he or she writes all the reasons against the decision. The customer then examines the reasons on each side and determines which reason is the best for his or her circumstances. At this point, you might want to remind the customer of the positive aspects he or she mentioned in earlier conversations.
2. Make note of each item with a check mark to track how many there are.
3. Set a goal for between 6 and 10 items on the plus side. If the customer hasn't listed 10 at this point, refer to your notes and remind the prospect of other items to add to this column. When you have a list of 10 reasons to make the decision, add up the positives and negatives. If the positives outnumber the negatives, you've helped your customer see the benefits of purchasing your product.
4. A question such as, "Isn't it obvious to you what the answer is?" Expect to wait through a long silence after you pose this question. The key here is to shut your mouth and not do or say anything that takes away from your request for a decision.

Your prospect should do one of three things:

▲ Try to stall, putting off making the decision by asking for more time or asking a question to change the subject.
▲ Decide to go ahead.
▲ Give you an objection.

10.1.2 Using Trial Closes to Gauge Interest

Closes call for decisions, but the **trial closes** technique involves asking questions for opinions that serve as indicators of how close the client is to making a purchase

++ 207d

LSL

decision. Your objective is to point your prospect toward ownership. You may, for example, ask the following questions:

▲ How does this look to you?
▲ How important is this to you?
▲ Is this what you had in mind?
▲ Will this equipment be consistent with what you have now?

If a prospect gives a positive response to one of these questions, the salesperson can assume that the person is leaning toward buying and can move directly to the final close. The salesperson should be prepared to continue the sales presentation. If the person does not appear ready to make a decision, the salesperson might ask, "Is there anything I presented that is unclear or doesn't meet your particular needs?" This question helps the salesperson uncover the prospect's real needs, which must happen before the salesperson can attempt any closing strategy.

A version of the trial close is the erroneous conclusion test close. An **erroneous conclusion** is an intentional error you make to test how serious the prospect is about going ahead with the sale. If the prospect doesn't correct you, you may have missed some information along the way that indicated the customer's seriousness about the purchase. If the customer does correct you, you know that he or she is looking to buy. In this kind of test, you want to take your prospect's buying temperature to see if it's warm enough to go ahead.

4
5

BT

FOR EXAMPLE

Some Mistakes Work in Your Favor

Larry works as a sales representative for a home renovation company. During a presentation to homeowners John and Cathy, Larry overhears Cathy tell John that her mother is visiting in July. "If we decide what we want today," says Cathy, "we ought to have it finished by then." Larry picks up on the comment and remembers it for his closing. Here's a look at Larry using the erroneous conclusion:

> LARRY: *I can see that you're kind of excited about this addition. Now, your mother is coming in August, isn't she?*
> CATHY: *No, in July.*
> LARRY: *So the first week in June would be the best time to get started?*
> CATHY: *Yes.*
> LARRY: *Let me make a note of that.*

The purpose of this method is not to tell a lie or trick the customer. It's simply a test for you to determine whether the prospect is sincere in moving ahead.

10.1.3 Asking a Reflex Question

It's a good idea to go into a closing sequence by asking a reflex question, which keeps the conversation moving forward. A **reflex question** is a question your prospect can answer without thinking. For instance, you have a prospect's first name. A good reflex question may be getting the prospect's middle initial. If you're dealing with a corporate executive, a good reflex question is to ask for the company's complete name and address. If the executive hands you a business card and lets you copy all the information, you get to move ahead.

10.1.4 Knowing What You Can Deliver

Before you ask a prospect, "Will you go ahead with the purchase?" you must be absolutely sure that you can deliver your product. You shouldn't say you can deliver the product if you can't. Overselling and over-promising are the two enemies of a professional salesperson.

If you are always honest, your reputation will bring you more business. One of the reasons trained salespeople outsell average salespeople is that the professionals know more about their products and what their companies can deliver. How do you get this information? It depends on your product, the company, and your attitude.

Salespeople often make enemies in production departments and on shipping docks by promising clients things the company can't deliver. When the client gets angry about a missed delivery date, the production department or the shipping dock usually takes the blame. You need to know what your company can deliver, and always thank the people in your company who help you get your job done, especially if fulfillment requires extra effort on their part in order for you to keep your sale.

10.1.5 Displaying Self-Confidence

Salespeople are often uncomfortable if they have to go beyond putting their offering out there. If a prospect doesn't quickly see the value of the product or service and jump right in to own it or to participate in some way, the salesperson may start to lose confidence. This wavering of confidence weakens the salesperson's desire to close the sale. In other words, the salesperson doesn't ask for the order, call for a decision, or otherwise try to get a commitment from the prospect.

One survey showed that many nonbuyers were simply not asked to buy.[2] The prospects were contacted, a product or service was demonstrated to them, and their questions (or objections or concerns) were answered. In some cases, they were convinced of the value of the offering and probably would have gone ahead, but nothing happened. The salespeople didn't ask the prospects to make a commitment or to part with their money, so they didn't.

Displaying a demeanor of self-confidence doesn't just mean showing the client your belief in yourself and your product. It also means asking for the order.

10.1.6 Asking for the Order More Than Once

You may indeed encounter "no" more frequently than "yes." In fact, the average consumer says "no" to a new product or service approximately five times before giving it serious consideration.[3] If a salesperson knows only one or two ways to ask for an order, he or she is likely to hear "no" much more frequently than a salesperson with a full arsenal of techniques. You need to learn how to ask for the order in a variety of ways. Mastering various closing techniques is key to your sales success.

10.1.7 Recognizing Closing Cues

In closing, as in many other aspects of life, timing is important. Successful salespeople learn to time their closing remarks on the basis of the customer's buying signals. These cues can take the form of gestures (e.g., the customer nods in agreement, picks up the product and examines it closely, leans back in his or her chair), or they can be verbal comments. The salesperson should recognize customer comments such as these as signs of interest and shift to a specific closing routine:

▲ "Shipments must be completed in five months?"
▲ "We like the speed-control feature."
▲ "Would we be able to install the custom model within three weeks?"

Notice that each of these signals suggests an action by the client, not just a problem.

Sometimes salespeople wait so long to ask for the sale that they miss the right time. To get past this timing challenge, you should figure out how to take a prospect's buying temperature. You need to watch for positive buying signs, including the following:

▲ The prospect has been moving along at a smooth pace then suddenly slows the pace significantly. The customer is making a final analysis or rationalizing the decision.
▲ The prospect speeds up the pace, showing an excitement to move ahead.
▲ The customer suddenly starts asking lots of questions. Customers ask questions only about things that interest them.

▲ The prospect asks questions about general terms of purchase before settling on one particular model. Some people start asking questions about initial investment, delivery, and so on as soon as they begin speaking with a salesperson; they feel safe doing this because they know you can't sell them everything. But if they ask these questions after you know exactly what they want, it's a good sign.

If you've noticed any of these positive signs, you should test the waters. If you think your prospect is ready to close the sale, ask a test question to make sure you've gotten the right impression. When you ask this question—to which you expect an answer confirming that the prospect wants to go ahead with the purchase—one of two things happens:

▲ The prospect gives you a "yes" or an answer that indirectly confirms his or her desire to go ahead with the sale.
▲ The prospect gives you an objection or asks for more information so that he or she can make a decision.

You shouldn't start talking before the prospect answers. You want to be sure to get either a confirmation to go ahead or an objection. If you get the former, you can go ahead with the close. If you get the latter, you need to answer the prospect's questions and address the person's concerns.

SELF-CHECK

1. Define **closing**.
2. Define **trial close**. What is the purpose of a trial close?
3. Define **erroneous conclusion**. Discuss how to use an erroneous conclusion as a trial close.
4. Discuss how to use the decision-making strategy of listing the positives and negatives of a buying decision.
5. What is a reflex question? What is its benefit?
6. Discuss the importance of salespeople knowing what they can deliver.
7. Describe the importance of a salesperson's demeanor of self-confidence.
8. Why should you know more than a couple closing techniques?
9. Describe the closing cues a salesperson might encounter.

10.2 Closing Techniques

Closing is where you and your client reap the rewards of your preparation and skills. You can use many different closing techniques, and salespeople have preferences for them, depending on the circumstances and what they're comfortable with. Salespeople need to be familiar with a number of closing techniques so that they can choose methods that are appropriate for each selling situation. This section describes some of the popular techniques.

10.2.1 The Basic Oral Close

When you're talking with your prospects in person, you have the perfect opportunity to close the sale through your conversation. The **basic oral close** is a simple statement asking for the order. Here's an example: "I'm excited to help you take this major step. We can do that right here, with your approval."

If you know everything is right, you can go ahead and ask for the order. One of the biggest mistakes novice salespeople make is to keep trying to sell. They don't always recognize when they can close. They simply continue to talk, re-demonstrate the product, or even change the subject while searching for a reason to continue in the company of their prospects.

10.2.2 The Basic Written Close

If you use order forms in your selling, the **basic written close** works especially well. This involves filling out an order form after determining preferences with your client. You ask the customer to check the order form. If the details are in order, you can have the client sign the form. In most cases, the forward momentum you develop while completing the form is enough to get it approved. If the prospect gets used to seeing you write on the order form, you're almost home.

10.2.3 The Alternative Choice Close

When the prospect is faced with a variety of colors and models, the **alternative choice** close may be effective. With this technique, the salesperson poses a series of questions designed to narrow the choice and help the prospect make a final selection. Here's an example: "These couplings can be packed in units of 24 or cases of 72. Which is more convenient for you?" This way, no matter which option your prospect chooses, the sale moves forward because you haven't given the prospect the option of saying no.

10.2.4 The Porcupine Method

Imagine that a prickly porcupine were tossed to you. What would you do? Instinctively, you would probably either jump out of its way or catch it and quickly toss it back. You can use a method of questioning called the **porcupine method** in much the same way: When your prospect asks you a question, you ask another question about that question.

Here's an example of the porcupine method in action at a car dealership. A young woman walks through a car lot, looking at convertibles. Suddenly she stops, points at a car, and says, "This is the convertible I'm interested in. Do you have it in red?" The average salesperson would answer her by saying, "If we don't have it in red, I can call around and get one for you in a hurry." Unlike the average salesperson, the champion salesperson would answer the customer's question this way: "Would you like it in Red-Hot Red or Cranberry Red?"

The client has already indicated that she's interested in a red convertible, so she'll most likely choose one color or the other. The salesperson is now one step closer to getting the customer's autograph on that dotted line and having a happy customer. The porcupine method illustrates that the real power in selling is in motivating the customer with questions.

10.2.5 The Summary Close

One of the most popular closes, the **summary close,** provides a summary of the benefits accepted and combines this list with an action plan that requires the customer's commitment. Here's an example of how one salesperson used the summary close:

> SALESPERSON: *George, you have said that our word processor has more memory, better graphics, and is easier to use than other machines you have seen. Is that correct?*
>
> PROSPECT: *Yes.*
>
> SALESPERSON: *I recommended that you lease one of our machines for three months, and the lease payments will apply to the purchase price if you decide to keep it.*

10.2.6 Sharp Angling

In some situations, a prospect might challenge you to give him exactly what he wants. The key is to accept the challenge. You also want an understanding that if you can provide the client's exact specifications, you win by getting the sale, and the prospect wins by owning the exact product or service desired. This method is referred to as **sharp angling** your prospect into ownership. Here's an example:

> PROSPECT: *If I decide I want this boat, can you handle delivery by Memorial Day?*
>
> SALESPERSON: *If I can guarantee delivery by Memorial Day, I bet you can guarantee me that you'll be prepared to have a great time enjoying the holiday on your new boat, can't you?*

An average salesperson would be tempted to answer the prospect's question with a simple "yes," even if the deadline is not feasible. Here's how a champion salesperson takes advantage of this same opportunity:

> SALESPERSON: *If I could guarantee delivery by May 15, and I am not certain yet that I can, are you prepared to approve the paperwork today?*

The champion salesperson then remains silent, which is key. The first person to speak owns the product. It will either be the salesperson keeping the product in inventory or the prospect keeping the product at his home or business.

Before you can use the sharp angling method, your prospect must first express a demand or desire that you can meet. To use your prospect's own demand as your way to get to a "yes" answer, you need to remember that sharp angling involves two pivotal points:

▲ You must know what benefits you can deliver.

▲ You must know when the delivery can be made.

A dangerous part of sharp angling is that you may be tempted to apply it before you've gathered enough qualification information or before you've built enough rapport. You shouldn't use this method too early in the selling process. If you do, you might offend some people because the method is not smooth and can be interpreted as overly aggressive. But if the prospect's thinking and the rapport you have with that person are in good shape, the sharp angle is a wonderful way to get agreement early in the sales process.

10.2.7 The Higher Authority Close

Every happy client is a potential higher authority, one you can use for the **higher authority close.** With this technique, you tell your client about one of your satisfied clients—a client that your prospect respects. The prospect doesn't have to know the higher authority personally, but the prospect does need to recognize the authority's name and position.

Here are the steps for using this close successfully:

1. Select your higher authority figure. You should constantly be on the lookout for higher authority figures. For example, imagine that you're the sales-record smasher for BuiltGreat Computer Systems. A prominent businessperson in the area invested in a computer system for her company, MarketShare, Inc., and she's very pleased with the system's performance and increased productivity. This businessperson, Katharine Steele, is an ideal higher authority figure for anyone interested in your computers.

2. Recruit your higher authority figure. Using the example in step 1, ask Katharine Steele if she'd be willing to share her knowledge of your product with other businesspeople. Katharine agrees because you've done a solid sales and service job for her on a good product, and you've assured her that you'll call her only when you need help with an occasional prospect who may be in a similar situation. In other words, you promise not to bother her if you're working on selling a two-computer system to a small business. (Be sure to give this person a small gift of appreciation.)

3. Schedule your higher authority figure for the sales situation. For example, determine whether Katharine Steele is available to take a phone call while you're with the client. With Katharine's cooperation, you complete your plans for a powerful presentation.

4. Use the higher authority figure confirmation effectively. For example, allow the client to ask questions of Katherine Steele. This way, the client gets answers from a respected figure.

5. Close after the call.

Don't settle for just one higher authority. You can wear out any one person if you rely on him or her too much. When you do your job with the utmost professionalism, most clients are happy to help you out. It's an ego boost for them to be considered a higher authority.

10.2.8 Advanced Closing Techniques

There are numerous variations on the closing techniques discussed in this chapter. The following are 10 especially good advanced closes[4]:   [Note 4]

▲ **The wish-ida close:** When you know what you're offering is truly good for your prospect and your prospect has agreed but just doesn't seem to want to make a decision, the **wish-ida close** is perfect. It's lighthearted, yet it makes a valid point: The prospect may regret not making the purchase. Here's one variation of the story: Everyone's a member of the Wish-Ida Club. Wish Ida bought real estate in Arizona 15 years ago. Wish Ida invested in some stock 20 years ago so I'd be rich today. Wish Ida grabbed a chance to gain an exclusive advantage. Wouldn't it be great to get rid of at least one Wish Ida by saying yes to something you really want?

▲ **The business-productivity close:** When marketing products or services to businesses, the company's main concern is always the bottom line and whether your product or service makes or saves them money. If your product does not clearly fall into one of those categories, the **business productivity close** helps the prospect view the decision from a different perspective—that of happier employees. Your goal is to show how your product benefits the employees. For instance, your product may boost employee morale, which usually increases productivity.

▲ **The best-things-in-life close:** Everyone wants to have the best things in life. Everyone wants to believe that he or she has made some of the best decisions when considering major purchases or investments. The **best-things-in-life close** gets the prospect's mind off the money objection and onto the enjoyment of benefits.

▲ **The lost-sale close:** If you think you've done everything and your prospect still doesn't decide to buy, admit defeat. Prepare to head for the door. Then use the lost-sale close. Ask the prospect to help you by showing you any mistakes in your presentation. More often than not, this reopens conversations enough that your prospect will give you something to grasp onto to tell you if he or she might say yes.

▲ **The my-dear-old-mother close:** The **my-dear-old-mother close** can be your salvation when you find yourself involved in a series of silences as you roll from close to close with the same prospect. If you have a clever way to break tension, pressure turns into humor. Lots of people can handle pressure, but laughter pops them wide open. So when the pressure has been on for several seconds after your last close and it's getting heavy in the room, you can suddenly grin and say, "My dear old mother once said, 'Silence means consent.' Was she right?"

▲ **The law-of-10 close:** The **law-of-10 close** works especially well for intangibles such as financial services, insurance, or education. It's also useful for large-ticket items, such as real estate or stocks—items that appreciate in value. Usually, a person has purchased an item that has appreciated in value over the years. A good test of the item's value is to determine whether it will stand the test of 10-times. For instance, you may have invested in a home, car, clothes, jewelry, or something that gave you great pleasure. But after you owned it for a while, could you answer this question positively: "Would I now be willing to pay 10 times more for it than I did then?" In other words, has it given you that much pleasure, increased mental attitude, or income? So, ask the prospect, "Ten years from now, will today's investment be worth more or less to you than you'll be investing today?"

▲ **The buyer-remorse close:** When people are making major decisions, you can expect them to have second thoughts about things after the decision is made. That's why so many contractual agreements for large-ticket items have a 72-hour clause that allows buyers to change their minds. If you're afraid a new client might try to later back out of the deal by invoking this clause, you should address head on by using the **buyer-remorse close**. Here's an example: "I feel good about the decision you have made tonight. I can tell you're both excited and somewhat relieved. From time to time, I have had people just like you who were positive about the decision they had made until they shared it with a friend or relative. The well-meaning friend of relative, not understanding all the facts and maybe even being a little envious, would discourage them to form their decision for one reason or another. Please don't let this happen to you. In fact, if you think you may change your mind, please tell me now."

▲ **The it's-not-in-the-budget close:** A standard line businesspeople use to get rid of average salespeople is, "It's not in the budget." They use this line because it works with average salespeople. However, businesspeople also understand that the budget is only a tool. If the product or service you're offering has enough value, most companies can find a way to loosen up that budget or take steps to own it. Here's a look at how you might use the **it's-not-in-the-budget close:** "I'm fully aware of the fact that every well-managed business controls the flow of its money with a carefully planned budget. The budget is a necessary tool for every company to give direction to its goals. However, the tool itself doesn't dictate how the company is run. It must be flexible. You, as the controller of that budget, retain for yourself the right to flex that budget in the best interest of the company's financial present and competitive future, don't you? What we have been examining here today is a system that will allow your company an immediate and continuing competitive edge. Tell me, under these conditions, will your budget flex, or will it dictate your actions?"

▲ **The take-it-away close:** Some people don't want to make a decision on ownership simply because they feel they can make the decision at any time. By subtly inferring that you have to see if your prospect qualifies before this person can own the product, you may entice a "yes." This close, called the **take-it-away close,** works especially well with products that involve financing or insurance or that require the client to meet a certain health standard.

▲ **The no close:** The **no close** can help you move beyond the word "no." Here's an example of how to use it: "Mr. Johnson, there are many salespeople in the world, and they're all confident they have opportunities that are good for you. And they have persuasive reasons for you to invest with them, haven't they? You, of course, can say no to any or all of them, can't you? You see, as a professional, my experience has taught me an overwhelming truth: No one can say no to me. All he can say no to is himself. Tell me, how can I accept this kind of no? In fact, if you were me, would you let Mr. Johnson say no to anything so critical to his success and happiness?"

SELF-CHECK

1. Define and list the benefits of each of the following closing techniques:

   (a) Basic oral close.

   (b) Basic written close.

   (c) Alternative choice.

   (d) Porcupine method.

   (e) Summary close.

   (f) Sharp angling.

   (g) Higher authority close.

2. List and describe the 10 advanced closes.

10.3 Dealing with "I Want to Think It Over"

In Chapter 9, you learned that one of most common stalling tactics is the phrase "I want to think it over." How do you handle this situation? One way is to ask about the benefits of the product. In most cases, the decision comes down to money. You should look for ways to provide financing or reducing the initial investment, if possible. Or, instead of addressing the total cost, you can examine the difference between the various options. For example, if your prospect plans to spend $20,000 for a car, and the car he's looking at is $22,000, the problem isn't $22,000. It's $2,000. When you know exactly the amount of money involved, you can work with your prospect to find ways to handle the investment and let the prospect have what he or she really wants—your product or service—at the same time.

You need to be sure to have a calculator ready. No matter how confident you are in your mathematical abilities, you should always use a calculator. You also need to know your formulas and figures so that you can quickly provide any numerical information your prospect requests.

A prospect who sees you punch numbers into your calculator—or one who does the punching—isn't likely to question the figures. But if you start furiously scratching numbers on paper with a pencil, the prospect gets uncomfortable sitting and watching you have all the fun with numbers. Even worse, if you rattle figures off the top of your head, your prospect may doubt you. Instead of paying attention to your presentation, the customer may look over your shoulder to double-check your math. Not using a calculator may raise doubts about your mathematical abilities.

SELF-CHECK

1. Describe a popular method for dealing with the stalling tactic "I want to think it over."

SUMMARY

Because prospects are people, they need help making decisions. Few people are persuaded to buy something they don't want. If your product or service is a major purchase, it may be difficult to sell prospects on it even if they do want it. Problems arise when unscrupulous salespeople lie about what a product is and what it can do. Through deceit, these salespeople violate the buyer's trust, and the buyer ends up owning something other than what was expected. It's important to never lie to a customer. However, there are techniques you can use to guide a prospect into buying your products instead of the competition's. Using the proper closing technique can help. This chapter examines many techniques and other considerations sales professionals can use to close a sale. Whatever closing techniques you choose, learning how to apply them properly can mean the difference between success and failure in sales.

KEY TERMS

Alternative choice	A closing technique in which the salesperson poses a series of questions designed to narrow the choice for a final selection.
Basic oral close	A closing technique involving a simple statement that directly asks for the order.
Basic written close	A closing method in which the salesperson fills out an order form after determining preferences with a client. The salesperson asks the client to check out the details and sign the form.
Best-things-in-life close	A closing technique that emphasizes the enjoyment of a product's benefits.
Business-productivity close	A closing technique that emphasizes the benefits of a product for a company's employees.
Buyer-remorse close	A closing technique that relieves remorse after a purchase.
Closing	The stage of selling when a salesperson asks for a commitment from the customer.

Erroneous conclusion	An intentional error a salesperson makes to test how serious the prospect is about going ahead with the sale.
Higher authority close	A closing technique in which you use the example of a higher authority who is respected by the client as one of your satisfied clients.
It's-not-in-the-budget close	A closing technique that allows a prospect to flex any budget constraints and disallows the easy dismissal of a salesperson.
Law-of-10 close	A closing technique that emphasizes a product's increased value in 10 years.
Lost-sale close	A closing technique that reopens the conversation between a salesperson and a prospect when the sale seems lost.
My-dear-old-mother close	A closing technique that emphasizes a mother's saying "Silence means consent, right?"
No close	A closing technique that helps the salesperson move beyond the word "no."
Porcupine method	A closing technique in which a salesperson responds to a prospect's question with another, related question.
Reflex question	A question a prospect can answer without thinking.
Sharp angling	A closing technique in which the salesperson accepts a prospect's challenge to provide exact specifications, with the understanding that the sale is made.
Summary close	A closing technique in which the salesperson provides a summary of the benefits accepted and combines it with an action plan that requires the customer's commitment.
Trial closes	A closing technique in which the salesperson asks questions whose answers serve as indicators of how close the client is to making a purchase decision.
Take-it-away close	A closing technique for dealing with people who don't want to make a decision on ownership simply because they feel they can make the decision at any time.
Wish-ida close	A closing technique that emphasizes that the prospect may regret not making the purchase.

ASSESS YOUR UNDERSTANDING

Go to www.wiley.com/college/hopkins to evaluate your knowledge of closing a sale. *Measure your learning by comparing pre-test and post-test results.*

Summary Questions

1. A common problem among salespeople is that they neglect to ask a prospect for an order. True or false?

2. Salespeople should learn one or two closing techniques. True or false?

3. Trial closes are used to discover whether the customer is leaning toward a buying decision. True or false?

4. An erroneous conclusion used by a salesperson tends to create doubts and mistrust. True or false?

5. The result of the technique in which a prospect lists positives and negatives about a buying decision is that the prospect:

   (a) makes the deal.

   (b) voices an objection.

   (c) stalls.

   (d) does any of the above.

6. Which of the following is *not* a positive buying signal?

   (a) The prospect smiles and nods a lot.

   (b) The prospect asks many questions.

   (c) The prospect slows the pace.

   (d) The prospect speeds up.

7. Using a series of questions used to narrow the choice for a prospect is called:

   (a) a basic oral close.

   (b) a summary close.

   (c) an alternative close.

   (d) sharp angling.

8. Every happy client is a potential higher authority. True or false?

9. A closing technique in which the salesperson asks the prospect to imagine the financial appreciation of an item in the future is called the:

   (a) business-productivity close.

   (b) law-of-10 close.

   (c) best-things-in-life close.

   (d) take-it-away close.

10. Professional salespeople should stop the selling process after hearing the customer express a desire to think about the decision. True or false?

Applying This Chapter

1. Visualize yourself as a sales representative for a home renovation company. You are working with a homeowner who has expressed a desire to completely renovate a kitchen, including replacing appliances. You're not sure that the person is completely sold on using your company for the renovation. Develop a set of at least five trial closing questions to gauge this person's interest in a purchasing decision.

2. Think about a time when you made a major purchase. Did the salesperson use one of the closing techniques described in this chapter? If so, describe the technique used. If not, describe the technique that might have been helpful in closing the deal.

3. Visualize working as a real estate agent and being assigned to sell an 80-acre farm. You think you have a buyer, who happens to be a housing developer. During your presentation, the developer stalls and voices a number of concerns. What closing techniques would you use to handle each of the following stalls or concerns?

    (a) "I want to think it over."

    (b) "I'm not sure I can afford it."

    (c) "I would need to develop the land within a year in order to meet my financial obligations."

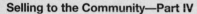

YOU TRY IT

Selling to the Community—Part IV

You've addressed the objections of the faction opposing the construction of the arts center. You're almost ready to pack up your visual aids and go back to the office. You don't have to obtain these residents' support in order to proceed with the building, but your client—the city's governing body—would like to have good feelings about the new project. Your job now is to "sell" this faction of the community on the benefits of the center. You sense that most people are willing to accept the arts center now because of the benefits you've outlined. You need to close the deal. Discuss how you will use trial closes and at least four closing techniques that could help you make the sale.

11

AFTER THE SALE: SERVICE TO BUILD A PARTNERSHIP
Following Up and Keeping in Touch

Starting Point

Go to www.wiley.com/college/hopkins to assess your knowledge of service to build a partnership.
Determine where you need to concentrate your effort.

What You'll Learn in This Chapter

▲ Keys to building long-term partnerships with customers
▲ Customer service methods that strengthen a partnership
▲ The importance of preplanning your service strategy
▲ Steps for getting referrals

After Studying This Chapter, You'll Be Able To

▲ Plan an effective strategy to maintain long-term partnerships with your customers

INTRODUCTION

A sale only begins the relationship between customer and supplier. After a salesperson helps a customer make a purchase, attention shifts to the follow-up activities. These are functions that lead to the ultimate goal of the salesperson: repeat business. This chapter examines the responsibilities of a salesperson after making a sale.

11.1 Building Long-Term Partnerships

The selling process is really a continuous one. After the immediate post-interaction activities are complete, the seller's focus shifts from the "attraction" part of the process to the "retention and growth" aspect. Retention activities may include performing customer market analysis, developing joint customer marketing programs, monitoring inventory, providing customer service, handling complaints, staying in touch, placing reorders, and providing ongoing training. These activities are perhaps the most important part of a long-term partnership. In fact, one study ranked the quality of customer service the highest in terms of contributions to growth and profits (see Figure 11-1). This shows that the salesperson's role in customer relationships shouldn't stop when the order form is filled out.

Figure 11-1

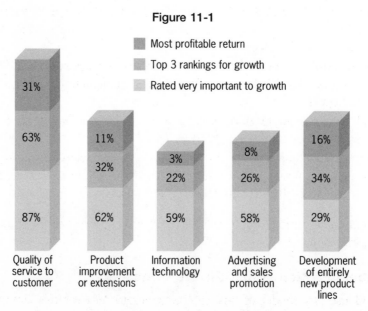

The role of customer service in sales.

Figure 11-2

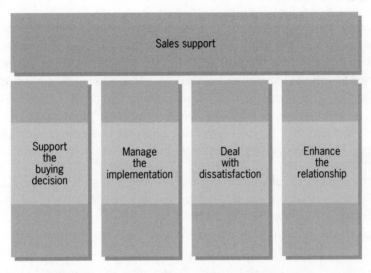

Servicing the sale: The four pillars of sales support.

Wilson Learning Worldwide provides one way to look at how to build long-term partnerships. This educational consulting firm developed the four pillars of sales support involved in after-sales follow-up (see Figure 11-2):

▲ **Support the buying decision** means reducing any anxiety that may arise with the purchasing decision. This may be accomplished through a follow-up sales call or by sending a card or letter thanking the customer for the order.

▲ **Manage the implementation** includes offering support services, assisting with any personnel training, and reporting implementation and utilization progress.

▲ **Deal with dissatisfaction** includes responding in an empathetic manner to any problems that arise.

▲ Salespeople should always try to **enhance the relationship** by being available, ensuring that the quality of the offering is maintained, and being a source of information, help, and ideas.

It is important to perform these activities successfully because the bulk of most salespeople's volume is in repeat business.

11.1.1 Creating More Value for the Customer

You could use any model of post-sale activities to uncover the same message: One of the keys in building a long-term partnership is that a company's sales force must create value for the customer. This holds true whether your client is an individual or a large corporation.

You may find yourself facing an analysis of how well you create more value. Many organizations evaluate their suppliers through a formal value analysis and/or a vendor analysis. A **value analysis,** the concept of which was developed by General Electric as a basis for cost reduction, is a detailed analysis of a product. It focuses on the relative cost of providing necessary function or service at the desired time and place with the necessary quality. Value analysis focuses on total cost, not just invoice cost. A **vendor analysis** is similar to a value analysis but focuses on the vendor by looking at such items as delivery reliability, product quality, price, service, and technical competence.

11.1.2 Achieving Successful Sales

As partnerships, alliances, and long-term customer relationships become more important in business, it is becoming increasingly necessary to distinguish between the deal and the relationship. To illustrate this concept, let's take a look at how Eastman Kodak and IBM looked at maintaining their long-term relationship. In a deal in which Eastman Kodak transferred its data center operations to IBM, executives from both companies developed two lists of specific issues that would ensure a successful relationship. Their lists were divided into issues on which they agreed related to the deal and to the relationship. Following are excerpts from the two lists[1]:

Deal Issues	Relationship Issues
Retirement and replacement of hardware	Reliability
Use of third-party software	Giving the benefit of the doubt
Service levels	Absence of coercion
Ease of communications	Understanding objectives
Record storage and maintenance	Timeliness of consultations

The lesson learned here is that every salesperson needs to pay attention to what the customer wants. You need to know the concerns that customers have about service and follow-up. Here's a list of customers' most pressing concerns about the selling and servicing of their accounts[2]:

▲ Receiving a call that a salesperson promised to make.
▲ Knowing contact numbers and the best available times to keep in touch with the sales and service people.
▲ Having the ability to talk to somebody in authority.

▲ Knowing that the salesperson and the salesperson's company appreciate their business.

▲ Spending minimal time on hold in order to speak to a real person.

▲ Being kept informed of ways to keep costs down and productivity up.

▲ Being informed promptly of potential challenges and getting any problems resolved quickly.

▲ Receiving acknowledgment of recognized challenges and accepting responsibility for errors.

▲ Being addressed politely and receiving personal attention.

▲ Being given realistic and honest information as it applies to delivery or problem-solving issues.

Understanding these issues is important to providing **follow-up**—all the efforts involved in servicing the sale and building a lasting and growing relationship. By making follow-up and service a regular part of your day, you can efficiently address all these customer concerns and possibly maintain an edge over your competitors.

SELF-CHECK

1. What are some of the retention activities for building long-term partnerships?
2. Describe the four pillars of sales support.
3. Define **value analysis** and **vendor analysis**.
4. List the most pressing concerns of customers.
5. Define follow-up.

11.2 Customer Service Methods That Strengthen a Partnership

You've learned the importance of customer service for a salesperson. Now take a look at some of the customer service methods you can use to strengthen your relationships:

▲ Cross-selling and up-selling.

▲ Follow-up.

▲ Thank-you notes.

11.2.1 Cross-Selling and Up-Selling to Grow Sales

To continue growth in your sales, you might be able to use the methods of cross-selling and up-selling.

Cross-selling involves selling additional products and services to an account, such as selling printers along with personal computers. For example, GE Medical Systems sells a large array of products to hospitals, including MRI machines, CT scanners, and x-ray imaging machines. In addition, the company can design the imaging rooms for the hospital and train the imaging personnel.

Up-selling is closely related to cross-selling and refers to selling bigger products or enhanced services to an account, which typically results in higher margins and greater dollar commitments. Referring again to GE Medical Systems, an example of up-selling would be for GE to offer to provide the personnel needed to run and manage a hospital's imaging department in addition to selling the equipment itself.

11.2.2 Following Up

Practicing consistent and persistent follow-up has proven to be one of the most important factors in successful selling. That's why developing an organized, systematic approach to follow-up, while individualizing your chosen methods with your own creative flair, works to your advantage. Here are some tips for providing effective follow-up:

▲ Make sure your methods and messages provide a memorable and interesting experience for the customers. If you see follow-up as boring, tedious repetition, you can expect your clients to feel the same way: bored and tired of your constant contacts. If you use follow-up with flair, you can expect higher percentages of response from your prospects.

▲ Make follow-up an important part of your regular selling routine.

▲ Know which methods work best for you and your client's responses to these methods. Of course, this takes time and experience, so don't get discouraged.

▲ Keep seeking ways to improve your follow-up program. You can contact other professional salespeople who are willing to listen, look at your follow-up, and offer advice. Good follow-up techniques can sometimes take as long to master as good selling techniques.

▲ Organize your follow-up time to ensure that your business stays productive. You can set up your follow-up system in several different ways. For example, you can use something as simple as index cards to keep track of your follow-ups. Or you might want or need to use a more sophisticated filing program. In today's world of high-tech equipment, keeping all your follow-up on a sales force automation software program designed to store the maximum amount of information in the minimum amount of space may be the most efficient system of all. Whatever way you choose to organize your time and the follow-up information, your method should enable you to systematically and periodically keep in touch with all your contacts.

▲ Inform your customers of the best times to contact you. It's important to then be accessible at the times you tell them to call.

▲ Avoid harassing customers. Sometimes knowing when keeping in touch with your client has crossed the line to downright bothering him or her is difficult. But you defeat the entire purpose of follow-up if you fail to recognize the signs of annoyance a customer may be sending your way. You need to be persistent, but you also need to be aware of when you are being a pest. That's a difference that perhaps only experience can show you. In most cases, however, you can let your clients know that you're not giving up and that you still hope to win their trust. And for the customers you obtained because of your effective follow-up, remain just as consistent and persistent in the service you provide.

▲ Keep your follow-up short and schedule follow-up for times that are most convenient for your prospects' schedules. Interruptions are sometimes unavoidable, but when too many interruptions occur, give your customers the opportunity to get back with you at a time better suited to their busy schedules.

▲ End each follow-up call on a positive note. If you know that a customer's answer was not based on your poor performance, you may still be able to get a referral for future business when the situation changes. In some cases, you may need to find out when the client expects a situation to change. You should therefore ask permission to call again.

▲ Be a fanatic in follow-up. Even if you haven't found the most creative or memorable way to follow up, practicing follow-up with zeal is better than not following up at all.

▲ Allow yourself a few mistakes and plenty of time to organize and maintain your chosen follow-up schedule.

You should also take a look at how to use the tools at your disposal for follow-up:

▲ **Telephone:** Telephone follow-up is perhaps the most common, least expensive, and most difficult method of follow-up to turn into a memorable experience. A primary reason for this is because people can just dismiss or ignore your call in numerous ways, such as using screening methods. To make your phone calls memorable, you should prepare a message that will get the person's attention. For example, you could pique a customer's interest by leaving a message on how upgrading the product can add profitability.

▲ **Mail:** Direct mail is a common method of follow-up, but your mailings don't have to be ordinary. You should personalize your follow-up to make it memorable for the person you're contacting. For example, you might include a special promotional discount on your offering or a coupon for the services included in your mailed package.

▲ **E-mail:** E-mail is a wonderful tool to use for follow-up if your client uses it regularly. For clients who do, you can send a note with an attached Web site address of an article or a piece of information that the client may find useful. But you need to make sure the information is relevant. If the new development has nothing to do with the client's needs, you shouldn't add to information overload.

11.2.3 Sending Thank-You Notes

Logically, the thank-you note is considered part of every salesperson's follow-up method. It is so important to customer service that it deserves its own section for consideration.

Everybody likes to be appreciated, and the deceptively modest "thank you," either by mail or in-person, is a powerful tool. Here are 10 instances in which thank-you notes are appropriate, followed by the exact words you can use for the occasion:

▲ **For telephone contact with a prospect:** "Thank you for talking with me on the telephone. In today's business world, time is precious. You can rest assured that I will always respect the time you invest as we discuss the possibility of a mutually beneficial business opportunity."

▲ **For in-person contact with a prospect:** "Thank you for taking time to meet with me. It was a pleasure meeting you, and I'm thankful for the time we shared. We have been fortunate to serve many happy clients, and I hope to someday be able to serve you. If you have any questions, please don't hesitate to call."

▲ **After a demonstration or presentation:** "Thank you for giving me the opportunity to discuss with you our potential association for the mutual benefit of our firms. We believe that quality, blended with excellent service, is the foundation for a successful business."

▲ **After a purchase:** "Thank you for giving me the opportunity to offer you our finest service. We are confident that you will be happy with this investment toward future growth. My goal now is to offer excellent follow-up service so that you will have no reservation about referring to me others who have needs similar to yours."

▲ **For a referral**: "Thank you for your kind referral. You can rest assured that anyone you refer to me will receive the highest degree of professional service possible."

▲ **After a final refusal**: "Thank you for taking the time to consider letting me serve you. I sincerely regret that your immediate plans do not include making the investment at this time. However, if you need further information or have any questions, please feel free to call. I will keep you posted on new developments and changes that may benefit you in the future."

▲ **After a prospect buys from someone else**: "Thank you for taking the time to analyze my services. I regret being unable at this time to help you appreciate the benefits that we can provide you. We keep constantly informed of new developments and changes in our industry, though, so I will keep in touch with you in the hope that, in the years ahead, we will be able to do business together."

▲ **After a prospect buys from someone else but offers you referrals**: "Thank you for your gracious offer to give me referrals. As we discussed, I am enclosing three of my business cards, and I thank you in advance for placing them in the hands of three of your friends, acquaintances, or relatives whom I might serve. I will keep in touch and be willing to render my services as needed."

▲ **To anyone who gives you service**: "Thank you for your continued and professional service. It is gratifying to meet someone dedicated to doing a good job. I sincerely appreciate your efforts. If my company or I can serve you in any way, please do not hesitate to call."

▲ **On an anniversary**: "With warm regards, I send this note to say hello and, again, thanks for your patronage. We are continually changing and improving our products and service. If you would like an update on our latest advancements, please give me a call."

As you can see, you have many reasons to say thank you. A thank-you note or two to the right person at the right time can go a long way toward building your success.

SELF-CHECK

1. Define **cross-selling** and **up-selling**.
2. Outline the steps of effective follow-up.
3. Discuss the importance of thank-you notes.

11.3 Preplanning Your Service Strategy

Your service strategy may not need to use anything more complicated than a set of index cards for recording your notes. You may not need to do more than send follow-up letters at predetermined intervals. But for successful long-term partnerships, you do need to preplan your service strategy. Studying the **customer relationship management (CRM)** model can provide some ideas in this area.

You read about CRM software in Chapter 6. But there is a vast realm of information involved in CRM. Although its implementation may differ among companies, CRM is essentially a comprehensive set of processes and technologies for managing relationships with potential and current customers and business partners across marketing, sales, and service, regardless of the communications channel. Successful CRM efforts depend on a combination of people, processes, technology, and knowledge.

Many companies are focusing their attention on CRM as strategic compliance for salespeople. This is a major shift in thinking for most companies, and it is being fostered by the investment community and enabled by technology. Figure 11-3 lists the major subprocesses involved in CRM. The sales force is involved in the subprocesses indicated by the arrows.

At the heart of the CRM process is information—the currency of the relationship. Information must be readily benchmarked, analyzed, critiqued, and shared among all the constituencies in the buying process. The processes

Figure 11-3

> Identifying high value prospects
>
> Learning about product usage and application
>
> Developing and executing advertising and promotion programs
>
> Developing and executing sales programs
>
> Developing and executing customer service programs
>
> Aquiring and leveraging customer contact information systems
>
> Managing customer contact teams
>
> Enhancing trust and customer loyalty
>
> Cross-selling and upselling of offerings

CRM subprocesses.

involved in customer relationship affected by CRM technology include the following:

▲ Targeting and acquiring prospects through data mining, campaign management, and distributing leads to sales and service.

▲ Developing effective selling processes, using proposal generators, knowledge management tools, contact managers, and forecasting aids.

▲ Addressing service and support issues with sophisticated call center applications and Internet-based customer service products.

As the functional unit often held responsible for all customer relationships, the sales force is intimately involved in a company's CRM efforts, and CRM has likewise had an important impact on the sales force. The nature of this impact, however, is likely to differ between companies, depending on how far the company has progressed in the CRM process.

According to the consulting firm CRM Group Ltd., CRM efforts tend to evolve through three phases. First, companies look to manage customer relationships as a driver of revenue. The focus is on utilizing cross-selling and up-selling opportunities, as well as on finding new solutions to customer situations that could be packaged as new offerings.

In the second phase, companies look for the possibility to manage customer relationships as drivers of profits. Successful CRM initiatives have focused on using customer knowledge and emerging new channels to decrease cost to serve and frequently on using advanced price mechanisms.

FOR EXAMPLE

Using the CRM Process

The major business division of BT plc (formerly known as British Telecom) concluded that it was relying too heavily on, and paying too much for, a long-standing, face-to-face selling model. Research indicated that many of BT's largest accounts were having difficulty resolving routine service and account management issues. For example, the field salesperson in charge of helping a customer implement a complex customer-contact system was also in charge of overseeing the addition of new phone lines. To solve the dilemma caused by balancing these two very different opportunities, BT decided to add low-cost, efficient channels such as the internet and tele-marketing to handle simple transactions and free up field sales time for larger, more complex deals. Integrating each of these channels to provide better service at a lower cost required that a complex information backbone be added to BT's CRM program.[3]

Some companies have now reached a third phase of CRM. At this stage, customer relationships and sales are regarded as a true driver of shareholder value. The idea is to improve the profitability of customers. A sales professional in the third phase of CRM adds value by being a customized solutions provider and a business relationship manager who oversees and nurtures the people and processes in the sales, marketing, and customer service areas.

These four skills are most important to top sales professionals in an environment in the third phase of CRM:

▲ **Collaboration:** With collaboration, the salesperson truly has in mind the interests of each stakeholder, including the customers, the selling team, and the enterprise.

▲ **Relationship management:** This includes skills in effective listening, analysis, and interpersonal communications.

▲ **Finance and business knowledge:** An effective salesperson must speak the vocabulary of business and analyze customer needs to come up with financially viable solutions.

▲ **Consultation:** The salesperson must apply consultative skills in analyzing customer needs, processes, and operational requirements.

Effective and successful selling over the next years in many companies will require an understanding of customer value, a consistent demonstration of behaviors that foster good customer relationships, and information technology literacy. In short, companies need to develop a CRM strategy and define the sales force's role in the organization's strategy.

SELF-CHECK

1. Define **CRM**.
2. List the major subprocesses involved in CRM.
3. What processes are affected by CRM technology?
4. What fundamental skills are important to top sales professionals in the third phase of CRM?

11.4 Getting Referrals

You've learned that you need to uncover your customer's needs and provide the necessary service for a long-lasting relationship. If you've done your job correctly, you should have a satisfied customer. It's time to ask for a referral.

For many seasoned salespeople, referrals are a major source of new business. Clients who contact you on an existing client's recommendation are usually more inclined than cold-call clients to own your product, service, or idea. They already have a positive feeling about you because you were referred by someone they already know and trust. With referrals, you enjoy tremendous credibility right from the start.

In fact, when it comes to qualified referrals, studies show a 60 percent closing rate. Compare that impressive figure to a closing rate of 10 percent with nonqualified nonreferrals, and you can see just how much harder you have to work on cold calls.[4]

Salespeople universally agree that prospects obtained through referrals are easier to convince than nonreferrals. But some salespeople think controlling referral business is impossible, so they refuse to give referral methods much attention. Such salespeople take the attitude that attaining referrals is just a haphazard, sometimes-it-happens-and-sometimes-it-doesn't way to prospect. Experts suggest that you choose a more take-charge philosophy toward referrals, which can involve the following steps:

1. Help a client think of specific people he or she knows.
2. Write the referrals' names on index cards. (When you get additional information about these people, you can make notations on those cards.)
3. Ask your client qualifying questions about the referrals. Jot down notes to help you remember specific things about them.
4. Ask for the referrals' addresses and phone numbers.
5. If the client doesn't know the referrals' addresses and phone numbers, get that information from the phone book.
6. Ask the client to call and set your appointments with the referrals. This step is where most novice salespeople balk. But keep in mind that this question is simply setting the stage for the final step. Few clients are comfortable calling to set an appointment for you. But they'll be so relieved that you offer them step 7 that they'll jump on it. If you went directly from step 5 to step 7, you may not get the same response.
7. If the client shows nervousness or refuses to call, ask if you can use the client's name when you contact the referral. Your client may not know the referral well or feel uncomfortable making the call. If this is the case, let the client know you understand this hesitation.

Salespeople must show referrals the same positive attitude, the same high energy level, the same respectful manner, and the same quality presentation that they show to cold calls. Referrals are only partially sold on you or your product. The important thing is that they're willing to give you the chance to convince them of how they'll benefit from your offering.

If you're successful, referrals just keep on coming. Before you know it, you'll create an endless chain of happily involved clients who want to do whatever they can to contribute to your success.

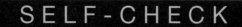

SELF-CHECK

1. Discuss the importance of getting referrals.
2. How can a salesperson effectively obtain referrals?

SUMMARY

Increasingly, a company's profitability and growth depend on establishing good relationships with the right customers and managing each relationship so as to deliver value to the customer. Plus, achieving successful sales is a continuous process in which the salesperson may need to take a more active role than just filling out an order form. A salesperson's activities may involve cross-selling, up-selling, and follow-up. A salesperson may also need the skills necessary for strategic planning efforts. Whatever the involvement, a salesperson needs to continue providing excellent service to build his or her partnerships with customers.

KEY TERMS

Cross-selling	Selling additional products and services to a customer.
Customer relationship management	A business strategy that involves a comprehensive set of processes and technologies for managing relationships with potential and current customers and business partners across marketing, sales, and service
Deal with dissatisfaction	One of pillars of sales support, which may include responding in an empathetic manner to any problems that arise.
Enhance the relationship	One of the pillars of sales support, which illustrates that salespeople should always try to be available, to ensure that the quality of the offering is maintained, and to be a source of information, help, and ideas.

Follow-up

All the efforts involved in servicing a sale and building a lasting and growing relationship with a customer.

Manage the implementation

One of the pillars of sales support, which involves offering support services, assisting with any personnel training, and reporting implementation and utilization progress.

Support the buying decision

One of the pillars of sales support, which means reducing any anxiety that may arise with the purchasing decision.

Up-selling

Selling bigger products or enhanced services to a customer, which typically results in higher margins and greater dollar commitments.

Value analysis

A detailed analysis of a product.

Vendor analysis

An analysis of a vendor that looks at such items as delivery reliability, product quality, price, service, and technical competence.

ASSESS YOUR UNDERSTANDING

Go to www.wiley.com/college/hopkins to evaluate your knowledge of service to build the partnership.

Measure your learning by comparing pre-test and post-test results.

Summary Questions

1. A salesperson's responsibility to a customer is finished when the purchase is finalized. True or false?

2. Which of the following has been ranked highest in terms of contribution to growth and profits?

   (a) product improvement or extensions

   (b) development of entirely new product lines

   (c) quality of service to the customer

   (d) advertising and sales promotion

3. Vendor analysis focuses on the relative cost of providing necessary function or service at the desired time and place with the necessary quality. True or false?

4. Distinguishing qualities and functions between a deal and a relationship is becoming increasingly important in business. True or false?

5. Which of the following is a pressing customer concern about service and follow-up?

   (a) spending minimal time on hold in order to speak to a real person

   (b) being kept informed of ways to keep costs down and productivity up

   (c) being informed promptly of potential challenges and getting any problems resolved quickly

   (d) all of the above

6. Cross-selling refers to selling bigger products or enhanced services to an account, which typically results in higher margins and greater dollar commitments. True or false?

7. An important aspect of follow-up is to make your conversation or correspondence as interesting as possible. True or false?

8. You should never send a thank-you note to someone who buys from your competition. True or false?

9. The heart of the CRM process is:

   (a) service.

   (b) information.

   (c) currency.

   (d) sales.

10. Which is *not* a competency listed as necessary the third phase of CRM?
    (a) consultation
    (b) relationship management
    (c) targeting a prospect
    (d) collaboration
11. Studies show that selling to qualified referrals has a closing rate of:
    (a) 80%.
    (b) 70%.
    (c) 60%.
    (d) 50%.

Applying This Chapter

1. Think again about a major purchase you have made recently. Did the salesperson apply a version of the four pillars of sales support involved in after-sales follow-up? Explain your answer.

2. Visualize yourself as a sales representative for a computer store that usually sells to individuals or small businesses. Most of your customers want systems they can install alone and use published training material to educate themselves. How would you create value after the sale for your customers?

3. Using the example in Question 2, develop your own list of at least three issues related to the deal and the relationship.

4. Using the example in Question 2, discuss customer service methods that are appropriate in this situation.

YOU TRY IT

Building Long-Term Partnerships

You recently accepted a job as a sales representative for a major computer manufacturer. Your primary targets are large corporations that need computers and software that easily interface with each other. You know that today's computer technology is rapidly changing. New software and hardware are introduced nearly every day. In fact, your company usually introduces at least one new major product or upgrade every year. You've already addressed how to find and qualify prospects, develop your presentation, and close the deal. Now you need to preplan your service strategy. Address the aspects you need in your strategy to build long-term partnerships.

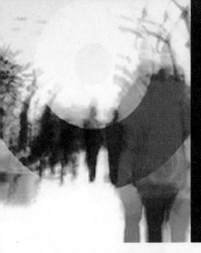

12

TIME AND TERRITORY MANAGEMENT: KEYS TO SUCCESS

Maintaining Self-Discipline and Organizational Skills

Starting Point

Go to www.wiley.com/college/hopkins to assess your knowledge of time management and territory management.
Determine where you need to concentrate your effort.

What You'll Learn in This Chapter

▲ The importance of managing yourself in sales
▲ How to avoid common time traps
▲ How to develop good time management habits
▲ How to manage a sales territory

After Studying This Chapter, You'll Be Able To

▲ Plan and implement effective time and territory management skills

INTRODUCTION

Salespeople constantly face time pressures that make it difficult for them to effectively allocate resources. For example, a study of 289 salespeople reported that 32 percent of the respondents spent fewer than five hours per week with customers.[1] Frequently, it is difficult to determine what is really important and what only seems important. Understanding the difference, however, often separates stellar from average performers. That's why enhancing time and territory management skills is important for all salespeople. This chapter examines the skills and pitfalls in both time and territory management.

12.1 Managing Yourself

In Chapter 1, you read that one of the qualities of top salespeople is learning how to manage time and obtain objectives. If you feel you don't believe you currently possess the skills to manage yourself, you need to learn them. Managing yourself involves both self-discipline and good habits.

To be successful, you need to be a finely tuned machine that can function over the long haul and face deadlines, rejection, the public, and your competition. You also must be able to meet your company's expectations and all the other demands you face as a professional salesperson and problem solver. You need to keep yourself tuned and in balance, physically and psychologically. And you should remember that balance starts with goals and productivity.

12.1.1 Self-Discipline

Salespeople typically work without direct supervision from their sales managers. With increasing layers of middle management being eliminated today, salespeople in many industries have learned to become even more self-reliant. One approach used to encourage self-management is called **behavioral self-management (BSM).** BSM consists of a series of steps involving monitoring, goal setting, rehearsal, rewards, and self-contracting. Figure 12-1 presents a summary of the techniques used in BSM.

To better understand how BSM can be used in sales management, consider a situation in which you are attempting to increase the number of calls you make on new accounts each week. Self-monitoring in this situation may mean recording the number of calls you make on new customers over a four-week period. After you establish the current level of effort, you set a goal for the number of new account calls you should make each week. Stimulus cues may include such things as a small note placed on the dashboard of your car that says "Have you met someone new today?" Or, you might use a special notebook for recording the new-customer calls you make each week. Consequence management may include stopping at a nicer place than

Figure 12-1

Technique	Method	Tools
Self-monitoring	Observe and record behavior.	Can use diaries, counters, tally sheets, charts.
Goal setting	Establish behavior change objectives.	Should be specific and with a short time horizon.
Stimulus control	Modify antecedents to behavior.	May involve introducing or removing cues.
Consequence management	Modify antecedents to behavior.	May involve reinforcement, punishment, or extinction.
Rehearsal	Conduct systematic practice of desired behavior.	May be overt or visualized.
Self-contracting	Specify the relationship between behaviors and their consequences.	May involve public commitment.

Self-management techniques.

usual for lunch when you meet your weekly objective or skipping lunch if you don't meet your objective by a certain day of the week. You can rehearse opening presentations with new accounts in the car while driving to an account. You can schedule such visits for the same time each day. Finally, it's a good idea to write a contract specifying the criteria for rewarding success and punishing failure and have someone witness it.

It's important to set goals that are challenging and achievable, while at the same time being consistent with overall organizational goals. An important factor in BSM is self-set goals. One of your goals may involve meeting your **quotas**, which are quantitative goals assigned to individual salespeople for a specified period of time. Or, your goal might be to meet a specific number of people within a week.

The primary point to remember is that your success in sales depends on how well you maintain self-discipline. Your effort directly affects your company. In fact, it's so important to the bottom line that some companies closely monitor sales force activities and direct and intervene to improve customer relations.

Many companies require salespeople to complete **call reports**, which detail who the salesperson called on, at what stage the prospect is within the sales cycle, and what follow-up activities are needed. Some sales managers use the **10-3-1 rule**, meaning that for every 10 qualified prospects, 3 will entertain a proposal, and 1 will become a customer. By monitoring call reports, managers can see how sales representatives are moving leads through the sales cycle.

> ## FOR EXAMPLE
>
> ### Monitoring Sales Calls
>
> The hotel company Swissôtel reviewed the activities of its 10 U.S. sales-people to see how they were allocating their time and how many calls they were making per week. The company found that salespeople were spending too much time in the office, preparing proposals and expense accounts, instead of talking to customers. Swissôtel set a new goal of six calls per day and expected these salespeople to spend 80 percent of their time in direct customer contact. To help make the salespeople more efficient, the company equipped them with mobile phones and laptop computers to provide up-to-the-minute inventory of hotel rooms. This provided salespeople with the information needed to close calls on the spot.

12.1.2 Good Habits

If you want to manage yourself and your time wisely, you need a planning device of some sort. Whether you prefer the pen-and-paper route or the high-tech one, you need to find an option that works well for you. You may want contact management software that includes a calendar section so you can have your contact information and meeting schedule all in one place. Many such programs even flag you if you try to enter a meeting that conflicts with another event you already have scheduled. Some contact management software is available online, so you don't have to be concerned about your laptop crashing and losing all your valuable information. Other programs are customized to the specific needs of sales-people—with forms for travel itineraries, charting activity and productivity, meeting notes, expense reports, and so on. You should take some time to find one you think you'll be comfortable using. If you're not comfortable, you won't use it, which will defeat the purpose of planning.

Another good idea is to set aside 15 minutes on the first day of every month at your desk or with your briefcase or laptop (wherever you keep all your pertinent information) to do your planning. You should use this time to review all unfinished business and plan how and when you'll get it done. You should write down everything you want to accomplish that month, and you need to be realistic and specific. You should include any family or social events you've committed to attend. Then you should add any important dates, such as family, friend, and client birthdays; your wedding anniversary, if it's this month; and activities you need to attend with your family (e.g., a child's school play or game, your spouse's company) picnic. Then you should note all the company meetings you must attend for the month and add any projects you're working on, their estimated completion dates, and reminders to follow up on them. If you're working on a large project, you should break it down into smaller pieces that you can accomplish each week. Taking large projects a week at a time helps you see your progress, and it prevents one big project from seeming so oppressive.

In daily time planning, you should keep track of all activities as you go instead of waiting until 4:00 p.m. and trying to remember what you did at 9:30 a.m. It's important to be truthful with yourself. You shouldn't play around with numbers or fake anything just so you can check it off. And you shouldn't overwhelm yourself with writing down every detail of your workday. You're not trying to write a book. You're just noting the key events and any information you simply wouldn't want to forget.

Finally, you should do your planning where you conduct your business. If you wait until you get home, you may not have a key phone number or other detail you need to record. You may need triggers to remember everything you need to plan, and those triggers are probably most available to you at your place of business.

4

SELF-CHECK

1. Define **BSM** and summarize the techniques of this approach.
2. Define **quota**.
3. Discuss how having good habits in managing yourself leads to good time management skills.
4. Define **call reports** and **10-3-1 rule**.

5 ## 12.2 Time Management

Time management is all about managing yourself. You can't really manage time, but you can manage what you do within a specific period of time. For example, you could be watching TV now instead of reading this book. But you have chosen to use your time in this manner. If you think that people who practice time management strategies are fanatical workaholics who leave no time for personal relaxation, you're mistaken; in operating more efficiently, they create more time for personal endeavors. If you invest time in planning your time, you'll think of dozens of ways to manage yourself more efficiently.

Most people in business are constantly seeking better time management skills. In fact, surveys of business training programs show that time management is one of the most frequently mentioned training topics. The reason is that significant productivity gains can be made through better time management. Figure 12-2 shows how salespeople spend their time. The amount of time spent selling, either face to face or over the phone, increased during the 1990s to 54 percent from

Figure 12-2

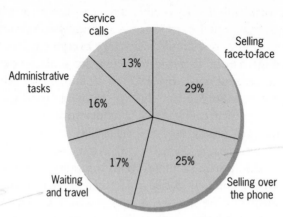

How salespeople spend their time.

only 50 percent in 1990. Most of this increase is due to a greater use of technology that enabled salespeople to free up more time.

Time is your most valuable resource, and until you realize that and learn how to manage your time, you'll always be wondering where all your time goes. The value of time has increased dramatically in recent years. Perhaps the quote by nationally known sales trainer Zig Ziglar illustrates the concept best: "When you do what you need to do when you need to do it, you will soon have the time to do what you want to do when you want to do it."

12.2.1 Time Traps

There is a difference between a time-consuming activity and a time trap. Many time-consuming activities are ones that you want to do and that give you pleasure (e.g., working on a hobby). On the other hand, you want to avoid time traps. These are the pitfalls that lead to frustration, particularly if you fall into them while working. This section explores some of the common time traps and how to avoid them.

Time traps can sap your energy and ability to serve your customers. When an occasional crisis comes up, you should deal with it quickly and then go right back to your original schedule. You don't have to become antisocial around the office, but you might be surprised at how much more efficient you can be when you start taking back stray minutes here and there.

Carelessness and Disorganization

Looking for lost items is a huge time waster. A scrap of paper with important contact information, your keys, your glasses—these are items that are commonly misplaced. Spending several minutes searching for each misplaced item can add up, so you should designate a specific place for every item you use regularly—and then always use it. If you always hang your keys on a hook by the door, you don't have to spend precious time searching for them. One of the main causes of wasted time and lost income is disorganized office space. You should place only immediate activities on your desk and keep everything but your most pressing tasks out of sight. You should also keep everything you need for accomplishing the immediate tasks somewhere nearby (in a place you can remember) so you don't waste time running hither and yon looking for what you need.

If you can't put your fingers on the contact information for all your clients within a matter of minutes, you should consider investing some time in using good contact management software. With today's technology, there's no good reason for a client or prospective client's information *not* to be at your fingertips. Entering the information takes only a few minutes, and then it's there forever.

Carelessness also applies to people who tend to rush through their paperwork and their planning of presentations without carefully checking or rechecking details. You need much less time to do something right the first time than if you have to go back and do it over. Also, you risk angering others with costly delays or mistakes when you have carelessly written paperwork. You should double-check everything for accuracy and clarity.

Another time-saver is to pick up paperwork only once. You should decide its importance and deal with it by passing it on or filing it. You shouldn't read it and put it in a pile that you plan to look at again later.

Procrastination

Most people procrastinate because of fear. They fear making a mistake, so instead they do nothing. Mistakes can and do happen. You need to learn to accept your mistakes and learn from them.

It's especially important that you not procrastinate about calling angry clients. The longer you wait, the more the situation worsens.

Unnecessary and Unnecessarily Long Phone Calls

The telephone can be your greatest ally or your greatest enemy, especially when it comes to time management. Here are some ideas to help you deal with wasted time on the phone:

▲ Set aside a specific time each day to take and make phone calls.
▲ Establish a total time limit for all your calls. Then limit your time on each call.
▲ Write down your objective for a phone call and focus on it.
▲ Have all your materials and information within reach before you pick up the phone.
▲ Find polite but effective exit lines to help you get off the phone without interrupting the other person or abruptly ending the conversation.
▲ Let all your customers know exactly when you're available for them to call you. You can have this information printed on your business card or

include it as a part of your e-mail signature information. If you have an unusually chatty customer, you should explain that you're in the middle of something extremely urgent and that you will call back. Then you can return the call just before the end of office hours. You'll be surprised how brief such conversations can become.

▲ If you spend great amounts of time on the phone, or if you're in tele-marketing, invest in a high-quality headset so you can use both hands to attend to other things while you're on the phone.

If you think of the phone as a business tool, not unlike your computer and calculator, you'll be able to form new habits for using it that should keep you out of this common time trap.

Unnecessary and Unnecessarily Long Meetings

Attending nonproductive meetings can be a major time waster. You should think carefully about whether a meeting is necessary and whether other means of communication could eliminate the need for meetings. Many people have found that holding meetings standing up is highly productive. When people don't settle into comfortable chairs for the duration, they finish their business much more quickly.

Long Client Lunches

When you're out for lunch with clients, you need to develop ways to let them know that you've finished your business for the day and that you must move on. Generally, a lunch meeting should not last more than two hours.

Negative Thinking

Negative thoughts that produce negative talk are a big waste of time for sales-people. Instead of focusing on things you don't like, you should think about the positive things you can do. Plus, if you surround yourself with positive thinkers, their positive energy will rub off on you.

Using Driving Time Unwisely

Most people in professional selling spend a lot of time in their cars driving from appointment to appointment. The average salesperson drives 25,000 miles per year for the job. That works out to about 500 hours a year. You can make good use of your driving time by listening to educational material on tape or disk. Remember that one of the characteristics of a top salesperson is the desire to be a life-long learner.

Neglecting to Confirm Appointments

Making a quick phone call before you leave for an appointment can save you valu-able selling time. A call also tells the prospect that you're a professional with some-thing valuable to say. If you handle it properly, your brief call to confirm may keep your appointment from being the one that gets canceled if your customer needs to change his or her decision-making schedule. Even if the decision maker does have to cancel, you have this person, or the person's assistant, on the phone to immediately schedule another appointment.

Watching Television

There may be programs you enjoy watching, but you need to limit your time. TV watching is one of the least-productive activities in the U.S. lifestyle.

Taking on Unwanted or Unproductive Tasks

Many people can't refuse when people want a chunk of their time. Top professionals recognize their limitations. If you're faced with a request that you feel unqualified to accomplish or believe will limit your ability to get your primary responsibilities done, you should say no. You can suggest someone more qualified or interested. You should carefully explain the fact that others are better suited to getting the job done properly. As you become more successful, your time becomes more valuable, making it all the more important to learn when and how to say no.

Allowing Excessive Interruptions

You should always allow part of your day to work with people, support your coworkers, or help your company solve problems. But you also need to allow yourself some solo time, both at work and in your personal life. It can be your time for emotional and physical health in your private life, as well as your most productive work time. During your solo work time, if someone asks, "Do you have a minute?" you can just answer, "Not right now. Can it wait until 11:00?" By that time, most people who were looking for your help will have solved the problem themselves, or they will have realized that their problem wasn't all that important anyway.

Here are some tips for handling interruptions to your valuable time:

▲ **Rearrange your office so that your desk is out of the line of sight from people who walk down the hallway:** If people don't see you as they're walking down the hall, they're less likely to stop in to chat.

▲ **Remove extra chairs from your office:** Position any necessary chairs as far away from your desk as possible. This way, people aren't tempted to sit down for long periods of time.

▲ **Place a large clock where you and any visitors can see it clearly:** A clock helps you—and your visitors—keep track of how much of your time they're taking up.

▲ **Don't look up when someone walks into your office:** This habit is hard to establish. If you appear to be extremely busy, however, and the potential interruption is nothing serious, most people simply walk away. This advice may sound cold, but if you can't get your work done, your inefficiency will cause your customers to receive less service. As a result, your inefficiency will cause you to earn a lower income.

12.2.2 Professional Selling Efficiency

Average salespeople often spend their time foolishly doing unproductive busy-work. Then they wonder where their day went, why they accomplished so little, and why they never seem to have time for any fun.

If you believe you fall into this category, a key word to consider is *spend*. Do you spend your time instead of investing it? The words *spending* and *investing* connote very different ideas. When you spend money, you probably think of the loss of that money rather than the benefits you'll enjoy from your purchase. On the other hand, the word *invest* signifies a payment from which you will derive a return. With an investment, you don't focus on the momentary loss of money but rather on the gain of the product or service you will receive. Similarly, when you spend your time instead of investing it, you focus on lost time rather than on personal gain.

If you've never put a dollar value on your time before, you should do it now. To determine what your time is worth, you can use this simple equation:

$$\text{Gross income} / \text{Total annual working hours} = \text{Hourly rate}$$

To see the value of this equation, suppose that your annual income is $30,000 and you work 40 hours a week for 50 weeks a year (allowing 2 weeks off for vacation). In this case, the value of each hour in your workweek is $15. In straight-commission sales, if you spend just 1 hour each day of each workweek on unproductive activity, you are spending about $3,750 a year for your time traps. When you choose not to manage your time, you may end up wasting 12 percent of your annual income or more. This amount doesn't even account for all the future business you lose by spending time instead of investing it. In sales, you often don't see immediate financial payoff from the time you invest. The longer the period between selling and payoff, the more difficult it is to stay focused on investing your time wisely. When you invest time in the people you're trying to persuade, thinking of the returns on your investment is normal.

12.2.3 Productivity Gains

Improving the amount of time spent selling is an opportunity for significant productivity gains. A task force for a Fortune 100 company estimated that a 10 percent improvement in the time its sales force spent selling would generate more than a 5 percent increase in overall sales volume. This helps to explain why, in a recent survey, 72 percent of sales executives listed mobile phones as the technology most essential to their salespeople's job.[2] The sales executives also ranked notebook computers and the internet as essential technologies.

This example also illustrates the use of technology to improve the efficiency of time and territory management, which has had a tremendous impact over the last few years. Sales force automation has been estimated to boost productivity by as

FOR EXAMPLE

Saving Time

In the 1980s, tracing a shipment of solvent for a client of the Quaker Oats chemical division required numerous hours of phone calls and plenty of headaches. Today, a Quaker Oats salesperson can simply open his or her laptop, go into the company's internal website, and click on a button that says "Shipment Information." In just a few minutes, they are able to tell the purchasing agent that the tank car is in Houston, 20 miles away. Salespeople are able to save time tracking down this information and invest that time in prospecting or strategic planning.[3]

much as 20 to 40 percent. For example, Pitney-Bowes recently put 3,000 of its salespeople through a sales automation training program to teach them how to use specific account management software. The results not only improved salesperson productivity by 30 percent but also improved customer satisfaction ratings.[4]

SELF-CHECK

1. Rank the areas in which salespeople spend their time.
2. Discuss how the following time traps affect a salesperson and steps to avoid these activities:
   (a) Carelessness and disorganization.
   (b) Procrastination.
   (c) Unnecessary or unnecessarily long phone calls and meetings.
   (d) Long lunches.
   (e) Negative thinking.
   (f) Using driving time unwisely.
   (g) Neglecting to confirm appointments.
   (h) Watching television.
   (i) Taking on unwanted or unproductive tasks.
   (j) Allowing excessive interruptions.
3. Explain the difference between the words *spending* and *investing* in discussing time management.
4. Discuss how increasing time spent selling affects sales volume.

12.3 Suggestions for Time Management

Despite all the emphasis companies are putting on increasing selling time, much of a salesperson's time is spent on administrative tasks. This has not changed much during the past two decades. A salesperson's time management is important to a company's, as well as that salesperson's, bottom line.

One aspect of time management that is particularly important in sales is knowing when the customer is available. This is the key selling time during the day, and salespeople should strictly adhere to contacting customers during these times. This time must be protected, with other duties and issues being handled at other times of the day.

A key step frequently recommended for improved time management is preparing a list of personal and professional goals and then pursuing the goals, one at a time. Planning does not have to be elaborate to be useful. Simply writing down a list of things you want to do tomorrow is a good place to start. The next step is to rank the tasks on the basis of their importance. When you start the day, you can begin task 1 and stay with it until it is complete. Then you should recheck your priorities and begin the next task. You should continue with the tasks that remain most important.

When you get into the habit of daily planning, you can begin to plan a week or more ahead. Many salespeople are required to prepare weekly call plans. The idea is to encourage salespeople to plan a series of calls for each day, to call ahead for appointments, and to make better use of their time. A useful device that helps with planning is a pocket- or purse-size diary. Carrying such a diary allows you to keep track of appointments and reschedule them as needed.

Stephen Covey, a well-known consultant in personal and professional development, advises people to analyze their time management by using a framework like the one shown in Figure 12-3.[5]

Figure 12-3

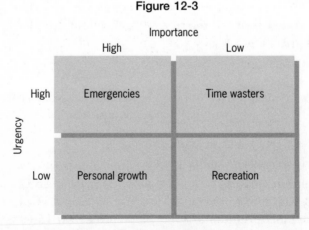

Time management.

Importance refers to activities that are of importance to you in meeting your objectives. *Urgency*, on the other hand, is the time pressure you feel to perform certain activities. Notice that you may feel this pressure for both important and relatively unimportant activities. According to Covey, activities in the Emergencies and Recreation sections of the framework generally take care of themselves. People can gain control over their lives by spending less time on time wasters and more on personal growth activities. Time wasters (which have high urgency but low importance) include phone calls, some meetings, and unnecessary administrative work—in other words, things that demand immediate attention. Personal growth activities (which have low urgency but high importance) are easily put off but are very important to your future growth and development. Activities in this category may include reading professional journals or books, enrolling in professional development or executive courses, learning how other functional areas operate, or prospecting for new customers. Notice that many people can postpone these activities indefinitely. Considering both urgency and importance may provide a useful perspective on how to spend time more productively.

Another way to examine time management is by separating your personal life into three areas in order to effectively organize your time:

▲ **Investigate your yesterday:** You should write down what you typically do with each of the 168 hours in your week. If you're like many other self-management beginners, you probably have habits that are serious time wasters. You can easily eliminate those habits when you become aware of them. You should try to be as honest and thorough as possible, and you should keep a daily log of your typical routine for seven days. Then you should review the log honestly and tally all the time wasters. The log will help you establish an accurate record of the habits you want to develop.

▲ **Analyze your today:** You should ask yourself, "Is what I'm doing right now the most productive thing I can do?" Some salespeople spend all their time getting organized and getting ready for persuasion situations that never come about. To them, getting organized itself has become the game. Time planning actually starts with goals because setting goals is the only way you can tell what tasks are the most productive at any given moment.

▲ **Discover your tomorrow:** You should assume that your goals and priorities are in line. You know what you want and how you want to get there. Your daily time planning should start at night, before you go to bed. You should go through your time planner and lay out the day to come. It's important to get a handle on your top six priorities, as well as who you will see or call, for the next day. Then you can add any personal areas you need to cover the next day. Writing down or entering the next day's top six priorities shouldn't take more than 10 to 15 minutes. When you've mapped out the next day, you can forget it and go to bed.

Whatever tools or philosophy you choose, you shouldn't try to plan for every minute of the day. Being inaccurate is too easy when you forecast time for task completion. Instead, you should start by planning just 75 percent of your total work time. That way, you allow for interruptions, delays, and unexpected emergencies. As your workday planning improves, you can increase to planning 90 percent of your day. But you should never plan for 100 percent. If you do, you don't leave room for the unexpected, and you'll just frustrate yourself when you can't accomplish your designated goals. You need to remain flexible.

When you plan your time, you should divide the things on which you choose to invest time into four categories:

▲ **Immediate activities:** These are the tasks you must complete today. Determine the immediacy of your activities and prioritize them by either the amount of relief you'll feel in getting them done or the amount of goodwill or income they'll generate. Have your immediate activities in front of you at all times. If you can't see what you need to accomplish today because you've buried your immediate activities under other less-important work, those activities can get lost in the shuffle—and you can lose sight of your goals.

▲ **Secondary activities:** These tasks are ones that are close to immediate but not quite. You probably need to complete them this week instead of today, for example. Identifying your secondary group of activities is usually easier than identifying immediate ones. Some secondary activities may be almost-but-not-quite immediate, and you should put them at the top of your secondary activity list. As for immediate activities, you need to prioritize your secondary list so you finish what's most important first.

It's a good idea to put any paperwork related to secondary activities in a desk drawer or a letter tray that you can move to your desk or even put on the floor, if necessary. You shouldn't let yourself get preoccupied with piles of paperwork. Paperwork overload causes stress and confuses you about what really needs immediate attention.

▲ **Relatively unimportant activities:** Some tasks don't need to be completed by a specific deadline. You can work them in when you have spare moments. Identifying which tasks fall into the "relatively unimportant" category is difficult. You may think everything needs your attention, but such thinking simply isn't true. By putting the right activities in your "relatively unimportant" category, you may be able to avoid spending time on these chores when you should be investing time on your immediate or secondary activities.

▲ **Emergencies:** Although emergencies are rare, you need to build time into your schedule to handle them. Planning your time efficiently can prevent some emergencies from happening in the first place, but you should always have an alternate approach to accomplishing your most important activities just in case an emergency arises. Planning ahead and being prepared can keep you from panicking and completely ruining your schedule, and those of others, when emergencies arise. It's important to have backup plans.

SELF-CHECK

1. How does goal setting affect time management?
2. Describe Stephen Covey's framework for analyzing time management.
3. Discuss how to use the following concepts to organize time:
   (a) Investigate your yesterday.
   (b) Analyze your today.
   (c) Discover your tomorrow.
4. Discuss how to divide tasks into the following categories:
   (a) Immediate activities.
   (b) Secondary activities.
   (c) Relatively unimportant activities.
   (d) Emergencies.

12.4 Territory Management

In many ways, time management and territory management are interrelated. Carefully scheduling calls in your territory can lead to substantial savings in travel time. A key difference between time management and territory management, however, is that you have some control over how you manage your time. Your supervisors often dictate territory management in the way that they divide an area among the sales representatives. Still, how and when you schedule calls in your territory is usually left up to you, the salesperson.

One of the most common territory structures is to assign salespeople all accounts in a particular geographic area. Even when sales forces are organized according to specialties, the responsibilities of various salespeople are often restricted to a particular geographic boundary or territory. So the majority of sales forces have some sort of exclusive territory alignment that specifies each salesperson's or sales team's account responsibility and activity mix.

12.4.1 What Territory Management Involves

A **territory** is defined as the customers, often located in a specified geographic area, that are assigned to an individual salesperson. Although territories are often referenced in geographic terms, the defining element of a territory is the set of customers in the geography.

A properly aligned sales territory is one in which customers receive the proper amount of attention and the workload is balanced across salespeople. Research by ZS Associates on territory alignment suggests that there are at least three reasons for properly aligning sales territories by bringing all territories within a proper workload tolerance level[6]:

▲ **Increased sales:** Rectifying a workload imbalance can improve sales by between 2 and 7 percent. Plus, in a properly aligned sales force, work shifts among salespeople so that all customers receive appropriate coverage.

▲ **Cost savings:** Having only one person cover each geographic area eliminates duplication of sales calls and related travel costs. Salespeople in well-designed territories spend less time traveling and more time selling, resulting in lower sales costs as a percentage of sales.

▲ **Increased morale:** Sales potential is the single best predictor of territory sales, regardless of any factors related to the salesperson. In other words, high sales potential leads to high sales, regardless of the salesperson's efforts. The reverse is true for low-sales potential territories. The strong sales-potential-territory sales relationship suggests that management must be careful to reward the salesperson and not the territory. Inequitable and unfair rewards are likely to result from improper territory alignment. Some very good salespeople may become dissatisfied with the jobs because they feel they are in a no-win situation or because they start questioning their own abilities and career choices. On the other hand, the salesperson who has been going on reward trips for the past 10 years may not really deserve the trips. His or her territory may simply have too much sales potential, so that it produces more sales than other territories, despite the salesperson's efforts. Compensation systems with a high percentage of incentive pay tend to accentuate the morale and turnover effects of poor territory alignment.

12.4.2 Territory Design

There are many ways to assign accounts to salespeople. In fact, there are more than 1,000 ways to assign 10 accounts to 2 salespeople. The number of solutions rises exponentially as the number of accounts and salespeople increases. Understandably, there are a number of potentially good alignments and an enormous number of poor ones. Fortunately, data and information processing technology advances can facilitate the process.

The task of selecting sales routes might be handled by a salesperson for a small firm, but at many large companies, a sales manager or staff specialists develop the routes. The rapidly increasing costs of automobiles, gasoline, and automobile repairs, as well as the possible savings in time, have encouraged many firms to employ more sophisticated technologies to find the best travel routes.

Techniques used to schedule and route salespeople have received considerable attention from management scientists. At the heart of the issue is the **traveling salesperson problem,** which is usually stated as a search for a route through the territory that allows a salesperson to visit each customer and return to the starting point with minimum expenditures of both time and money. A simple way to find a good sales call route, and one that is often very effective in minimizing travel time and costs, is to plan a travel route based on four basic rules:

▲ The route should be circular.
▲ The route should never cross itself.
▲ The same route should not be used to travel to and from a customer.
▲ Customers in neighboring areas should be visited in sequence.

Circular routes are reasonable because salespeople usually start at a home base and then return to it at the end of the sales trip. Similarly, if sales routes cross, a salesperson knows that a shorter route was overlooked. Sometimes a salesperson is forced to use the same route to travel to and from a customer because of local road conditions or scheduled appointments, but this should be avoided when possible.

In reality, factors often interfere with plans that appear to be ideal on paper. In geographic routing problems, circumstances such as availability of good roads, traffic flows at different times of the day, traffic lights, and congestion often require the use of a different route than originally planned. This does not mean that operations research approaches are not of value; they are an excellent starting point for analysis.

One additional factor to consider in territory design is the work schedule of the accounts. The best approach is to travel when clients are not available in order to avoid wasting valuable selling time. If customers are not available early in the morning, this might be a good time to get in the most travel miles. As a result, you may make your first call on the customer farthest from your home rather than making a circular route. Improved routing usually depends on experience and increased familiarity with the territory.

12.4.3 Sales Call Plans

One way to manage your territory when you have to spend time traveling is to cluster your appointments. By organizing your presentations or customer service appointments by geographic area, you can save a lot of travel time—and if you live in a rather large metropolitan area, you saving time sitting in traffic as well. If your travel time is primarily within major cities, you might want to schedule it so that you don't get stuck in rush-hour traffic. In addition, taking side streets and back roads may lead you to new opportunities if you keep your eyes open and remain aware of your surroundings.

SELF-CHECK

1. How are time management and territory management interrelated?
2. Define **territory**. How is a territory usually structured?
3. Why is proper division of territories important?
4. What is the traveling salesperson problem?
5. List the four basic rules for planning a travel route.
6. What other factors should be considered in designing a territory?

SUMMARY

A salesperson who feels the proper balance in life probably knows how to manage time effectively. This means avoiding the unproductive time traps common in life and concentrating instead on activities that enhance productivity for achieving professional and personal goals. A salesperson who manages time effectively has also learned the importance of effective territory management, a skill closely linked to managing time. In this chapter, you've learned how managing your time and territory can be key to your sales success.

KEY TERMS

10-3-1 rule	A guide for sales which says that for every 10 qualified prospects, 3 will entertain a proposal, and 1 will become a customer.
Behavioral self-management (BSM)	A series of steps involving monitoring, goal setting, rehearsal, rewards, and self-contracting.
Call reports	Reports completed by salespeople that detail who the salesperson called on, at what stage the prospect is within the sales cycle, and what follow-up activities are needed.

Quotas	Quantitative goals assigned to individual sales-people for a specified period of time.
Territory	Customers, often located in a specified geographic area, that are assigned to an individual salesperson.
Traveling salesperson problem	A dilemma usually stated as a search for a route through a territory that allows a salesperson to visit each customer and return to the starting point with minimum expenditures of both time or money.

ASSESS YOUR UNDERSTANDING

Go to www.wiley.com/college/hopkins to evaluate your knowledge of time management and territory management.

Measure your learning by comparing pre-test and post-test results.

Summary Questions

1. Time management and territory management rely heavily on your own self-discipline. True or false?
2. Which is *not* a step in the BSM model?
   (a) goal setting
   (b) rewards
   (c) rehearsal
   (d) managing time
3. An important tip for time management is to review and update your to-do list every month, every week, and every day. True or false?
4. As a salesperson, your most valuable resource is your territory. True or false?
5. A time trap is an unproductive activity that you should avoid. True or false?
6. How much of a salesperson's time do administrative tasks usually consume?
   (a) 6 percent
   (b) 16 percent
   (c) 26 percent
   (d) 36 percent
7. Which of the following is an activity area addressed by Covey's method for time management?
   (a) emergencies
   (b) time wasters
   (c) personal growth areas
   (d) all of the above
8. Time wasters include:
   (a) some phone calls.
   (b) some meetings.
   (c) some administrative work.
   (d) all of the above.

9. In planning how to manage your time, you need to consider:
   (a) immediate activities.
   (b) secondary activities.
   (c) relatively unimportant activities.
   (d) all of the above.
10. A salesperson is always responsible for territory and sales route designs. True or false?
11. Properly aligned territories improve morale among sales forces. True or false?
12. A salesperson should always follow a circular route in covering sales calls. True or false?

Applying This Chapter

1. You have a job raising funds for the local chapter of the Red Cross. In this job, you have to "sell" the public on the Red Cross. Your goal is to raise 10 percent more in private donations this year than last year. You've found that one of the most effective ways of raising money is to give presentations to civic groups. Explain how you would use the BSM model to manage yourself and your time in achieving this goal.
2. Everybody has a time trap to either overcome or continue to suppress. Describe at least two time traps in your present or past. What do you plan to do (or have you done) to overcome them?
3. List at least three personal and three professional goals you want to achieve. For each of these goals, describe a step you plan to take tomorrow, next week, and next month to achieve this goal.
4. Start a daily log of your activities. Note any time wasters that you hope to eliminate.
5. Start planning for next week. List your immediate activities and secondary activities. Are there any relatively unimportant activities you can eliminate? Do you have any backup plans in case of emergencies (i.e., a babysitter fails to show up)?
6. Visualize yourself working as a sales representative for a new tire wholesaler that sells tires to retail outlets. The wholesaler has just established itself in your current area. Your job includes devising a sales route for yourself so that you can call on prospects in your territory at least once a month. Take a look in your local Yellow Pages to determine the addresses of five retail outlets. Then outline an efficient circular route. (You may want to use the Mapquest Web site or obtain a map of your area to assist in this assignment.)

YOU TRY IT

Managing Job and Family Priorities

You have accepted a new job selling advertising for a local television station. In addition, you and your spouse recently had your first child. Selling advertising sometimes means working at night or on the week-ends, at times when your customers are available. Plus, your territory covers a circumference of 100 miles, which means many hours on the road. You want to be able to do your job well and also spend time every day with your new baby.

1. How do you plan to balance your work and family priorities?
2. How do you plan to manage your time?
3. What are some of the elements you need to consider in managing your territory?

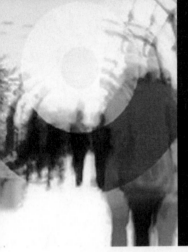

13

MANAGING AND TRAINING OTHERS
Being a Good Sales Manager

Starting Point

Go to www.wiley.com/college/hopkins to assess your knowledge of managing and training others.
Determine where you need to concentrate your effort.

What You'll Learn in This Chapter

▲ The responsibilities of a sales manager's job and the competencies needed
▲ Important considerations in recruiting and selecting salespeople
▲ The need for proper orientation and training of salespeople
▲ Tools that can be used in motivating a sales force
▲ Important considerations in compensation plans
▲ Primary elements in assessing sales force productivity

After Studying This Chapter, You'll Be Able To

▲ Understand the fundamental functions of a sales manager's job

INTRODUCTION

Sales skills provide an entry into many fields and careers. Some salespeople choose never to leave the exciting opportunities presented in sales. Others view the occupation as a springboard into other positions. Many move on to become sales managers. In fact, most sales managers begin their careers as salespeople. It's important to understand the competencies needed for advancement into sales management. This chapter reviews the functions and areas of responsibilities in managing and training others.

13.1 Sales Management Functions

A **sales manager** is responsible for management of the field sales operations. This individual may be a first-line manager, directly responsible for the day-to-day management of salespeople, or may be positioned at a higher level in the management hierarchy, responsible for directing the activities of other managers. In either case, **sales management** focuses on the administration of the personal selling function in the marketing mix. This role includes the planning, management, and control of sales programs, as well as the recruiting, training, compensation, motivation, and evaluation of field sales personnel. Therefore, sales management can be defined as the planning, organizing, leading, and controlling of personal contact programs designed to achieve the sales and profit objectives of a firm.

Regardless of whether a sales manager directs salespeople or other sales managers, all managers have two types of responsibilities:

▲ Achieving or exceeding the goals established for performance in the current period.

▲ Developing the people who report to them.

Each of these responsibilities includes a number of specific functions and activities that are discussed throughout this chapter.

Let's look more closely at the competencies that managers need in order to succeed. **Sales management competencies** are defined as sets of knowledge, skills, behaviors, and attitudes that a person needs to be effective in a wide range of industries and various types of organizations. People use many types of competencies in their everyday lives. The following are six competencies needed for today's sales management responsibilities:

▲ **Strategic action competency** involves understanding the industry and the organization and then taking strategic actions. One dimension of strategic thinking is to anticipate strategic trends in the industry and to make the appropriate adjustments to take advantage of these changes.

▲ **Coaching competency** is defined as a sequence of conversations and activities that provide ongoing feedback and encouragement to a salesperson, with the goal of improving that person's performance.

▲ **Team building competency** means accomplishing tasks by using small groups of people who are collectively responsible and whose work is interdependent.

▲ **Self-management competency** refers to taking responsibility for your actions at work and elsewhere. This includes integrity and ethics, managing your own personal drive, and self-awareness.

▲ **Global perspective competency** means a manager must draw on human, financial, information, and material resources from multiple countries and serve customers who span multiple cultures.

▲ **Technology competency** involves understanding the potential for technology to improve sales force efficiency and effectiveness and knowing how to implement technology into the sales force.

SELF-CHECK

1. Define **sales manager** and **sales management**.
2. What are the two primary functions of a sales manager?
3. List and describe the six competencies needed in an effective sales manager.

13.2 Recruitment and Selection of Salespeople

Sales managers usually have a major role in recruiting and selecting their sales forces. The costs associated with a poor hiring decision are significant. An often-quoted figure is that out-of-pocket costs associated with recruiting and selection range from 20 to 80 percent of a salesperson's annual salary. Experts estimate that the value of sales lost by a single ineffective salesperson could be as much as $300,000 to several million dollars per year.

In addition to direct costs, a poor hiring decision can negatively affect a company's culture and productivity. Especially in the case of a termination, the morale among the salespeople who stay may suffer because these people might be required to pick up the slack caused by the colleague's departure. Plus, higher turnover leads to a sales force being low on the productivity and learning curves, thus potentially damaging client relationships. Selection of good salespeople represents an important opportunity to gain a competitive advantage.

Before reviewing the necessary tools for recruiting, you need to understand the preliminaries. The recruiting and selection process should emphasize proper planning. You need to determine the number of people to recruit, and you need to analyze each sales job. A careful review of the activities to be performed by salespeople helps you prepare a list of specific job qualifications, and you can then use that list to build a profile to guide the search for successful recruits. Next, you must decide where to look for recruits. From a pool of recruits, you then need to select job candidates. Finally, you need to validate the selection criteria and salesperson success.

13.2.1 The Planning Process

In recruiting and selection, the planning process should include a preliminary analysis of personnel needs, company culture, a job analysis, and a job description that lists the necessary job qualifications. Based on the results of these analyses, sources of sales recruits and selection procedures should be planned. Proper planning helps ensure the success of the recruiting process and provides more time for locating the best candidates.

A well-composed **job description** that focuses on the activities and responsibilities of the job is vital. **Job qualifications** refer to the aptitudes, skills, knowledge, and personality traits necessary to perform the job successfully. A statement of job qualifications typically includes desired education, previous work experience, technical expertise, aptitudes, and interests. These qualifications, based on the job description, serve as a set of selection criteria that help sales managers choose the best prospects from among those who apply.

Although lists of qualifications are useful in recruiting for sales positions, they must be used with caution. The main concern is to avoid employment discrimination that results when qualifications are used to exclude some individuals from certain jobs. Figure 13-1 outlines laws designed to prevent illegal employment discrimination.

13.2.2 Recruiting Salespeople

The goal of recruiting is to find and attract the best-qualified applicants for sales positions. The following are some of the common tools used for recruiting:

▲ Classified and online advertising, which have the advantage of reaching a wide audience for relatively little cost and may attract candidates who are not actively looking for a job.

▲ Present employees, who are good candidates for sales jobs because they are familiar with the company's products and procedures and do not require as much training as prospects recruited from outside sources.

▲ Referrals/networking, which are among the top conduits for effective recruiting in today's workplace.

Figure 13-1

Legislation	Purpose
Civil Rights Act (1964)	Prevents employment discrimination based on race, color, religion, national origin, or sex.
Age Discrimination in Employment Act (1967)	Prohibits discrimination against people ages 40 to 70.
Fair Employment Opportunity Act (1972)	Founded the Equal Employment Opportunity Commission to ensure compliance with the Civil Rights Act.
Rehabilitation Act (1973)	Requires affirmative action to hire and promote handicapped persons if the firm employees 50 or more workers and is seeking a federal contract in excess of $50,000.
Vietnam Veterans' Readjustment Assistance Act (1974)	Requires affirmative action to hire Vietnam veterans and disabled veterans of any war by firms holding federal contracts in excess of $25,000.
Americans with Disabilities Act (1990)	Prohibits discrimination based on physical or mental handicaps or disabilities.

Legal issues affecting recruitment and selection.

▲ Employment agencies, which are frequently used sources because they can save busy sales managers time and money.

▲ Schools and colleges, which provide graduates who tend to be more easily trained and are often more poised and mature than those without college training.

▲ Customers, suppliers and competitors, who are familiar with the company and may know what is expected of a salesperson. Care should be taken to ensure that the customer or supplier is aware of the recruiting process and willing to cooperate.

13.2.3 Selecting Salespeople

After recruiting a pool of sales candidates, managers must screen out candidates who do not meet the hiring criteria. The procedure for selecting prospects is a sequential filtering process, as illustrated in Figure 13-2.

The recruiter begins the selection process by evaluating application blanks and résumés and proceeds to interviews and background checks. In this way, the sales manager can eliminate obviously unsuitable prospects by using low-cost methods. The sales manager can save more expensive testing procedures for a smaller group of promising candidates.

Figure 13-2

```
                  ┌─────────────────────────┐
                  │   Direct recruit to control │
                  │  location or phone number │
                  └─────────────────────────┘
                              ↓
┌──────────┐      ┌─────────────────────────┐
│          │ ───→ │   Complete application   │ ──────────→
│          │      │          blanks          │
│          │      └─────────────────────────┘
│          │                 ↓
│          │ ───→ ┌─────────────────────────┐
│          │      │    Conduct screening     │ ──────────→
│          │      │       interviews         │
│ Hiring   │      └─────────────────────────┘
│ criteria │                 ↓
│ for      │ ───→ ┌─────────────────────────┐
│ sales    │      │    Check credit and      │ ──────────→
│ jobs     │      │      background          │
│ used     │      └─────────────────────────┘
│ to       │                 ↓
│ guide    │ ───→ ┌─────────────────────────┐
│ selection│      │  Complete psychological  │ ──────────→
│ process  │      │  and achievement tests   │
│          │      └─────────────────────────┘
│          │                 ↓
│          │ ───→ ┌─────────────────────────┐
│          │      │   Secondary interviews   │ ──────────→
│          │      └─────────────────────────┘
│          │                 ↓
│          │ ───→ ┌─────────────────────────┐
│          │      │   Make offer for sales   │ ──────────→
│          │      │        position          │
│          │      └─────────────────────────┘
│          │                 ↓
│          │ ───→ ┌─────────────────────────┐   ┌──────────┐
│          │      │      Physical exam       │   │  Reject  │
└──────────┘      └─────────────────────────┘   └──────────┘
      ↑                      ↓
┌──────────┐      ┌─────────────────────────┐
│  Modify  │      │   Measure subsequent     │
│  hiring  │ ←─── │   success on the job     │
│ criteria,│      └─────────────────────────┘
│ tests or │
│interview │
│procedures│
└──────────┘
```

A model for selecting salespeople.

The following are the major selection tools:

▲ **Application form:** Using an application form is a popular way to gather personal history data on applicants. Providing application forms is easy and requires very little executive time because of the standardized format.

▲ **Personal interview:** The interview is a crucial part of the selection process because interpersonal skills are so important in sales. Figure 13-3 lists common questions to ask during an interview.

Figure 13-3

Why should we hire you?

Regardless of the company and type of sales position for which you may interview, there are some interview questions that are typically asked. You may not be asked each of these questions in every interview, but you should be prepared to answer them all. After reading each question, think about what the interviewer's purpose may be in asking the question. What is he or she trying to determine? What should your response be to each question?

- What was the most monotonous job you ever had to do?
- In thinking about the people you like, what is it you like most about them?
- Up to this point in your life, what do you consider to be your biggest disappointment?
- How willing are you to relocate? To what extent are you willing to travel?
- How do you feel about the way your previous employer treated you?
- What are your long-term financial objectives, and how do you propose to achieve them?
- What was the most difficult decision you ever had to make as a leader?
- Why should we hire you?

Typical interview questions.

▲ **Background and credit checks:** These provide verification of information on the interviewee's application form.

▲ **Testing:** Testing uncovers more objective information than can be obtained from subjective conversation.

13.2.4 Interviewing Salespeople

Interviews are typically conducted at two levels—the initial interview and the call-back interview.

The initial interview is used primarily to inform the candidate about the job and to look for **knockout factors**—that is, characteristics that eliminate a person from further consideration, such as poor speech patterns, unacceptable appearance, or lack of necessary maturity. This initial interview is followed by the main interview, or call-back interview, in which the candidate is screened in order to identify people who best match the job's qualifications. The main interviewing process may include a series of interviews with sales managers, typically including the person to whom the candidate would report. The types of interview can vary widely, depending on the company.

One benefit of interviews is that they allow managers to follow up on information obtained from applications. For example, they can ask candidates to explain gaps in their employment or educational record and defend decisions to leave previous employers. A second advantage of interviews is that they allow sales managers to assess the applicant's level of interest and desire for the job. Interviews also allow managers to observe a candidate's conversational ability and social skills.

A problem with personal interviews, however, is that managers fall into a trap of assessing how easy the candidate would be to manage instead of assessing how effective the candidate would be in selling.

Recruiters must avoid asking questions during a personal interview that could be used to discriminate by hiring on the basis of race, sex, religion, age, or national origin. This is sometimes easier said than done because some seemingly innocent questions can be viewed as attempts to gain information that might be used to discriminate against a candidate. Figure 13-3 includes some typical questions asked in sales interviews.

The candidates for any professional selling position should be prepared to briefly present their background and career goals in approximately 2 minutes. Typically, an interviewer opens with "Tell me about yourself."

Interviewing is a subjective process, and there are bound to be a few mistakes in any interview. Applicant ratings based on personal interviews vary dramatically among interviewers because some interviewers stress unimportant job attributes during face-to-face interviews. Worse yet, studies have found that personal interview ratings are a very poor predictor of subsequent job success. However, because of the personal nature of selling, the interview has remained the preferred selection tool of most sales managers.

13.2.5 Avoiding Nine Common Recruiting Mistakes

Previous chapters discuss learning from others' mistakes. Here is a list of nine common mistakes managers make in recruiting employees.

Relying Solely on Interviews to Evaluate a Candidate

A typical interview only slightly increases a company's chances of selecting the best candidate. Interviews are poor predictors of sales success for two main reasons:

▲ Most managers do not take the time to structure an interview beforehand and determine the ideal answers to questions.

▲ Candidates do much more interviewing than most managers and are more adept at presenting themselves than many managers are at seeing through the candidates' fronts.

However, interviews remain the most common selection technique because a typical interview helps managers evaluate personal chemistry and determine how well candidates might work together with others.

Using a Generalized "Success" Model for Selection

While measuring the success characteristics of top performers may seem like a good idea, understanding differences between top performers and low achievers is more important for developing a selection model. In addition, validating the critical success skills by comparing large enough samples of top performers and weak performers helps you determine the factors that consistently distinguish the winners from the "also rans." Duplicating success may seem like a good idea, but the reasons people succeed cannot be determined simply by measuring the characteristics of top performers. You could select well-spoken, energetic candidates who fail quickly but with style.

Using Too Many Criteria

It's important to avoid getting caught up in looking for a large number of success factors. You need to be sure to validate those that you do select. Usually, the most critical factor for predicting success in a particular job is as important as or more important than all other factors combined. To hire winners, you should decide on six to eight factors that separate them from losers. You should ignore any factors that are not validated.

Evaluating Personality Instead of Job Skills

Although certain personality traits—such as high energy, honesty, and a solid work ethic—seem to practically guarantee success, they don't. While some research has shown a slight positive correlation between extraversion and conscientiousness and job performance, other factors may affect a person's performance in a particular job. Understanding how these factors fit into the overall recruiting picture is more important than knowing whether your sales candidates are outgoing and thoughtful.

Using Yourself As an Example

Your own sales success might lead you to believe you can spot candidates with potential, but you can't count on it. Many managers who reached their position by virtue of their sales success believe they can instinctively recognize a good candidate, when they are unconsciously just using themselves as a template. In these instances, one's ego often gets in the way, which can skew one's objectivity in judging others.

Failure to Use Statistically Validated Testing to Predict the Job Skills Most Critical to Success

In some companies, committees use deductive reasoning or brainstorming to identify criteria for candidate selection. Although this technique may encourage cooperation and participation, it has the potential to result in too many nonessential success characteristics. In other words, using statistically validated selling skills and abilities should be the goal. Often, committees and common-sense attitudinal and personality criteria are used because using them is easier than measuring candidates' skills. Gauging skill levels requires carefully developed tests or on-the-job trials, which many managers are unwilling or unable to conduct.

Not Researching Why People Have Failed in a Job

The reasons people fail in a job are often different from the criteria used to select them. Most managers can list the most common reasons people have failed, yet they seldom incorporate the information into developing new criteria for future candidates. There would be a significant reduction of hiring mistakes if managers would incorporate the identified failure points into the selection process. In most competitive sales situations, for example, the average prospect buys from a new salesperson only after six contacts. The average unsuccessful salesperson tends to give up after three contacts. Although some of the salesperson's techniques may be adequate, the tendency to give up after three rejections is not easily uncovered or evaluated.

Relying on General "Good Guy" Criteria

Everyone may want to hire good people, but being a good person does not ensure success on the job. You may be able to get away with using broad "good guy" criteria for entry-level hiring, but more specialized criteria are needed for sales positions that require experience or specialized sales skills.

Bypassing the Reference Check

Various recruiting and placement agencies report a fairly high percentage of false information presented in résumés and job applications. In fact, as many as 15 to 20 percent of job applicants are likely to provide false information on their résumés. It's important to make the extra effort to verify the information your applicants provide. An individual who twists the facts to get a job is likely to bend the rules on the job. Checking references may seem tedious, but it beats the frustration and cost of hiring someone you have to fire in two weeks.

13.2.6 Validating the Hiring Process

The last step in the hiring process is to validate the relationship between the selection criteria used and job success. **Validation** is generally most useful in large samples where information is collected on the progress of sales personnel and is fed back into the system to modify the factors considered in the hiring process. Validation requires that managers specify exactly what distinguishes top performers from poor performers.

Validation seeks to build a set of hiring criteria that filters out poor prospects and makes offers to those who have a high probability of success. No system can be 100 percent correct, but a carefully designed program can improve the ratio of successful hires to failures.

The depth of the hiring criteria depends on the type of sales job for which someone is being recruited. For some routine sales jobs, a set of fairly easy hiring criteria may be adequate. In more specialized industrial selling jobs where a heavy investment in training is required, a more rigorous set of experience and educational criteria may be justified. The goal of validation is to learn what factors are related to success so that they can be used to select new additions to the sales force.

SELF-CHECK

1. Discuss the elements of the planning process in recruitment.
2. Describe the common tools used in recruiting salespeople.
3. Discuss the selection process. Why is the selection of the right employees so important to a company?
4. Describe the two levels of the interview process. Why is the interview the preferred selection tool among sales managers?
5. List the nine common recruiting mistakes. How can a manager avoid them?
6. Discuss validating the hiring process

13.3 Orientation and Training

Sales executives and purchasing agents generally agree that inadequate training of salespeople is one of the most common problems they encounter. When asked what qualities make a top salesperson, purchasing agents frequently mention qualities that can be influenced by training. This is why some of the most respected companies are willing to spend a great deal on sales training. The average new hire for a business-to-business sales job costs approximately $13,000 to train over an average of four months.[1] When you add in the costs of pulling in experienced salespeople from the field and lost productivity of the entire sales force, the costs can escalate into the millions. Most of the best sales organizations, however, consider training costs as an investment in the future success of the firm rather than simply as a current expense.

13.3.1 The Benefits of a Training Program

The returns from a training program are judged as follows:

▲ **Increased productivity:** The ultimate objective of any training program is to produce profitable results.

FOR EXAMPLE

Training Pays Off

The Nabisco Biscuit Company estimated that it realized a return of 122-to-1 on a program that teaches salespeople to plan for and make professional sales presentations to retail customers. Nabisco paid $1,008 to put each salesperson through the program, and preliminary results equate to an increase of $122,640 in sales per year per salesperson.[2]

Although money spent on poorly conceived and executed training programs is largely wasted, the Nabisco example illustrates the potential for significant returns on money spent on training. Unfortunately, most firms today do not formally evaluate the financial impact of their sales training because of the perceived difficulties and added expenses.[3] However, useful cost/benefit analytical models are becoming available for managers to systematically evaluate the financial impact of a sales training program. One benefit of these models is that they allow managers to translate the skills and knowledge gained in a specific training context into a dollar-based estimate of the resulting revenues. Sales trainers report that companies are increasingly requiring this type of justification from training investments.

▲ **Reduced turnover:** Salespeople who go into the field without adequate training typically find it difficult to see buyers, answer questions, or close orders. The resulting confusion and disappointment often cause novices to quit before they have a chance to learn how to sell effectively. The company may, therefore, experience a high rate of **turnover,** which is the ratio of the number of people who leave the company to the average size of the sales team. A study of the insurance industry, for example, found that the likelihood of turnover peaks at 15 months of employment and is highest among low-productivity agents.[4] Although these results may not surprise you, the question remains: Does training really help with turnover? The results of a multiple-industry study revealed that sales managers may be able to reduce job stress (an indicator of turnover intentions) and increase job satisfaction by providing new agents with a quality sales training program.[5]

▲ **Improved customer relations:** Industrial buyers, in particular, complain that too much of their time is wasted in dealing with untrained salespeople. Buyers do not like to spend their time counseling salespeople on market conditions and product needs. They prefer to work with trained salespeople who have a thorough knowledge of the industry, their firm's business, and their own product lines. With more and more buyers requiring vendors to provide a total business solution, the number of a sales rep's contact points within the buying firm is also increasing. Today's sales training programs are responding by providing information about the buying motives for other potential key influencers, such as finance executives, operating officers, and accountants.

▲ **Better morale:** The majority of sales training is designed to increase product knowledge and improve selling skills. One by-product of acquiring these skills is increased self-confidence and enthusiasm among the sales force. When salespeople know what is expected of them, they are in a better position to withstand the disappointments and meet the challenges of a sales career. Trained salespeople produce orders faster, and their increased earnings help boost morale. The significance of this objective is reinforced by a recent study of sales trainees in which attitude was the most frequently mentioned characteristic of successful salespeople. When brought together for training, people get a sense of belonging to a team in which they can exchange successful selling techniques and ideas.

▲ **Improved time and territory efficiency:** Enhancing salesperson time and territory management skills is important for all sales organizations. Salespeople are constantly faced with time pressures that make it difficult for them to effectively allocate resources. Frequently, it is difficult to determine what is really important and what only seems important. Understanding the difference, however, is often what separates the stellar performers from the average performers.

13.3.2 Planning for Training

Planning for sales training involves three related processes:

▲ **Assessing sales training needs:** To simplify the issue, sales force productivity needs generally break down into three elements. The sales force (1) does not know what to do, (2) how to do it, or (3) why they should do it. A **training needs analysis** is a tool for determining where problems and opportunities exist and whether training can best address the issues. A complete training needs analysis includes a review of the firm's strategic objectives, management observation and survey of salespeople, customer input, and review of company records.

▲ **Setting objectives:** After assessing the training needs of the sales force, specific sales training objectives should be established and put in writing. Like all other good objectives, training objectives should be specific enough and measurable so that the extent to which they have been met can be evaluated following the training program. This also helps avoid the problem of training for training's sake. Written objectives are also helpful in gaining top management's commitment and willingness to provide budget support for training. In fact, a lack of management commitment is often cited as one of the major reasons sales training fails to produce meaningful results.[6]

▲ **Setting a training budget:** Companies spend millions of dollars every year on training for new salespeople. It should come as no surprise that the more technically oriented industrial and service industries spend more money than average and take more time to train new salespeople. A computer manufacturer, for instance, might hire engineers for sales positions and put them through a two-year training program before deploying them to its field offices. Most managers believe that the need to learn is never-ending and that even the most successful sales representatives can benefit from refresher training. Products change, markets shift, and territories are reorganized. As a result, salespeople need continuing training to help adjust to the new environmental situations.

After determining the needs of the sales force and setting specific objectives and a budget for training, a number of decisions critical to the success of the individual training program must be addressed. These decisions include what topics to cover, where to conduct the training, what training methods to use, and who should do the training. These four decisions are interrelated, and one decision affects the others.

SELF-CHECK

1. List and describe the five benefits of a training program.
2. Describe how assessing sales training needs is necessary for an effective training program.
3. Describe how setting objectives is necessary for an effective training program.
4. Describe how setting a training budget is necessary for an effective training program.

13.4 Team Building

Effective sales managers are good leaders and know how to help their teams of sales professionals achieve the company's goals and their own goals. In fact, today's workforce is becoming increasingly oriented toward teams of sales representatives working together to serve their clients. Companies are realizing that they are not selling just products; to remain competitive, they must provide system-oriented solutions to a customer's business problems. Teams of individuals, each with expertise in areas different from their team members, are becoming the way of the future.

Despite the fact that teamwork has become more important for effective selling, companies have difficulties maintaining productive sales teams. The following are the most common reasons for a lack of sales team cooperation:

▲ Rewards and compensation focus on individual performance rather than team effort.
▲ Information systems often do not keep team members supplied with pertinent data.
▲ Organizational structures foster internal competition rather than cooperation.
▲ The mind-set of some people makes them unwilling to set aside position and power for mutual gains.

A sales manager needs to help break down these barriers and reduce destructive competition among reps. A well-designed team is capable of high performance, but it needs a supportive environment to achieve its full potential. In a supportive environment, team members are empowered to take actions based on their best judgment. This means that it is very important to hire people who can get along with others and who work well in a team environment. These salespeople are quite different from traditional salespersons, who survived by relying on their own abilities. Successful team development requires team training, which is necessary to allow team members to assume each other's roles and to work interdependently.

Conflicts and disagreements among team members are natural, so managing team dynamics is necessary for effective team building. Essentially, this means maintaining cooperative relationships while pursuing a common goal. If managed well, conflict can be productive; if managed poorly, however, it can destroy a team.

SELF-CHECK

1. Discuss elements for effective team building.
2. Why is team building important to a modern-day sales manager?

13.5 Sales Force Motivation

Sales force motivation is a hot topic with sales managers. If the product or service is right, and if sales force selection, organization, and training are right, then motivation is the critical determinant of success. Another reason sales managers are concerned about motivation is the demanding environment in which salespeople operate. Field salespeople are continually moving between the exhilaration of making a sale to the disappointment of being turned down. Salespeople must frequently talk with strangers who are not always ready or willing to buy what they have to sell; some must routinely spend long hours on the road, away from their families and friends. Faced with these conditions, it is understandable that salespeople often need extra support to do an effective job.

A second reason motivation is critical is that most salespeople are not under direct supervision, in the physical presence of their manager. Veteran salespeople often meet with their immediate sales managers fewer than six times per year. In the absence of direct supervision, self-motivation is critical.

Third, motivation affects not only what activities salespeople perform but also their enthusiasm and the quality of their work. A salesperson's conviction that a product or service is best for the customer has a profound influence on a customer's purchasing decision. Customers are unlikely to purchase if they feel that a salesperson is not really motivated to help them.

More than 30 years ago, in a classic article on motivation, Frederick Herzberg noted that a KITP, which he coyly explained stood for "kick in the pants," may produce compliance, but it never produces motivation.[7] When describing someone as being motivated, sales managers are talking about three characteristics of effort:

▲ **The drive to initiate action on a task:** A common concern among sales managers is to get salespeople to call on targeted prospects.

▲ **The quality of effort on a task:** It's not enough to get people to call on prospects; they must also be motivated to put forth the effort to prepare to prospect properly and call on qualified prospects.

▲ **The persistence to expend effort over a period of time sufficient to meet or exceed objectives:** It is not enough to make the effort some of the time. Top performers show up to win every time.

No one can motivate a salesperson to do anything, but a good sales manager can help salespeople motivate themselves. Behavior is not random; it is caused. What causes people to exhibit certain behaviors in defined circumstances? To address this question, let's take a look at individual needs, what they are, and how they are related.

13.5.1 Individual Needs

In sales, the future of a business—and possibly even a sales manager's job—depends on managers' ability to understand the psychology of their salespeople. Good sales managers know what their salespeople want—what drives them. If a sales manager feels that the need for status, control, respect, and routine are most important, a number of actions can be taken to motivate the sales force, as shown in Figure 13-4.

Figure 13-4

Sales Force Needs	Company Actions to Fill Needs
Status	Change title from "salesperson" to "area manager." Buy salespeople more luxurious cars to drive.
Control	Allow salespeople to help plan sales quotas and sequences of calls.
Respect	Invite salespeople to gatherings of top executives. Put pictures of top salespeople in company ads and newsletters.
Routine	Assign each salesperson a core of loyal customers that are called on regularly.
Accomplishment	Set reasonable goals for the number of calls and sales.
Stimulation	Run short-term sales contests. Schedule sales meetings in exotic locations.
Honesty	Deliver promptly all rewards and benefits promised.

Sales force needs and ways to fulfill them.

A number of formal theories have been developed to understand differences in individual needs. Some of the classic theories are reviewed in Figure 13-5. Keep in mind that these theories may have very different implications for selling in other cultures.

These classic motivation theories are concerned with unique needs. Although each individual is unique, motivational and personality profiles of salespeople's

Figure 13-5

Theory	Author	Description
Hierarchy of needs	Abraham Maslow	Physiological, safety, belonging, esteem, and self-actualization needs are ranked in a hierarchy from lowest to highest. An individual moves up the hierarchy as a need is substantially realized.
ERG theory	Clayton P. Alderfer	Hierarchically classifies needs as existence, relatedness, and growth needs. Like Maslow, suggests that people will focus on higher needs as lower needs are satisfied but, unlike Maslow, suggests that people will focus on lower needs if their higher needs are not satisfied.
Motivation-hygiene	Frederick Herzberg	Argues that intrinsic job factors (e.g., challenging work, achievement) motivate, whereas extrinsic factors (e.g., pay) only placate employees.
Theory of learned needs	David McClelland	Proposes that there are three major professional needs: achievement, affiliation, and power. A high need for achievement and affiliation has been related to higher sales force performance. A high need for power has been related to higher sales manager performance.
Equity theory	J. Stacy Adams	Proposes that people will evaluate their treatment in comparison to that of "relevant others" and that motivation will suffer if treatment is perceived to be inequitable.

Summary of classic motivation theories.

Figure 13-6

The Competitor	This type not only wants to win, but derives satisfaction from beating specific rivals—another company or even colleagues. They tend to verbalize what they are going to do, and then do it.
The Ego-driven	They are not interested in beating specific opponents; they just want to win. They like to be considered experts but are prone to feeling slighted, change jobs frequently, and take things too personally.
The Achiever	This type is almost completely self-motivated. They usually set high goals, and as soon as they hit one goal, they move the bar higher. They like accomplishment, regardless of who receives the credit.
The Service-oriented	Their strengths lie in building and cultivating relationships.

Motivating personalities.

wants and patterns of behavior have been identified. After interviewing more than half a million salespeople, the Gallup Management Consulting Group's research has revealed that high performers tend to exhibit one of four personality types, each with different drives: competitor, ego-driven, achiever, and service-oriented.[8] (See Figure 13-6.) Although no person is purely one type of personality, you might think about how you would motivate each type of person and identify the potential pitfalls associated with each type of person.

13.5.2 Career Stages

Experienced sales managers have long understood that motivation varies according to the age and experience of the salesperson. Career stages provide a framework to understand how individual salespeople differ and how their approach to work is likely to change over time. These stages—exploration, establishment, maintenance and disengagement—are summarized in Figure 13-7.

13.5.3 Incentive and Recognition Programs

Incentive programs are short-term promotional events intended to inspire salespeople to greater-than-usual performance levels and provide them with rewards. Incentives are a proven motivational device with widespread acceptance. It is estimated that two-thirds of all consumer goods companies and more than half of all industrial goods companies have sponsored incentive programs. Incentive budgets can range in size from under $5,000 to much more.

Figure 13-7

	Exploration	Establishment	Maintenance	Disengagement
Career Concerns	Finding an appropriate occupational field.	Successfully establishing a career in a certain occupation.	Holding on to what has been achieved; reassessing career, with possible redirection.	Completing one's career.
Motivational Needs Job Related	Learning the skills required to do job well. Becoming a contributing member of an organization.	Using skills to produce results. Adjusting to working with greater autonomy.	Developing broader view of work and organization. Maintaining a high performance level.	Establishing a stronger self-identity outside of work. Maintaining an acceptable performance level.
Personal Challenges	Establishing a good initial professional self-concept.	Producing superior results on the job in order to be promoted.	Maintaining motivation, though possible rewards have changed. Facing concerns about aging.	Acceptance of career accomplishments.
Psychological Needs	Support Peer acceptance Challenging position	Achievement Esteem Autonomy Competition	Reduced competiveness Security Helping younger colleagues.	Detachment from the organization and organizational life.

Career stage characteristics.

A **recognition program** is similar to an incentive program in that an individual or a group of salespeople receives an award for exceptional performance. However, recognition programs differ from incentive programs in several important ways. Although some monetary award may be involved, the primary award is recognition by management for exceptional performance. Without a doubt, recognition and prizes push people closer to their potential than envelopes stuffed with money. This is why almost all sales managers have some sort of recognition program.

There are also timing differences between incentive and recognition programs. Whereas incentive programs are usually short in duration, a recognition program can be based on performance over a year or longer. In addition, recognition programs usually focus on overall performance rather than the sale of targeted products.

FOR EXAMPLE

Rewarding the Best

Pitney Bowes, a leading supplier of mailing equipment and office automation, has one of the most professional and successful sales forces in the world. One key to its success is the company's many recognition programs. These programs are based on two principles: (1) generate enthusiasm and motivation for as many salespeople as possible and (2) get useful feedback from the sales force to improve performance opportunities even more. Three Pitney Bowes programs illustrate these principles:

- ▲ **Pace-Maker Conference:** This week-long conference is an all-expenses-paid trip to an exotic location for the senior salespeople and their spouses or partners who have been in the top 10 percent of sales in the company for the past year. In addition to the recognition award ceremonies and other activities, the salespeople are provided a forum with senior managers, including the CEO, to learn more about the company's strategic plans, express problems or concerns, and ask questions.

- ▲ **Top Honors Conference:** This conference is designed to recognize the top new salespeople in the company. The top rookie salespeople are given a vacation trip, which includes motivational and recognition activities.

- ▲ **Walter Wheeler Award:** This award is given to any person in the company, including salespeople, who has had an extraordinary accomplishment or exhibited a strong sense of the company's vision over the past year. One person from each country where Pitney Bowes is located can be nominated for this award. All the nominees, including the overall winner, are invited to a lavish vacation.[9]

To be successful, recognition programs must become part of the company's culture. They should be long-standing, anticipated, and have lasting value. Recognition programs focus on the drive to persistently put forth exceptional effort. Successful recognition programs also appeal to the highest of Maslow's needs, self-actualization.

Recognition motivates salespeople primarily because most people strive for recognition from management and peers and cannot get enough recognition. For high performance to lead to positive job attitudes and subsequent high performance, individuals must have a positive emotional reaction to their performance.[10] A well-administered recognition program can help foster a strong, positive reaction to high performance.

SELF-CHECK

1. Why is a motivational program important to a sales force?
2. Discuss the three characteristics of effort related to someone being motivated.
3. List the actions that can be taken to motivate a sales force.
4. What four personality types are common among high performers?
5. Describe the four career stages. How does motivation vary among these stages?
6. Define **incentive program** and **recognition programs**. Why are they important?

13.6 Compensation Plans

Compensation is one of the most important tools for motivating and retaining field salespeople. However, sales force compensation is a cost that can quickly spiral out of control in a compensation plan that is designed improperly. To maintain profitability, managers must design compensation plans that encourage salespeople to work efficiently, and this is not easy to do. In fact, salesperson compensation has long been an issue marked by trial and error. Many companies have struggled for years to discover just the right formula or approach.[11]

A good starting point in developing the optimal pay plan is to define the goals of the company and how the sales force can support those goals. Although the most important goal of senior-level managers, according to a recent survey, is to increase sales and revenues,[12] a manager has access to many short- and long-term sales force tactics. For example, do you want reps to sell more premium items in certain product lines? increase long-term customer relationships? or increase salesperson motivation? Each required a different tactic.

Compensation plans must be custom designed to not only meet the goals of individual firms but also provide competitive compensation packages to the marketplace. They must balance the natural desire of salespeople to earn more money with the firm's need to control expenses. This means that you have the difficult task of designing compensation programs that motivate salespeople to reach company goals and satisfy customers without bankrupting the firm. And because 20 to 30 percent of all sales reps are unhappy with their compensation plans at any one time, you may be constantly challenged to come up with a better program.

Several theories can guide you in designing sales compensation plans that fit the needs of a specific firm. Building a program is a combination of art and sci-

---

FOR EXAMPLE

Motivating Compensation

For the past several years, the sales compensation plan for Liberty Courier, Inc., a delivery company in Woburn, Massachusetts, had stunted the company's growth. Salespeople, who were paid a straight salary, expected a raise each time they increased their business. When the raise was not forthcoming, they began calculating what their earnings might look like if they worked for competitors, many of which offered commission-based plans. As a result, reps' motivation dropped, and turnover increased. In response, Liberty completely revamped its compensation plan to align it with its goal of increasing profits with the customers who were expected to produce the most revenue. Soon after the new plan was implemented, motivation increased, turnover dropped, and Liberty's sales exploded to 130 percent of those from the previous year.[13]

---

ence, and sales managers often feel the need to review or alter compensation plans regularly to increase their efficiency. By far the most common compensation plan combines a base salary with some type of incentives. Table 13-1 shows that approximately 83 percent of firms use combination plans for intermediate-level salespeople. One advantage of a combination plan is that the incentive portion can be used to influence specific salesperson behaviors, such as focusing on a particular segment of customers or a specific product line. A useful rule of thumb for any company thinking of exerting some behavioral control using incentives is to make sure that the incentive component is between 15 and 30 percent of total compensation.[14]

Table 13-1: Use of Compensation Plans

	Percentage of Companies Using
Straight salary	18
Straight commission	19
Combination plans (63%):	
Salary plus bonus	24
Salary plus commission	20
Salary plus bonus plus commission	18
Commission plus bonus	1
Total	100%

13.6.1 Expense Reimbursement

No discussion of sales force compensation would be complete without mention of expense accounts and other benefits. Almost all firms that pay straight salaries or some combination of salary, commission, and/or bonus cover expenses for salespeople. Typical expenses paid by firms include those for automobiles and other travel, tips, lodging, food, samples, telephone, postage, and tickets for sporting and theater events.

Three types of expense plans can be used:

▲ **Unlimited plans:** With an **unlimited plan,** salespeople submit itemized forms showing their expenditures. The firm simply pays all reported expenses.

▲ **Per diem plans:** A **per diem plan** pays the salesperson a fixed dollar amount for each day or week spent in the field. The amount is designed to cover food, gasoline, lodging, telephone calls, and other expenses.

▲ **Limited repayment plans:** With a **limited repayment plan,** the firm sets dollar limits on each category of sales expenses.

13.6.2 Benefits

Benefits packages can be used to attract and reward salespeople. These programs include a variety of hospitalization, insurance, and pension plans. One study found that salespeople prefer benefits to recognition and incentive awards.[15] Benefits packages range from $4,300 for insurance salespeople to $21,000 for rubber and plastics reps, with a typical program costing $7,600.[16] The recent explosion in medical care costs has made it difficult for many firms to control the expenses of benefits packages. One approach has been to raise the medical deductible levels so that employees pay more of the costs. Another popular solution is to allocate a certain number of benefit dollars to each employee and let each person choose from a cafeteria plan of possible benefits. This allows reps to select benefits packages that fit their individual needs.

SELF-CHECK

1. Why are properly designed compensation plans important for motivating and retaining salespeople?
2. Discuss important considerations in designing a compensation plan.
3. List and describe the three types of expense reimbursement plans.
4. What are the important considerations in developing a benefits package?

13.7 Assessing Sales Force Productivity

At first glance, evaluating a salesperson's performance seems simple: You merely measure sales volume. The thinking behind this theory is that higher volume means increased performance. But the focus on sales volume can be misleading. Consider the following scenario: A district sales manager recently asked one of his first-line sales managers, "How good is your sales force?" The sales manager quickly responded, "We are very good." The district manager followed up with the question, "How do you know?" "Because we made our performance goal the last three years," replied the sales manager.

Does three years of goal attainment make a sales team "very good"? One salesperson may generate a high sales volume made up of low-profit items. Another may have high volume with a few customers but may make too few calls. Still another high-volume salesperson may spend too much time and money on each call. The point is that increased volume may not represent an increased level of profit for a business. Properly evaluating sales personnel requires looking at many factors that influence their value to the company.

Evaluation is defined as a comparison of sales force goals and objectives with actual achievements in the field. To begin the evaluation process, management must first decide what it wants the sales force to accomplish. The most common objectives are the attainment of specific sales revenues, contribution profits, market shares, and expense levels. Then, a sales plan must be prepared to show how the goals are to be achieved. The next step is to set performance standards for individual products for different levels in the organization. This typically requires setting goals for total sales, as well as sales by regions, by product, by salesperson, and for each separate account. At the conclusion of an evaluation period, differences between the performance standards and the results attained are determined. Reasons for above- and below-standard performance are analyzed, and modifications are made in the plans for the future.

The task of selecting a set of sales performance measures for a firm is difficult because so many unique factors can be used. Most experts agree that performance measures should be tailored to the goals and objectives of each organization.[17] This leads to the observation that different sets of evaluation criteria can be successful in separate sales environments.[18]

Performance reviews are usually conducted annually, although many firms conduct evaluations semiannually or quarterly. While these reviews are difficult to administer, they provide valuable information for staffing decisions and serve as a basis to improve salesperson performance. The results of performance reviews can be used to answer a number of important questions, such as these:

▲ Who should receive raises, bonuses, and prizes?
▲ Who should be promoted?
▲ What criteria should be used in hiring?

▲ Who needs retraining?

▲ What subjects should be emphasized in training classes?

▲ Have the company's strategic selling objectives been met?

▲ How should sales territories be adjusted?

▲ Who should be terminated?

Each of these questions requires you to look at a slightly different set of evaluative criteria.

Historically, sales performance metrics were simple: Increase revenue over the previous year. Sales managers typically rewarded and compensated salespeople by evaluating sales volume over a certain period of time. Although sales volume is still important, companies are discovering that not all sales are equally profitable. Profitability often depends on the following:

▲ The amount of time necessary to complete a sale.

▲ The gross margins associated with a sale.

▲ The level of price discounting.

▲ The amount of promotional support.

▲ The amount of post-sale support.

▲ The impact of future product sales.

The sales force has an important influence on all these issues, through its account selection, account penetration, account retention, pricing, and servicing decisions. In effect, salespeople are resource allocators. First, they decide which customers and prospects they will spend time selling and how much time they will allocate to each customer. Second, the sales force also has an important role in the allocation of marketing resources to individual customers. For example, sales forces for large food manufacturers selling through grocery stores are responsible for trade promotion spending decisions, such as coupon promotions, newspaper advertising, display racks, and price promotions. Studies have found that trade promotion spending consumes approximately 50 percent of the marketing budgets of these companies and represents about 12 percent of sales.[19] Spending this money effectively is critical to these firms' profitability. As a result, salespeople are being evaluated on a wider array of performance metrics, which places greater emphasis on gathering more and better performance data.

13.7.1 Six Insights for Evaluation and Control Systems

Experts suggest that sales managers are more likely to spend time in the evaluation process and use the results if a similar process is used to manage their own performance as well as others in the sales organization. The following are six insights for evaluation and control systems:

▲ **The evaluation system is used at all levels of the company:** First-line sales managers (as well as salespeople) are more likely to take the process seriously and use it if a similar process is used to manage their own performance.

▲ **A good evaluation system reflects the company's culture:** An evaluation system needs to be consistent with the sales force culture.

▲ **Peer influence is powerful in helping manage performance:** Most evaluation interactions occur between a salesperson and his or her superior. That is, the evaluation system is hierarchical. Some companies that use team selling have discovered a powerful way to influence performance: horizontal (i.e., peer) evaluations. Team selling naturally lends itself to horizontal evaluations because team members expect good performances and encouragement from one another.

▲ **Evaluation systems must leverage a person's motivators:** It is important to remember that people are motivated by positive feedback, specific and understandable goals, and a compensation system that reinforces these goals. In addition to these factors, the manager must also take the role of a coach by appealing to the achievement, power, ego gratification, social affiliation, and survival needs of the salespeople.

▲ **Empowerment and direction:** It's not just a question of either empowerment or direction but a question of when. A person may need to be empowered in one area and directed in another. For example, a salesperson may have excellent prospecting and relationship-building skills but poor closing skills. Thus, an evaluation system that permits a manager to tailor the evaluation procedure to an individual is recommended.

▲ **The evaluation system itself must evolve:** High-performing sales organizations are able to change with the marketplace. These changes include salesperson success factors. The evaluation system must also evolve to adapt and reflect these changes.

SELF-CHECK

1. Define **evaluation**. What are important considerations in developing the evaluation process?

2. Discuss the various factors affecting profitability. How could these factors affect metrics used to measure sales performance?

3. Describe six insights for designing and implementing evaluation and control systems.

SUMMARY

The responsibility of a sales manager may cover a vast array of competencies, from strategic planning to team building and self-management. In order to be successful, a sales manager must not only develop these competencies but also learn how to recruit and select the right salespeople. The manager must also uncover each salesperson's motivational drive. Developing a satisfactory compensation package may also be part of the job. With all these elements in place, the manager must then assess sales productivity and make any necessary adjustments. This chapter examines these fundamentals in managing and training others.

KEY TERMS

Benefits package	Incentives used to attract new employees and reward salespeople. A benefits package generally includes hospitalization, insurance, and pension plans.
Coaching competency	A sequence of conversations and activities that provide ongoing feedback and encouragement to a salesperson or sales team member, with the goal of improving that person's performance.
Evaluation	A comparison of sales force goals and objectives with actual achievements in the field.
Global perspective competency	Drawing on human, financial, information, and material resources from multiple countries and serving customers who span multiple cultures.
Incentive programs	Short-term promotional events intended to inspire salespeople to a greater-than-usual performance level and provide them with rewards.
Job description	A set of rules or practices that define the role of an employee.
Job qualifications	The aptitudes, skills, knowledge, and personality traits necessary to perform a particular job successfully.
Knockout factors	Characteristics, uncovered during an interview, that eliminate a person from further consideration, such as poor speech patterns, unacceptable appearance, or lack of necessary maturity.
Limited repayment plan	An expense plan in which the firm sets dollar limits on each category of sales expenses.
Per diem plan	An expense plan that pays a salesperson a fixed dollar amount for each day or week spent in the field. The

	amount is designed to cover food, gasoline, lodging, telephone calls, and other expenses.
Recognition program	A program similar to incentives in that an individual or group of salespeople receives an award for exceptional performance, but the primary award is recognition by management for exceptional performance.
Sales management	The planning, organizing, leading, and controlling of personal contact programs designed to achieve the sales and profit objectives of a firm.
Sales manager	The person responsible for management of the field sales operation.
Sales management competencies	Sets of knowledge, skills, behaviors, and attitudes that a person needs to be effective in a wide range of industries and various types of organizations.
Self-management competency	Taking responsibility for your actions at work and elsewhere.
Strategic action competency	Understanding the industry and the organization and then taking strategic actions.
Team building competency	Accomplishing tasks through small groups of people who are collectively responsible and whose work is interdependent.
Technology competency	Understanding the potential for technology to improve sales force efficiency and effectiveness and knowing how to implement the integration of technology into the sales force
Training needs analysis	A process for determining where problems and opportunities exist and whether training can best address the issues.
Turnover	The ratio of the number of people who leave to the average size of the sales team.
Unlimited plan	A type of expense reimbursement plan in which salespeople submit itemized forms showing their expenditures, and the firm simply pays all reported expenses.
Validation	The last step in the hiring process, which involves validating the relationship between the selection criteria used by the firm and job success.

ASSESS YOUR UNDERSTANDING

Go to www.wiley.com/college/hopkins to evaluate your knowledge of managing and training others.
Measure your learning by comparing pre-test and post-test results.

Summary Questions

1. Sales management includes recruiting, training, motivating, and evaluating sales personnel. True or false?
2. Which of the following is *not* a competency for sales managers?
   (a) coaching
   (b) technology
   (c) recruiting and selecting employees
   (d) self-management
3. The planning process in recruiting and selecting personnel should include:
   (a) a job description.
   (b) analysis of personnel needs.
   (c) a look at the company culture.
   (d) all of the above.
4. A common source used in recruiting is:
   (a) an employment agency.
   (b) referrals.
   (c) schools and colleges.
   (d) all of the above.
5. An important aspect of an interview for selecting an employee is the evaluation of the applicant's interpersonal skills. True or false?
6. During the interview, a person applying for a sales representative job should be able to state his or her experience and skills within:
   (a) one minute.
   (b) two minutes.
   (c) three minutes.
   (d) four minutes.
7. A generalized success model is an important tool in recruiting employees. True or false?
8. You should rely solely on your instincts in hiring an employee. True or false?
9. The purpose of validation is to build effective hiring criteria. True or false?

10. Top salespeople don't need additional training after achieving their pinnacle. True or false?

11. The benefits of an effective training program is:
    (a) better morale.
    (b) reduced turnover.
    (c) increased productivity.
    (d) all of the above.

12. A training needs analysis determines how training can address specified problems and opportunities. True or false?

13. An effective sales manager relies on a salesperson's self-management skills to keep motivation high. True or false?

14. The same motivation techniques can be used for everyone in the same sales force. True or false?

15. A recognition program differs from an incentive program in its duration of time. True or false?

16. The success of compensation plans relies heavily on designs that meet the demands of the firm, marketplace, and individual employees. True or false?

17. A limited reimbursement plan pays a fixed dollar amount for each day or week. True or false?

18. Effectively evaluating a salesperson's performance involves measuring only that person's annual sales volume. True or false?

19. Sales teams are becoming increasingly abundant in today's business environment. True or false?

Applying This Chapter

1. Take a look at the six competencies needed for today's sales managers. In which area do you believe you have an inclination or a talent? Why?

2. Discuss how you would recruit and select a salesperson for work in a highly technical field, such as robotics. Which recruitment tool do you believe would be most effective in this case? Why?

3. Visualize yourself as a sales manager for a small company with a sales force of five representatives. Your sales training budget is extremely low. In fact, you need each salesperson out in the field as soon as possible. Describe at least three training means you could implement that cost little or no money.

4. How would you motivate each of the following personality types: competitor, ego-driven, achiever, and service-oriented. Describe at least one pitfall associated with each type.

5. Think of one of your past (or present) jobs. In that job, what were (or are) some of the benefits or incentives offered by management?

6. Visualize yourself as a sales manager for a food manufacturer. Your company is launching a new product that upper management believes has great potential. You've decided to provide extra monetary incentives for salespeople who sell a specified amount of this new product. What considerations would you add in evaluating your salespeople to reflect this new product?

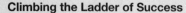

Climbing the Ladder of Success

For seven years you've been one of the top salespeople for your company. You've worked particularly hard to develop your sales skill and have received superior evaluations from your superiors. In other words, you know the right stuff for a successful career in sales. Now, however, you believe you want to advance into sales management. You've just learned that a highly respected sales manager is retiring in two years. You want that job. What steps would you take to be considered for that position?

ENDNOTES

Chapter 1

1. Hopkins, Tom. 2001. *Selling for Dummies, 2nd edition*, pp. 331–333. Wiley Publishing, Inc., Indianapolis, IN.

Chapter 2

1. Bridget O'Brian, "Prudential Fined $20 Million by NASD over Its Sales of Variable Life Insurance, *The Wall Street Journal* (July 9, 1999), pp. C1, C11.
2. Dawn Blalock, "For Many Executives, Ethics Appear to be a Write-Off," *The Wall Street Journal* (March 26, 1996), p. C1.
3. Eric Strout, "To Tell the Truth," *Sales & Marketing Management* (July 2002), pp. 40–47.
4. Sean Valentine and Tim Barnett, "Ethics Codes and Sales Professionals: Perceptions of Their Organizations—Ethical Values." *Journal of Business Ethics* (October 2002), pp. 191–200.
5. Alan J. Dubinsky, Marvin A. Jolson, Ronald E. Michaels, Masaaki Kotabe, and Chae Un Lim, "Ethical Perceptions of Field Sales Personnel: An Empirical Assessment," *Journal of Sales & Marketing Management* (Fall 1992), p. 18.
6. *The Wall Street Journal* (May 14, 1996), p. A1.
7. Gabriella Stern and Joann S. Lublin, "New GM Rules Curb Wining and Dining," *The Wall Street Journal* (May 5, 1996), p. B1.
8. Rolph Anderson, Rajiv Mehta, and James Strong, "An Empirical Investigation of Sales Management Training Programs for Sales Managers," *Journal of Personal Selling & Sales Management,* 17 (Summer 1997), p. 61.
9. Rosemary R. Lagace, Robert Dahlstrom, and Jule B. Gassenheimer, "The Relevance of Ethical Salesperson Behavior on Relationship

Quality: The Pharmaceutical Industry," *Journal of Personal Selling & Sales Management* (Fall 1991), p. 44.

10. Ken Bass, Tim Barnett, and Gene Brown, "The Moral Philosophy of Sales Managers and Its Influence on Ethical Decision Making," *Journal of Personal Selling & Sales Management,* 18 (Spring 1998) p. 11.

11. Bass et al., "The Moral Philosophy of Sales Managers and Its Influence on Ethical Decision Making" p. 1–17.

12. Niccol Machiavelli, The Prince (New York: Mentor Classics, 1952).

13. Anusorn Singhapakdi and Scott J. Vitell "Analyzing the Ethical Decision Making of Sales Professionals," *Journal of Personal Selling & Sales Management* (Fall 1991), p. 9.

14. Melinda Ligos, "Are Your Reps Bribing Customers," *Sales & Marketing Management* (March 2002) pp. 126–130.

15. Rob Zeiger, "Sex, Sales & Stereotypes," *Sales & Marketing Management* (July 1995), pp. 46–56.

16. Leslie M. Fine, C. David Shepard, and Susan L. Josephs, " Insights into Sexual Harassment of Salespeople by Customers: The Role of Gender and Customer Power," *Journal of Personal Selling & Sales Management,* 19, No. 2 (Spring 1999), p. 29.

17. Charles Haddad and Amy Barett, "A Whistle-Blower Rocks an Industry," *Business Week* (June 24, 2002), pp. 126–130.

Chapter 3

1. Nicole Coviello, Roderick Brodie, Peter Danaher, and Wesley Johnston, "How Firms Relate to Their Markets: An Empirical Examination of Contemporary Marketing Practices," *Journal of Marketing,* 66 (July 2002), pp. 33–46.

2. Kevin Hoffberg and Kevin Corcoran, "Selling at the Speed of Change," *Harvard Business Review,* 77 (November–December 1999), p. 22.

Chapter 4

1. http://www.dictionary.com

2. *Webster's New World Dictionary,* August 1983, Warner Books, Inc., 666 Fifth Avenue, New York, NY 10103.

3. Ibid.

4. Tom Hopkins, 2001. *Selling for Dummies, 2nd edition,* p 56–64.Wiley Publishing, Indianapolis, IN.

5. For more on relationship development, see James C. Anderson, "Relationships in Business Markets: Exchange Episodes, Value Creation, and Their Empirical Assessment," *Journal of the Academy of Marketing Science,* 23 (1996), pp. 346–350.

6. Michael Dorsch, Scott Swanson, and Scott Kelley, "The Role of Relationship Quality in the Stratification of Vendors as Perceived by Customers," *Journal of the Academy of Marketing Science,* 26, 2 (1998), pp. 128–142.

7. Douglas Bowman and Das Narayandas, "Linking Customer Management Effort to Customer Profitability in Business Markets," *Journal of Marketing Research,* 41 (November 2004), pp. 433–447.

8. For more on building trust, see Carolyn Nicholson, Larry Compeau, and Rajesh Sethi, "The Role of Interpersonal Liking in Building Trust in Long-Term Channel Relationships," *Journal of the Academy of Marketing Science,* 29 (2001), pp. 3–15; Patricia Doney and Joseph Cannon, "An Examination of the Nature of Trust in Buyer-Seller Relationships," *Journal of Marketing,* 61 (April 1997), pp. 35–51; and Robert Morgan and Shelby Hunt, "The Commitment-Trust Theory of Relationship Marketing," *Journal of Marketing,* 58 (July 1994), pp. 20–38.

9. Lan Xia, Kent Monroe, and Jennifer Cox, "The Price is Unfair! A Conceptual Framework of Price Fairness Perceptions," *Journal of Marketing,* 68 (October 2004), pp. 1–15; and Roy Lweicki and Barbara Bunker, "Trust in Relationships: A Model of Development and Decline," in Conflict, Cooperation, and Justice: Essays Inspired by the Work of Morton Deutsch, The Jossey-Bass Management Series and The Jossey-Bass Conflict Series, vol. 33, Barbara Benedict Bunker and Jeffrey Rubin, eds. (San Francisco: Jossey-Bass), 1995, pp. 133–173.

10. Willem Verbeke and Richard Bagozzi, "Sales Call Anxiety: Exploring What It Means When Fear Rules a Sales Encounter," *Journal of Marketing,* 64 (July 2000), pp. 88–101.

Chapter 5

1. "Data Watch," *Velocity* (1st Quarter 2002), p. 5.
2. Theodore Kinmi, "How Strategic Is Your Sales Strategy?" *Harvard Management Update* (February 2004), p. 5.
3. David Reid, Ellen Pullins, and Richard Plank, "The Impact of Purchase Situation on Salesperson Communication Behaviors in Business Markets," *Industrial Marketing Management,* 31 (2002), pp. 205–213.

Chapter 6

1. Betsy Cummings, "Wake Up, Salespeople," *Sales & Marketing Management* (June 2002), p. 11.
2. Theodore Kinmi, "How Strategic Is Your Sales Strategy?" *Harvard Management Update* (February 2004), p. 5.

3. Tom Mitchell, "Cisco Resellers Add Value," *Industrial Marketing Management,* 30 (2001), pp. 115–118.

4. Annie Liu and Mark Leach, "Developing Loyal Customers with a Value-adding Sales Force: Examining Customer Satisfaction and the Perceived Credibility of Consultative Salespeople," *Journal of Selling & Sales Management,* 21 (Spring 2001), pp. 147–156.

Chapter 7

1. Mehrabian, Albert. 1971. *Silent Messages,* Wadsworth Publishing, Belmont, CA.

Chapter 8

1. Tim Minahan, "Chrysler Elects Procurement Team Leader as Its New President," *Purchasing Magazine* (January 1998), pp. 22–25.

Chapter 9

1. William L. Cron and Thomas E. DeCarlo, *Dalrymple's Sales Management, Ninth Edition,* p. 156. John Wiley & Sons., Inc., Hoboken, NJ.

2. Cron and DeCarlo, *Dalrymple's Sales Management,* p. 157.

Chapter 10

1. Cron and DeCarlo, *Dalrymple's Sales Management,* p. 155.

2. Hopkins, *Selling for Dummies,* p. 200.

3. Hopkins, *Selling for Dummies,* p. 205.

4. Hopkins, *Selling for Dummies,* pp. 333–340.

Chapter 11

1. Cron and DeCarlo, *Dalyrymple's Sales Managemet,* p. 136.

2. Hopkins, *Selling for Dummies,* p. 241.

3. Lesley Abery, Colleen Chirsten, and Erin Kriessmann, "Customers Talk, BT Listens," *Velocity* (1st and 2nd Quarter 2002), p. 14.

4. Hopkins, *Selling for Dummies,* p. 225.

Chapter 12

1. Erin Strout, "Prisoners of Paperwork," *Sales & Marketing Management* (December 2002), pp. 41–45.
2. Ginger Conlon, "Plug and Play," *Sales & Marketing Management* (December 1998), p. 65.
3. Cron and DeCarlo, *Dalrymple's Sales Management,* p. 112.
4. Thayer C. Taylor, "Does This Compute?" *Sales & Marketing Management* (September 1994), pp. 115–119.
5. Stephen Covey, *Principle-Centered Leadership* (New York: Simon & Schuster, 1992).
6. Andris Zoltners, Prabhakant Sinha, and Greggor Zoltners, *The Complete Guide to Accelerating Sales Force Performance* (New York: AMACOM, 2001), p. 117.

Chapter 13

1. *Sales Force Compensation Survey* (Chicago: Dartnell Corporation, 1999), p. 143.
2. Robert Klein, "Nabisco Sales Soar after Sales Training," *Marketing News* (January 6, 1997), p. 23.
3. Christine Galea and Carl Wiens, "2002 Sales Training Survey," *Sales & Marketing Management* (July 2002), pp. 34–37; also, for more information about the difficulties in evaluating sales training, see Ashraf M. Attia, Earl D. Honeycutt, and Magdy Mohamed Attia, "The Difficulties of Evaluating Sales Training," *Industrial Marketing Management,* 31 (2002), pp. 253–259.
4. William Moncrief, Ronald Hoverstad, and George Lucas, "Survival Analysis: A New Approach to Analyzing Sales Force Retention," *Journal of Personal Selling & Sales Management,* 9 (Summer 1989), p. 26.
5. Frederick A. Russ, Kevin M. McNeilly, James M. Comer, and Theodore B. Light, "Exploring the Impact of Critical Sales Events," *Journal of Personal Selling & Sales Management,* 18 (Spring 1998), p. 26.
6. Mark McMaster, "Is Your Training a Waste of Money?" *Sales & Marketing Management* (January 2001), p. 40-48.
7. For further discussion of expectancy theory, see Gordon T. Gray and Stacia Wert-Gray, "Research Note: Decision-Making Processes and Formation of Salespeople's Expectancies, Instrumentalities, and Valences," *Journal of Personal Selling & Sales Management* (Summer 1999), pp. 53–59; Thomas E. DeCarlo, R. Kenneth Teas, and James C. McElroy, "Salesperson Performance Attribution Processes and the Formation of Expectancy Estimates," *Journal of Personal Selling & Sales Management,* 27 (Summer 1997), pp. 1–17; and Wesley J. Johnston and Keysuk Kim, "Performance Attribution and Expectancy Linkages

in Personal Selling," *Journal of Marketing,* 58 (October 1994), pp. 68–81.

8. Geoffrey Brewer, "What Makes Great Salespeople?" *Sales & Marketing Management* (May 1994), pp. 82–92.

9. Based on discussions with Liz Crute, Vice President, Pitney Bowes' Credit Corporation (February 2003).

10. Steven Brown, William Cron, and Thomas Leigh, "Do Feelings of Success Mediate Sales Performance-Work Attitude Relationships?" *Journal of the Academy of Marketing Science,* 21 (Spring 1993), pp. 91–100.

11. Donald L. Caruth and Gail D. Handlogten-Caruth, "Compensating Sales Personnel," *The American Salesman* (April 2002), pp. 6–15.

12. *BFOB Magazine* (January 14, 2002) p. 1 and p. 23.

13. Michele Marchetti, "Compensation Is Kid Stuff," *Sales & Marketing Management* (April 1999), pp. 53–59.

14. Andris Zoltners, Prabhakant Sinha, and Greggor Zoltners, *The Complete Guide to Accelerating Sales Force Performance* (New York: AMACOM, 2001), p. 301.

15. Lawrence B. Chonko, John F. Tanner, and William A. Weeks, "Selling and Sales Management in Action: Reward Preferences of Salespeople," *Journal of Personal Selling & Sales Management* (Summer 1992), p. 69.

16. *Sales Force Compensation Survey* (Chicago: Dartnell Corporation, 1999), p. 119.

17. Donald W. Jackson, John L. Schlacter, and William G. Wolfe, "Examining the Bases Utilized for Evaluating Salespeoples' Performance," *Journal of Personal Selling & Sales Management,* 15, No. 4. (Fall 1995), p. 65.

18. Vlasis Stathakopoulos, "Sales Force Control: A Synthesis of Three Theories," *Journal of Personal Selling & Sales Management,* 16, No. 2 (Spring 1996), p. 1.

19. Donald W. Jackson, John L. Schlacter, and William G. Wolfe, "Examining the Bases Utilized for Evaluating Salespeoples' Performance," *Journal of Personal Selling & Sales Management,* 15, No. 4. (Fall 1995), p. 65.

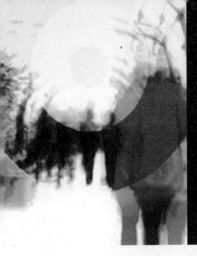

GLOSSARY

10-3-1 rule A guide for sales which says that for every 10 qualified prospects, 3 will entertain a proposal, and 1 will become a customer.

Addressing concerns The sales strategy's fifth step, in which the salesperson answers the prospect's questions satisfactorily and fulfills any needs.

Advocating skills The ability to clearly and fully present a solution that customers can see helps address their needs.

Alternate of choice questioning A strategy used to involve prospects by presenting two acceptable suggestions for the client's choice.

Alternative choice A closing technique in which the salesperson poses a series of questions designed to narrow the choice for a final selection.

Analyzers A type of buyers who study every detail and want an organized salesperson.

Assumptive selling The process of giving a prospect the ownership of your idea, product, or service to help move that person closer to making a decision.

Attention-getters Verbal and nonverbal messages that can project a positive or negative image.

Basic oral close A closing technique involving a simple statement that directly asks for the order.

Basic written close A closing method in which the salesperson fills out an order form after determining preferences with a client. The salesperson asks the client to check out the details and sign the form.

Behavioral self-management (BSM) A series of steps involving monitoring, goal setting, rehearsal, rewards, and self-contracting.

Believers A type of buyers who are easygoing, believe in the salesperson and company, and remain loyal customers.

Benefitizing   Translating features of a product into benefits believed to be of value to the customer.

Benefits package   Incentives used to attract new employees and reward salespeople. A benefits package generally includes hospitalization, insurance, and pension plans.

Best-things-in-life close   A closing technique that emphasizes the enjoyment of a product's benefits.

Brand identity   The consumer's perception of who you and your company are.

Brand meaning   The consumer's perception of what you are.

Brand relationships   Consumers' preferences for associating with you.

Brand responses   Consumers' answers about how they think or feel about you.

Bribe   An agreed-upon payment to obtain a customer's business.

Brief recap   A restatement of the major points during a presentation.

Business-productivity close   A closing technique that emphasizes the benefits of a product for a company's employees.

Buyer-remorse close   A closing technique that relieves remorse after a purchase.

Buying Power Index (BPI)   The multifactor index of area demand, which is published each year by *Sales & Marketing Management* magazine.

Call reluctance   The fear of making contact with a customer.

Call reports   Reports completed by salespeople that detail who the salesperson called on, at what stage the prospect is within the sales cycle, and what follow-up activities are needed.

Canned presentation   The same basic presentation given to every customer.

Closed-ended questions   Questions to be answered with a simple "yes" or "no" response or by selecting from a list of responses. Also known as alternate-of-choice questions.

Closing   The stage of selling when a salesperson asks for a commitment from the customer.

Closing the sale   The sales strategy's sixth step, in which the salesperson meets the prospect's needs and concerns.

Coaching competency   A sequence of conversations and activities that provide ongoing feedback and encouragement to a salesperson or sales team member, with the goal of improving that person's performance.

Complainers   A type of buyers who focus on negatives.

Conscious competence   The third phase of the learning curve, in which a person realizes the skills he or she has acquired.

Conscious incompetence   The second phase of the learning curve, in which a person chooses to learn specific skills and knowledge.

Consultative relationship   A high-investment approach to relationship building that focuses on problem solving for the client.

Contact management software   Software that works with a database of information to organize information about present and future clients.

Conventional morality   A standard in which emphasis shifts from the individual to what society thinks about the ethical issue. Also known as *situation ethics*.

Core Based Statistical Areas (CBSAs)   922 geographic areas used by *Sales & Marketing Management* magazine in its Buying Power Index

Cross-selling   Selling additional products and services to a customer.

Customer relationship management   A business strategy that involves a comprehensive set of processes and technologies for managing relationships with potential and current customers and business partners across marketing, sales, and service.

Customer relationship management software   Software designed to ensure that every person from a supplier's organization who comes into contact with a customer has access to all the latest information on the customer.

Cynics   A type of buyers who fight change, are suspicious, and question everything.

Deal with dissatisfaction   One of the pillars of sales support, which may include responding in an empathetic manner to any problems that arise.

Decision maker   The person who has the ability or power to make decisions about the products or services you sell.

De-motivators   Factors that keep salespeople from advancing in their careers.

Direct mail   Mail, such as catalogs and flyers, sent for sales purposes.

Disorganized and controlling buyers   A type of buyers who are self-proclaimed experts but poor at delegating authority.

E-mail approach   An electronic sales approach for reaching prospects.

Enhance the relationship   One of the pillars of sales support, which illustrates that salespeople should always try to be available, to ensure that the quality of the offering is maintained, and to be a source of information, help, and ideas.

Erroneous conclusion   An intentional error a salesperson makes to test how serious the prospect is about going ahead with the sale.

Ethics   A code of moral behavior that governs the conduct of an individual or a business community.

Ethics policy statement   A document prepared by a company that indicates to the sales force that the company believes in playing fair with customers and competitors.

Evaders   A type of buyers who refuse to return a salesperson's calls and are difficult to reach.

Evaluation   A comparison of sales force goals and objectives with actual achievements in the field.

Expectations   Rules or norms, with respect to acceptable conduct and performance.

Follow-up   All the efforts involved in servicing a sale and building a lasting and growing relationship with a customer.

Foreign Corrupt Practices Act   U.S. legislation that makes it a criminal offense to offer a payment to a foreign government official to obtain or retain foreign business.

Gift   An unexpected item given to a customer, primarily to thank the client for his or her business.

Global perspective competency   Drawing on human, financial, information, and material resources from multiple countries and serving customers who span multiple cultures.

Go-to-market participants   Avenues used to access customers, such as the internet, telemarketing, advertising, direct mail, and person-to-person selling.

Go-to-market strategy   Identification of who will perform sales activities and for which customers.

Higher authority close   A closing technique in which you use the example of a higher authority who is respected by the client as one of your satisfied clients.

Idealism   A pattern of moral reasoning that accepts moral codes and believes that positive outcomes are possible through morally correct actions.

Incentive programs   Short-term promotional events intended to inspire salespeople to a greater-than-usual performance level and provide them with rewards.

Interaction   Actions initiated while interacting with decision makers, calling on such skills as relating and needs discovery.

Internet approach   Use of Web sites to sell to a global audience.

It's-not-in-the-budget close   A closing technique that allows a prospect to flex any budget constraints and disallows the easy dismissal of a salesperson.

Jargon   Words and phrases particular to a given field of work.

Job description   1. A set of rules or practices that define the role of an employee.
2. A summary that describes the activities and responsibilities of a job.

Job qualifications   The aptitudes, skills, knowledge, and personality traits necessary to perform a particular job successfully.

Jury of executive opinion technique   A forecasting technique that involves soliciting the judgment of a group of experienced managers to give sales estimates for proposed and current products.

Knockout factors   Characteristics, uncovered during an interview, that eliminate a person from further consideration, such as poor speech patterns, unacceptable appearance, or lack of necessary maturity.

Law-of-10 close   A closing technique that emphasizes a product's increased value in 10 years.

Lay language   Language, or words, that most people understand.

Leading indicators   A tool used in forecasting that is particularly useful in predicting changes in sales trends. Examples of leading indicators include prices of common stocks, new orders for durable goods, new building permits, contracts and orders for plant and equipment, and changes in consumer installment debt.

Learning curve   The time needed to progress from being a complete beginner to an expert.

Limited repayment plan   An expense plan in which the firm sets dollar limits on each category of sales expenses.

List broker   An individual or a company that sorts through lists, sometimes separating them into demographic needs, and offers these lists for sale.

Lost-sale close   A closing technique that reopens the conversation between a salesperson and a prospect when the sale seems lost.

LSCPA   An acronym that describes the process for responding to customer concerns. Stands for listen, share, clarify, problem-solve, and ask for action.

Machiavellianism   A pattern of moral reasoning that is usually defined as the principles and methods of craftiness, duplicity, and deceit. Machiavellianism is based on realism.

Manage the implementation   One of the pillars of sales support, which involves offering support services, assisting with any personnel training, and reporting implementation and utilization progress.

Market segmentation   The part of a marketing strategy that involves aggregating customers into groups that have one or more common characteristics, have similar needs, and will respond similarly to a marketing program.

Marketing mix   Marketing considerations regarding the blending of price, product, promotion, and channels.

Marketing strategy   The set of integrated decisions and actions a business undertakes to achieve its marketing objectives by addressing the value requirements of its customers.

Mentor   A person who has experience in a specific field of endeavor who serves as a guide for a less experienced person.

Money terms   Terms such as *initial investment, initial amount, monthly investment,* and *monthly amount.*

Motivators   Factors that keep salespeople moving forward in their careers.

My-dear-old-mother close   A closing technique that emphasizes a mother's saying "Silence means consent, right?"

NEADS   An acronym for now, enjoy, alter, decision, and solutions, with each letter representing an aspect of a prospect's needs.

Need-satisfaction model   An approach used for buyers who best respond to an investment of more time and resources in the buyer–seller relationship and discovery process.

Nepotism   A practice in which relatives are favored or hired.

No close   A closing technique that helps the salesperson move beyond the word "no."

No-nonsense buyers   A type of buyers who are distant and want an all-business relationship.

North American Industry Classification System (NAICS)   Codes used by the Census of Manufacturers to combine businesses according to products produced to operations performed.

One-time close   A technique used in telemarketing to sell a product during the first call.

Open-ended questions   Questions to be answered with a simple "yes" or no" response that are used to identify a topic.

Opt-in e-mail lists   Lists of people who have agreed to have information about certain things they're interested in sent to them via e-mail

Original contact   The sales strategy's second step, in which the salesperson first spends time with a prospect.

Per diem plan   An expense plan that pays a salesperson a fixed dollar amount for each day or week spent in the field. The amount is designed to cover food, gasoline, lodging, telephone calls, and other expenses.

Personal motives   An individual's preferences that spur that person to buy.

Personal selling   The direct communications between paid representatives and prospects that lead to transactions, customer satisfaction, account development, and profitable relationships.

Personal space   The distance between people during a conversation.

Person-to-person selling   A sales method in which the salesperson has face-to-face contact with the prospect.

Piggybacking   A rapport-building technique in which a question is asked, the answer is acknowledged, and another question is asked, based on the response.

Porcupine method   A closing technique in which a salesperson responds to a prospect's question with another, related question.

Positioning   The consumer's perception of your product, brand, company, and competition.

Post-interaction   The activities following a transaction involving supporting skills.

Power-seekers   A type of buyers who want to advance in their company and tend to trust salespeople who have done extensive research to uncover the customer's needs.

Pre-interaction   The actions initiated prior to interaction with key decision makers, requiring skills in pre-call planning.

Prequalification   Behind-the-scenes activity of learning about a prospect.

Presentation   The sales strategy's fourth step, in which a salesperson shows the benefits of a product or service to a prospect.

Problem-solution model   An approach that is similar to the need-satisfaction model but that is based on more formal studies of the customer's operations.

Product specifications   A precise statement of the client's requirements and tolerances.

Professional selling   The process of moving goods and services from the hands of those who produce them into the hands of those who benefit from them.

Prospecting   1. The sales strategy's first step, in which a salesperson finds the right potential buyer.
2. The search for people who will buy products or services.

Qualification   The sales strategy's third step, in which a salesperson meets with a prospect, learns details about the prospect, and determines how the product can fulfill a need.

Qualitative methods   Forecasting techniques focused on subjective methods that are based on interpretations of business conditions by executives and salespeople.

Quantitative techniques   Forecasting procedures that are based on the use of historical data.

Quotas   Quantitative goals assigned to individual salespeople for a specified period of time.

Realist   A person who focuses on what is rather than on what ought to be.

Receptionist   A person who knows what each employee's area of responsibility is in order to direct calls properly.

Recognition program   A program similar to incentives in that an individual or group of salespeople receives an award for exceptional performance, but the primary award is recognition by management for exceptional performance.

Referral   The sales strategy's seventh step, or a satisfied customer's recommendation of another prospect for the salesperson.

Reflex question   A question a prospect can answer without thinking.

Relating skills   The ability to put the other person at ease in a potentially tense situation.

Relationship anxiety   A fear that a customer has in meeting a salesperson.

Relationship evolution   A five-stage process in which a relationship progresses.

Relativism   A pattern of moral reasoning that rejects universal moral rules and makes decisions on the basis of personal values and the ramifications of each situation.

Request for Proposal (RFP)   A notice that a customer sends out to qualified suppliers, asking them to bid on a project with a certain set of specifications.

Role morality   A code that demands the loyalty of employees and their silence when faced with unethical situations.

Sales force composite method   A forecasting procedure in which salespeople project volume for their customers.

Sales forecasting   The predication of future levels of demand for a product.

Sales management   The planning, organizing, leading, and controlling of personal contact programs designed to achieve the sales and profit objectives of a firm.

Sales management competencies   Sets of knowledge, skills, behaviors, and attitudes that a person needs to be effective in a wide range of industries and various types of organizations.

Sales manager   The person responsible for management of the field sales operation.

Sales process activities   The activities needed to serve a customer properly.

Sales proposal   A written offer by a seller to provide a product or service to a purchasing organization.

Self-management competency   Taking responsibility for your actions at work and elsewhere.

Selling instincts   Messages your brain sends out, telling you what's right and what's not in a selling situation.

Selling vocabulary   A list of powerful but easy-to-understand words and phrases that is specific to your product or service.

Sexual harassment   Unwelcome sexual advances, requests for sexual favors, and other verbal or physical conduct of a sexual nature.

Sharp angling   A closing technique in which the salesperson accepts a prospect's challenge to provide exact specifications, with the understanding that the sale is made.

Solution presentation   A sales presentation structure that is used to convince customers that the goods and services offered match their requirements and satisfy their needs.

Standardized model   An approach for a buyer who responds most positively to a series of statements constructed about an offering.

Strategic action competency   Understanding the industry and the organization and then taking strategic actions.

Success journal   A tool in which a salesperson records specific instances and details of successfully using new selling techniques. A success journal reinforces successful sales habits.

Suggestive selling   A process in which a salesperson offers something the prospect hasn't yet asked for or about.

Summary close   A closing technique in which the salesperson provides a summary of the benefits accepted and combines it with an action plan that requires the customer's commitment.

Support the buying decision   One of the pillars of sales support, which means reducing any anxiety that may arise with the purchasing decision.

Survey approach   A telemarketing method you can use to establish rapport and qualify a prospect.

Take-it-away close   A closing technique for dealing with people who don't want to make a decision on ownership simply because they feel they can make the decision at any time.

Target marketing   The part of a marketing strategy that refers to the selection and prioritization of segments to which the company will market.

Task motives   The logical, practical, or functional reasons for buying.

Team building competency   Accomplishing tasks through small groups of people who are collectively responsible and whose work is interdependent.

Technology competency   Understanding the potential for technology to improve sales force efficiency and effectiveness and knowing how to implement the integration of technology into the sales force

Telemarketing   A sales method in which the salesperson contacts a prospect by phone.

Territory   Customers, often located in a specified geographic area, that are assigned to an individual salesperson.

Third-party harassment   Harassment by someone outside the boundaries of a firm, such as a customer, vendor, or service person.

Tie-down technique   A technique that involves making a statement and then asking for agreement by adding a question to the end.

Training needs analysis   A process for determining where problems and opportunities exist and whether training can best address the issues.

Transactional relationship   A low-investment approach to relationship building that concentrates on explaining product features.

Traveling salesperson problem   A dilemma usually stated as a search for a route through a territory that allows a salesperson to visit each customer and return to the starting point with minimum expenditures of both time or money.

Trial closes   A closing technique in which the salesperson asks questions whose answers serve as indicators of how close the client is to making a purchase decision.

Trust   The belief that an individual's word or promise can be believed and that the long-term interests of the customer will be served.

Turnover   The ratio of the number of people who leave to the average size of the sales team.

Unconscious competence   The fourth stage of the learning curve, in which the person has learned specific skills and knowledge and applies them in an unconscious manner.

Unconscious incompetence   The first stage of the learning curve, in which a person is unaware of the amount of knowledge needed to accomplish a task.

Unlimited plan   A type of expense reimbursement plan in which sales-people submit itemized forms showing their expenditures, and the firm simply pays all reported expenses.

Up-selling   Selling bigger products or enhanced services to a customer, which typically results in higher margins and greater dollar commitments.

Validation   The last step in the hiring process, which involves validating the relationship between the selection criteria used by the firm and job success.

Value   The perception that the rewards exceed the costs associated with establishing and/or expanding a relationship.

Value analysis   A detailed analysis of a product.

Vendor analysis   An analysis of a vendor that looks at such items as delivery reliability, product quality, price, service, and technical competence.

Wheeler-dealers   A type of buyers who like to bargain and gain an advantage over the salesperson.

Whistle-blowing   A last-resort action to inform the public about an employer's or a supervisor's immoral or illegal behavior.

Wish-ida close   A closing technique that emphasizes that the prospect may regret not making the purchase.

A

Acceptance from others, 154–55
Accessible, making yourself less, 107
Accomplishment, sales force need for, 278
Achievement, as a motivator, 154
Achiever personality type, 280
Acquaintances, listing of, 98
Activities, relatively unimportant, 254
Adams, J. Stacy, 279
Address book software, 17, 107–8
Addressing concerns sales strategy step, 60
Adversarial relationship, not building, 205
Advertising agency, hiring, 100
Advocating skills, 140, 141
Age Discrimination in Employment Act
        (1967), 267
Alderfer, Clayton P., 279
Alternate-of-choice questions, 103–4, 119
Alternative choice close, 211, 218
Americans with Disabilities Act (1990), 267
Analyzers, 69, 87
Anniversary, thank-you note on, 231
Anxiety, during a sales call, 154–55
Application form, 268
Appointments
    confirming details about, 155
    getting, 147–51
    neglecting to confirm, 248–49
    setting a time limit on, 149
    with someone from another culture, 77
Approaches
    to customers, 152–56
    to prospective clients, 147–51
    used in sales, 4–6
Arguing with a prospect, 198
Arms, folded, 72
Asking, more than once, 209
Assessment of key customers, 83, 84
Assistants to decision makers, 153
Assumptive selling, 172, 183
Assurance in a sales proposal, 178

Attention-getters, 158–59, 160
Attention span, 166
Attire, 151–52
Attitude and goal setting, 8
Automobile Information Disclosure
        Act, 39
Awareness relationship stage, 81, 82

B

Background and credit checks, 269
Baja Fresh, 59
Barriers, hiding behind, 72
Base salary, combining with
        incentives, 284
Basic oral close, 211, 218
Basic written close, 211, 218
BCC (blind carbon copy) field, 99
Behavioral self-management (BSM),
        242–43, 258
Believers, 67, 87
Benefitizing, 56, 60
Benefits, tying to a product or service, 176
Benefits packages, 285, 289
Best-things-in-life close, 215, 218
Blind carbon copy (BCC) field, 99
Body language
    deciphering, 173–74
    fear shown in, 190
    during the first appointment, 152
    positive gestures, 71–72
BPI (Buying Power Index), 115, 119
Brand identity, 136, 141
Brand meaning, 136, 141
Brand relationships, 136, 141
Brand responses, 136, 141
Breaks, during a sales presentation, 167
Bribes, 34–35, 40
Brief recap, 167, 183
BSM (behavioral self-management),
        242–43, 258
BT plc (British Telecom), 233

Budget
    as a necessary tool, 216
    for training, 275–76
Business cards, 77–78, 95
Business card scanners, 109
Business contacts, prospecting, 99
Business environment, role in ethics, 27–28
Business-productivity close, 214–15, 218
Buyer(s). *See also* Customer(s)
    creating value for, 81
    disorganized and controlling, 69–70
    estimating the number of, 114
    finding for your product or service, 49
    gifts for, 34
    motives, uncovering systematically,
        49–52
Buyer concerns
    about selling and servicing of accounts,
        226–27
    negotiating, 188–89, 194, 195–200
    sources of, 189–94
Buyer-remorse close, 215–16, 218
Buyer/seller relationship, stages in, 81, 82
Buying
    decision, 56–58, 225, 237
    motives for, 52–56, 206
    positive signs, 209–10
    situations, 137–38
Buying Power Index (BPI), 115, 119

C
Calculator, using for computations, 217
Call reluctance, 85, 87
Call reports, 243, 258
Canned presentations, 56, 60
Career stages, 280, 281
Carelessness, 246–47
Catalogs, getting copies of a company's, 48
CBSAs (core-based statistical areas), 115,
    119
Chairs, removing from your office, 249
Chambers of Commerce, finding
        prospects, 96–97
Change
    as a de-motivator, 155
    fear of, 190

Checking questions, 104
Circular routes, 257
Cisco, repositioning of, 136
Civil Rights Act (1964), 267
Clarifying the real issue, 196
Clients
    addressing concerns of, 13
    demeanor with each, 175
    listening to, 73–75
    perceptions of needs, 53
    preparing for the first, 13
    qualifying prospective, 102
    researching prospective, 47–48
Closed-ended questions, 103–4,
    119
Closes, using multiple, 205
Closing
    cues, 209–10
    defined, 205, 218
    techniques, 211–17
Closing the sale
    defined, 60
    described, 51–52
    guidelines, 205–10
    mistakes during, 159
Clothing. *see* Attire
Coaching competency, 265, 289
Collaboration, 234
Colleagues
    consulting, 131–32
    getting advice from, 99–100
Colors of your product, 127
Commitment
    determining, 200
    maintaining, 15
Commitment relationship stage,
    81, 82
Common ground, establishing, 156
Communication
    cultural aspects of, 75–80
    do's and don'ts, 71–72
    as an exchange of ideas, 66
    selling as a two-way, 13–14
    skills, 66–67
Communication-style flexibility,
    67–70

Companies
  finding information on, 47
  identifying yours through visual aids, 180
  policies on receiving gifts, 80
Company-led prospecting program, 96
Company potential
  calculating, 116
  examining, 114
Company software, 108
Compensation, 283–85
Competence of salespeople, 83
Competencies
  phases or levels of, 6–7
  for sales management responsibilities, 264–65
Competition
  knowledge of, 130
  reducing among sales reps, 276–77
Competitive intelligence, assessing, 84
Competitor personality type, 280
Competitors, hiring from, 33
Complainers, 68–69, 87
Computer literacy, 16
Concerns
  addressing, 13, 51, 188
  getting the client to answer, 197–98
  negotiating buyer, 188–89, 194, 195–200
  sharing without judgment, 196
  showing interest, 188
  sources of buyer, 189–94
Conditions, valid, 198
Conferences, attending, 131
Confidence, 9, 152
Confirming details, 14
Conscious competence, 7, 19
Conscious incompetence, 7, 19
Consequence management, 242–43
Consultation, 234
Consultative relationships
  defined, 60
  described, 54
  product specifications developed in, 177
  vs. transactional, 54–56
Consumer Credit Protection Act, 39
Consumer demand, 115

Consumer goods, market potentials for, 115
Contact management software, 107–8, 119, 244, 247
Contacts, prospecting current, 97–99
Contract, as a negative word, 171
Control, sales force need for, 278
Controlling buyers, 69–70
Control systems, insights for, 287–88
Controversy, avoiding, 157
Conventional morality, 31–32, 40
Core-based statistical areas (CBSAs), 115, 119
Cost(s)
  negotiations on, 191
  other words for, 171
  savings from aligning territories, 256
Couldn't we? tie-down, 105
Countries, doing business in other, 75–76
Courtesy in securing appointments, 155
Covey, Stephen, 252–53
Credibility of referrals, 235
Credit checks, 269
Criteria in recruiting, 271
CRM (customer relationship management)
  described, 236
  model, 232–34
  software, 129, 141
Crossed arms, indicating doubt, 173
Cross-selling, 228, 236
Cultural aspects of communication, 75–80
Cultural needs, unique, 75–76
Current contacts, prospecting, 97–99
Current customers, prospecting, 95–96
Customer(s). See also Buyer(s)
  aggregating into groups, 133–35
  approaching, 152–56
  avoiding harassing, 229
  characteristics of, 134
  contacting past, 96
  creating more value for, 225–26
  current as a source of information, 131
  gaining knowledge of, 128–30
  intelligence, 83, 84
  interaction techniques, 126
  making buying decisions, 56–58
  needs, discovering and matching, 54–55

orientation, 83
prospecting current, 95–96
relations, 274
retention and growth, 138
Customer relationship management. *see* CRM
Customer service, 224, 227–31
Cycle, selling as a, 46
Cynics, 70, 87

D
Daily planning, 252
Daily time planning, 245
Daimler-Chrysler, 178
Data banks, mining, 114
Deception, fear of, 192
Decision(s)
    asking the client for, 14
    on ethical problems, 25–26
    knowing who will be making the final, 103
Decision makers
    defined, 87
    determining, 66–67
    face-to-face prospecting, 110
    getting to, 94
    meeting with, 152–53
Decision-making strategy, 206
Delivery dates
    client anger about missed, 208
    for your product, 127
Demand, predicting future levels of, 113
Demonstrations
    performed by prospects, 182
    proving problem-solving claims, 177
    thank-you notes after, 230
De-motivators, 155, 160
Dependability of salespeople, 83
Desk
    clearing, 107
    moving, 249
Details
    confirming, 14
    not paying enough attention to, 159
Detective, salesperson like a, 159
Diary, 252

Didn't you? tie-down, 105
Digital cameras, 17
Direction, 288
Direct mail
    defined, 19
    follow-up, 230
    as a selling approach, 5
    using for prospecting, 111
Direct supervision, 277
Discipline, maintaining, 15
Discomfort, avoiding, 174
Discrimination, laws prohibiting, 32–33
Disengagement career stage, 280, 281
Disorganization, 246–47
Disorganized and controlling buyers, 69–70, 87
Dissatisfaction, dealing with, 225, 236
Dissolution relationship stage, 81, 82
Distribution of your product, 128
Doesn't it? tie-down, 105
Don't you? tie-down, 105
Door, closing, 107
Down payment, 171
Dress code, 151–52
Driving time, 248
Dun's Marketing Services, 114

E
Eastman Kodak, 226
Ego-driven personality type, 280
Electrical outlets for a sales presentation, 168
E-mail
    address for each prospect, 150
    approach, 5–6, 19
    follow-up, 230
    prospecting, 111–12
Embarrassment, fear of, 192–93
Emergencies, 254–55
Empathy
    of a sales professional, 9
    in a sales proposal, 178
Empowerment, 288
Entertainment, 35–36
Enthusiasm
    of a sales professional, 9
    from sincerity, 71

Environment, knowledge of, 131–32
Equipment for a sales presentation, 168
Equity theory, 279
ERG theory, 279
Erroneous conclusion, 219
Erroneous conclusion test close, 207–8
Establishment career stage, 280, 281
Ethical decisions, making, 24–29
Ethical environment, 27
Ethics
    defined, 24, 41
    role of a job description in ensuring,
        26–27
    role of the business environment in,
        27–28
    training, 29
Ethics policy statement
    defined, 41
    having a written, 27–28
    monitoring, 28
Evaders, 68, 87
Evaluation
    defined, 286, 289
    of yourself, 15–16
Evaluation and control systems, 287–88
Executives, setting the moral climate, 27
Exit lines, 247
Expansion relationship stage, 81, 82
Expectations
    defined, 87
    meeting, 82–83
    realistic, 14–15
Expense accounts
    described, 285
    ethical abuse involving, 33–34
    padding, 31
Exploration career stage, 280, 281
Exploration relationship stage, 81, 82
Eye contact
    combined with smiling, 71
    making good, 152
    using, 174

F
Face-to-face appointment, 149
Fact-finding questions, 104

Failure
    fear of, 191
    as a learning experience, 155
Failure points in the selection process, 272
Fair Employment Opportunity Act
        (1972), 267
Fair Packaging and Labeling Act, 39
Families, finding information on, 47
Family members, contacting, 98
Fear
    of failure, 155
    as the greatest enemy, 190
    helping prospects overcome, 190–94
Federal fines, against unethical practices, 36
Federal Trade Commission (FTC), 39
Feeling-finding questions, 104
Feelings, client's, 195
Feng shui, 77
Final refusal, thank-you note after, 231
Finance and business knowledge, 234
Financial commitment, 102
Financial intelligence, 84
Financial motives, 53
Financial report, 48
Financing
    providing, 217
    of your product, 127
First impression
    importance of a good, 11
    on prospective clients, 151–52
Flexibility, communication-style, 67–70
Folded arms, 72
Follow-up
    consistent and persistent, 228–30
    defined, 237
    methods of, 229–30
    providing, 227
    system to organize, 228–29
Forecasting software, 118
Forecasts, adjusting computer-generated,
        117
Foreign Corrupt Practices Act (1977),
        35, 41
Formal studies of the customer's operation,
        58
Franklin, Benjamin, 206

Friends, contacting, 98
FTC (Federal Trade Commission), 39

G

General Motors (GM), 28
Gestures, open-handed, 72
Gifts
    for buyers, 34
    defined, 41
    in different cultures, 78–80
Glancing away, 173
Global perspective competency, 265, 289
Goal setting
    for new account calls, 242, 243
    of a sales professional, 9
    in the selling triangle, 8
Good guy criteria, 272
Go-to-market participants, 135, 141
Go-to-market strategy, 133–34, 141
Government regulation of sales ethics,
        39–40
Graham Company, 135
Gratitude to a prospective client, 148
Grease payments, 35
Greeting to a prospective client, 147–48

H

Habits, 244–45
Hamm, Mia, 59
Hands in pockets, 72
Hasn't he? tie-down, 105
Head nodding, 71
Headset, 248
Herzberg, Frederick, 277, 279
Hewlett-Packard, 112
Hierarchy of needs theory, 279
Higher authority close, 213–14, 219
High performers, personality types of, 280
Hiring practices, 32–33
Hiring process, validation of, 272
Honesty
    in every selling situation, 192
    sales force need for, 278
    of salespeople, 83
Horizontal (peer) evaluations, 288
House accounts, 33

I

IBM, 135, 226
Idealism, 30, 41
Images, created by words, 170
Immediate activities, 254
Implementation, 225, 237
Importance in the Covey framework,
        252, 253
Improvement, taking steps to, 159
Incentive programs, 280–82, 289
Indifference in failed interactions, 188
Individual needs, 278–80
Individuals, finding information on, 47
Information
    based on prospect interaction, 189
    as the heart of CRM, 232
In-person calls to prospective clients, 150
In-person contact, thank-you note after,
        230
Insurance industry, target marketing in,
        135
Integrity. *see* Honesty
Interaction phase, 125, 141
Interactions, successful, 188
Interest
    gauging with trial closes, 206–8
    in others, 8
    showed by concerns, 188
Internet
    as an approach to sales, 6
    arranging travel plans, 18, 19
    finding prospects, 97
Interpreter, meeting with in advance, 75
Interruptions
    allowing excessive, 249
    limiting during study, 12
Interviewing salespeople, 269–70
Introductions
    personal, 85, 148
    third-party to prospective clients, 151
Investing time, 250
Investment
    reducing the initial, 217
    in your product, 127
Isn't it? tie-down, 105
It's-not-in-the-budget close, 216, 219

"I want to think it over" stalling tactic
   dealing with, 217–18
   described, 189–90
   money usually involved, 197

J

Jargon
   defined, 183
   using carefully, 173
Job description, 26, 41, 266, 289
Job qualifications, 266, 289
Johnson Controls, Inc., 178
Journaling for success, 15–16
Judgmental procedures, adjusting
            forecasts, 117
Jury of executive opinion technique,
            113, 119

K

Keeping in touch with customers, 160
Key selling time, 252
Knockout factors, 269, 289
Knowledge, obtaining prior to a sales call,
            125–32

L

Laptop computers, 17
Law-of-10 close, 215, 219
Laws, employment discrimination, 266,
            267
Lay language, 169, 183
Leading indicators, 115, 117, 119
Leaning back, 173
Leaning forward
   as positive, 72
   showing interest and attention, 173
Learners, lifelong, 9
Learning curve, 6–8, 19
Learning environment, 11
Letters to prospective clients, 150
Liberty Courier, Inc., 284
Limited repayment expense plan, 285, 289
List brokers
   contacting, 97
   defined, 119
   information from, 47
Listening to clients, 73–75, 195

Long-distance sales presentations, 174–75
Long-term partnership, building, 224–27
Lost items, looking for, 246
Lost-sale close, 215, 219
LSCPA method, 195, 201
Lunches, long client, 248

M

Machiavelli, Niccolo, 30–31
Machiavellianism, 30–31, 41
Magnuson-Moss Warranty Act, 39
Mailing address for each prospect, 150
Maintenance career stage, 280, 281
Managers, responsibilities of, 264
Managing yourself, 242–45
Marketing
   mix, 136, 141
   programs, 3
   strategy, 133–38, 141
Market intelligence, assessing, 84
Market opportunities, 112
Market potential
   annual measures of, 116
   examining, 113–14
Market segmentation, 133–35, 141
Maslow, Abraham, 279
McClelland, David, 279
Medical care costs, 285
Meetings
   confirming details about, 155
   unnecessary and unnecessarily long, 248
Memorization, reflecting your personality, 13
Mentor, 99–100, 119
Messages, nonverbal, 71–72
Microsoft PowerPoint, 17, 180–81
Mistakes
   biggest sales, 159–60
   fear of repeating past, 193
Mobile phones, 17–18, 109, 250
Models, 58–59
Modified rebuy, 137–38
Money
   fear of owing, 191–92
   handling concerns about, 198–99
   as a motivator, 154
   terms, 171–72, 183

Monthly payment, 171
Moral decisions, 26–27
Moral dilemmas, 29
Morale
    improved by a training program,
        274–75
    increased by aligning territories, 256
Morality, conventional, 31–32
Moral reasoning, 30–32
Motivation-hygiene theory, 279
Motivation of the sales force, 277–83
Motivators, 154–55, 160
Motives for buying, 52–56
My-dear-mother close, 215, 219

N

Nabisco Biscuit Company, 273
NAICS (North American Industry
        Classification System), 115, 119
Names, pronouncing correctly, 76–77
NEADS formula, 102–3, 119
Needs
    related to selling success, 53
    shifting to meet the client's, 14
    uncovering, 46–48
Need-satisfaction model, 57–58, 60
Negative body language, 72
Negative thinking, 248
Negative words and phrases, 73
Nepotism, 32, 41
Networking into an appointment, 153
New buy, 138
News, keeping up-to-date on, 131
News articles on a business, 48
Newspaper, as a prospecting tool, 101
No close, 216, 219
Nodding, 71
No-nonsense buyers, 68, 87
Nonverbal interaction cues, 75
Nonverbal messages, positive, 71–72
Norms. *see* Expectations
North American Industry Classification
        System (NAICS), 115, 119

O

Objections. *see* Concerns

Objectives
    for a sales presentation, 138–40, 166–67
    for training, 275
Observant, being during a sales call, 156
Older employees, discriminating against, 33
One-time close, 5, 19
Open-ended questions, 104, 119
Open-handed gestures, 72, 174
Operational intelligence, assessing, 84
Operation of your product, 127
Oprah Winfrey's TV show, 59
Opt-in e-mail list, 97, 111, 119
Options in the problem-solving stage,
        197–200
Oral close, 211, 218
Organization, knowledge of your, 130
Organizational intelligence, assessing, 84
Original contact, 50, 60
Over-promising, as an enemy, 208
Overseas, selling, 79
Overselling, as an enemy, 208

P

Pace-maker conference at Pitney Bowes, 282
Paperwork overload, causing stress, 254
Partnerships
    building long-term, 224–27
    strengthening customer, 227–31
Passion for selling, 10
Past customers, contacting, 96
PDAs (personal digital assistants), 17,
        108–9
Per diem expense plan, 285, 289–90
Performance expectations, perceptions of
        buyers', 83
Performance measures for a firm, 286
Performance reviews, conducting, 286–87
Permission questions, 104
Persistence, 9
Personal commitment, 102
Personal growth activities, 252, 253
Personal interview, 268, 269
Personality, evaluating, 271
Personality types
    of high performers, 280
    relating to different, 67–70

Personal life, 253
Personal motives
    defined, 53, 60
    vs. task motives, 53–54
Personal selling, 3, 19
Personal space, 78, 87
Personal stories, including, 71
Personnel intelligence, assessing, 84
Person-to-person selling, 4–5, 19, 109–10
Phone calls. see Telephone calls
Phrases, negative, 73
Piggybacking, 157, 160
Pitch, as a negative word, 73
Pitney Bowes, 251, 282
Planning
    daily, 245, 252
    on the first day of every month, 244–45
    recruiting and selection, 266
    training, 275–76
Politics, avoiding the discussion of, 157
Porcupine method, 211–12, 219
Positioning, 136, 141
Positioning strategy, 136–37
Positive attitude, 9
Positive body language gestures, 71–72
Positive impression, 158
Post-interaction phase, 125, 141
Post-purchase phase, 138
Power cords for a sales presentation, 168
Power players, finding, 166
PowerPoint software program, 17, 180–81
Power seekers, 69, 87
Pre-interaction phase, 125–26, 142
Preparation, prior to the sales pitch, 11–12
Preplanning service strategy, 232–34
Prequalification, 46, 60
Presentations. See also Sales presentation
    defined, 60
    guidelines for, 51
    before opening, 157–58
    professionalism in, 12–13
    thank-you notes after, 230
Price, 171. See also Investment
Prices, regulating, 40
Problem analysis study, 58
Problem-solution model, 58, 60

Problem solving, 197–200
Problem-solving approach, 54
Procrastination, 247
Product
    brochures, getting copies of, 48
    delivery of, 208
    knowledge, 8, 127–28
    not being able to afford, 198
    number of possible users of, 114
    offering on a sample or trial basis, 193
    specifications, 177, 183
    as the star of your presentations, 179–80
    warranties, 39
Productivity
    assessing for the sales force, 286–88
    gains in, 250–51
    increased by a training program, 273–74
    motives, 53
Profanity, 157
Professional selling, 4, 19. See also Sales
        professional
Professional vocabulary, 73
Profitability of sales, 287
Profits, customer relationships as drivers
        of, 233
Promotion component of a marketing
        program, 3
Prospect(s)
    actual contact with, 147
    approaches to, 147–51
    building rapport with, 156
    contacting, 109–12
    finding, 95–101
    learning all you can about, 46
    organizing information on, 106–12
    qualifying, 13, 101–6
Prospecting
    defined, 61, 94, 119
    described, 49–50
    introduction to, 94–95
Prospecting and sales forecasting plan,
        112–18
Protective pad for a sales presentation, 169
Prudential Insurance Company of America,
        24
Public libraries, 96–97

Public relations firm, 100
Purchase, thank-you note after, 230
Purchase rate, maximum expected, 114
Purchasing
    person responsible, 66–67
    understanding, 137–38
Purchasing agents, 165
Purpose of call, stating, 149

Q

Quaker Oats chemical division, 251
Qualifications for a job, 266
Qualification stage in the selling cycle, 101–6
Qualifying a prospect, 13, 50–51, 61, 101–6
Qualitative methods
    data needed to use, 113–15, 117
    defined, 119
Quantitative techniques, 117–18, 119
Questioning
    techniques, 106
    your way to success, 103–6
Questions
    clarifying the real issue, 196
    directing and redirecting, 189
    motivating the customer, 212
Quotas, 243, 259

R

Rapport, 156, 157
Realism, 30
Realist, 30–31, 41
Receptionist
    as a contact, 109–10
    defined, 160
    knowing areas of responsibility, 153
Recognition, 154
Recognition program, 281–82, 290
Recording yourself, 74
Recruiting
    common mistakes in, 270–72
    salespeople, 266–67
Reference checks, bypassing, 272
Referrals
    defined, 61
    getting, 52, 234–36
    thank-you notes after, 231

Reflex question, 208, 219
Regulations, 39–40
Rehabilitation Act (1973), 267
Rehearsal, 243
Rehearsing your sales pitch, 12
Relating skills, 85–86, 87
Relationship(s)
    binders, 81–85
    building, 25, 80–86
    enhancing, 225, 236
    evolution of, 81, 88
    managing, 234
Relationship anxiety, 85, 86, 87
Relativism, 30, 41
Reliability in a sales proposal, 178
Religion, 157
Request for proposal (RFP), 178, 183
Researching prospective clients, 47–48
Resource allocators, 287
Respect, sales force need for, 278
Response rate for direct mail, 5
Responsiveness, 178
Résumés, 272
Retention activities, 224
Revenue, customer relationships driving, 233
Reverse discrimination, 33
RFP (request for proposal), 178, 183
Role morality, 37, 41
Rookie rules, 12
Routine, sales force need for, 278
Rules. *see* Expectations

S

Sales. *See also* Closing
    achieving successful, 226–27
    communication skills in, 66–67
    continuing growth in, 228
    increased by aligning territories, 256
    number of people working in, 2
    person-to-person, 4–5, 19, 109–10
    primary approaches used in, 4–6
    universal need for, 2–4
    using technology in, 16–18
Sales & Marketing Management magazine, 114

Sales acceptance, prospect's level of, 52
Sales calls
    managing anxiety and motivation, 154–55
    monitoring, 244
    plans for, 257–58
Sales ethics, 24–29, 39–40
Sales ethics program, 27
Sales force
    compensation, 283
    evaluation of, 286
    motivation, 277–83
    productivity, 286–88
    value-added role, 137
Sales force composite method, 113, 119
Sales forecasting, 112–18, 119
Sales goals, assigning realistic, 27
Sales managers
    defined, 264, 290
    as good leaders, 276
    recruiting and selecting sales forces, 265
Sales mistakes, biggest, 159–60
Sales models, 58–59
Salespeople
    attributes of trusted, 83
    covering expenses for, 285
    ethical problems faced by, 32–38
    factors influencing ethics of, 30–32
    fear of, 190
    hiring from competitors, 33
    interviewing, 269–70
    listening to others selling, 74
    mistakes of, 132
    psychology of, 278
    recruiting, 266–67
    selecting, 267–69, 270–71
    as a source of prospects, 100
    time spent by, 245–46
    vocabulary of great, 72–74
Sales pitch
    airing out, 47
    preparing before, 11–12
Sales potential, predicting territory sales, 256
Sales practices, deceptive, 24
Sales presentation. See also Presentations
    adjuncts to, 177–79
    breaks in, 167
    components of a successful, 165–76
    customizing materials for, 169
    establishing objectives, 138–40
    importance of, 165
    items causing problems for, 168–69
    keeping as brief as possible, 166–67
    long-distance, 174–75
    preparation for, 167–69
    proof devices for effective, 179–82
    selling vocabulary for, 169–73
Sales process activities, 134–35, 142
Sales professional. See also Professional selling
    characteristics of a successful, 8–10
    describing the ideal, 8–10
    skills important to, 234
    steps in becoming and remaining, 11–16
Sales proposal, 178, 183
Sales routes, selecting, 257
Sales strategy, 49–52
Sales success, interviews as poor predictors of, 270
Sales support, pillars of, 225
Sales teams, maintaining productive, 276
Sales territories, 256
Sales training. See also Training
    assessing needs, 275
    cost of, 273
Sales trends, predicting, 117
Sales volume, focus on, 286
Scanners of business cards, 109
SCORE (Service Corps of Retired Executives), 100
Scott Paper Company, 130
Seasonal adjustments, 117
Secondary activities, 254
Segmenting a market, 134
Self-acceptance, 155
Self-actualization, 279, 282
Self-assurance, 152
Self-confidence, 208–9
Self-contracting, 243
Self-discipline, 242–44

Self-doubts, 155
Self-management competency, 265, 290
Self-monitoring, 242, 243
Self-set goals, 243
Selling
   approaches, 56–58
   concept of, 3–4
   as a continuous process, 224
   as a cycle, 46
   efficiency, 250
   instincts, 194, 201
   overseas, 79
   passion for, 10
   preparing for, 46
   skills, 2–3, 271
   tactics and strategies, 8
   triangle, 8
   understanding, 159
   vocabulary, 169–73, 183
Senses
   evoking all, 182
   involvement of, 181
Service, offering on a sample or trial basis, 193
Service Corps of Retired Executives (SCORE), 100
Service-oriented personality type, 280
Service strategy, preplanning, 232–34
17-minute time constraint on sales presentations, 167
Sexual harassment, 36, 36–37, 41
Shareholder value, drivers of, 234
Sharing concerns without judgment, 196
Sharp angling, 212–13, 219
Shouldn't we? tie-down, 105
Sincerity
   enthusiasm coming from, 71
   lacking, 159
Situation ethics. see Conventional morality
Skills, relating, 85–86
Slang, 157
Slump in sales, correcting, 160
Smart phones, 109
Smiling, 71, 152
Software
   address book, 17, 107–8

company, 108
contact management, 107–8, 119, 244, 247
CRM (customer relationship management), 129, 141
for forecasting, 118
PowerPoint, 17, 180–81
Solution presentations, 176–77, 183
Solutions
   creating, 103
   customers buying, 52
   in the problem-solving stage, 197–200
Specifications, working together on, 178
Spending time, vs. investing, 250
Spiel, as a negative word, 73
Standardized model, 56–57, 61
Status, sales force need for, 278
Stimulation, sales force need for, 278
Stimulus control, 242, 243
Story, telling a good, 165–66
Straight rebuy, 137
Strategic action competency, 264, 290
Strength of a sales professional, 9
Student, master sales person as, 11
Studying, pace of, 12
Subordinates, deferring to power players, 166
Succeed, desire and passion to, 8
Success
   definition of, 16
   questioning your way to, 103–6
Success journal, 15–16, 19
Suggestive selling, 172, 183
Summary close, 212, 219
Superiors. see Executives
Suppliers, evaluating, 226
Surname, determining, 76
Survey approach, 110, 119
Swissôtel, 244

T
Take-it-away close, 216, 219
Talking
   rate of, matching with the prospect, 157–58
   on someone else's level, 175

Tangibles, 178
TAP Pharmaceutical Products, Inc., 36
Target marketing, 135, 142
Task motives
    defined, 53, 61
    vs. personal buying motives, 53–54
Tasks, unwanted or unproductive, 249
Teachers, former as the best salespeople, 193
Team building, 265, 276–77, 290
Technology
    competency, 265, 290
    organizing contacts, 107
    in sales, 16–18
    in time and territory management,
        250–51
Telemarketing
    defined, 19
    described, 5
    goals of a call, 111
    using for prospecting, 110–11
Telephone, not answering, 107
Telephone calls, 147–50, 247–48
Telephone contact, thank-you note after, 230
Telephone follow-up, 229–30
Television, watching, 249
10-3-1 rule, 243, 258
Tension, relieving, 106
Territory
    defined, 256, 259
    design, 256–57
    efficiency, 275
    estimate, 113
    management, 255–58
Testing of recruits, 269
Thanking the prospective client, 149–50
Thank-you notes, sending, 150, 230–31
Theories of individual needs, 279–80
Theory of learned needs, 279
Third-party harassment, 36–37, 41
Third-party information, fear based on, 194
Third-party introductions to prospective
        clients, 151
Tie-down technique, 105, 119
Time
    categories of investment, 254–355
    determining the worth of, 250

Time and territory efficiency, 275
Time management, 245–46, 252–55
Time series, seasonally adjusting, 117
Time traps, 246–49
Time wasters, 252, 253
Today, analyzing, 253
Toll-free directories, 99
Tomorrow, discovering, 253
Top Honors Conference at Pitney Bowes, 282
Trade promotion spending, 287
Training
    benefits of a program, 273–75
    budget for, 275–76
    planning for, 275–76
    of salespeople, 273
    sessions in your organization, 130
Training needs analysis, 275, 290
Transactional relationships
    vs. consultative, 54–56
    defined, 61
Traveling salesperson problem, 257, 259
Travel plans, arranging on the
        Internet, 18
Trial closes, 206–8, 219
Trust
    building with customers, 83–85
    defined, 88
    establishing during the sales
        presentation, 175
Truth-in-lending laws, 39
Turnover, 274, 290

U
Unconscious competence, 7, 19
Unconscious incompetence, 6–7, 19
United States, regional differences, 76
U.S. Census of Manufacturers, 115
Unknown, fear of, 193
Unlimited expense plan, 285, 290
Up-selling, 228, 237
Urgency in the Covey framework, 252,
        253

V
Validation in the hiring process, 272, 290
Valid conditions, 198

Value
 to a buyer, 81
 creating, 81
 defined, 88
 of time, 246
Value-added role of a sales force, 137
Value analysis, 226, 237
Vendor analysis, 226, 237
Videotapes in presentations, 181
Vietnam Veterans' Readjustment Assistance
  Act (1974), 267
Visual aids
 for a sales presentation, 168
 during a sales presentation, 180–82
 sending prior to a long-distance
  presentation, 174
Visualization
 as an effective technique, 9–10
 of a successful sales encounter, 139
Vocabulary of a great salesperson, 72–74

W

Walter Wheeler Award at Pitney Bowes,
 282

Wants, uncovering, 46–48
Web sites
 selling via, 6
 visiting, 48, 97
Weekly call plans, preparing, 252
Wheeler-dealers, 67–68, 88
Whistle-blowing, 37–38, 41
Wish-ida close, 214, 219
Words
 choosing for each client, 80
 killing sales, 159
 negative, 73, 170–72
 pictures painted by, 170
Workshops, attending, 131
Workspace, organizing, 107
Written close, 211, 218
Written ethics policy, 28
Written proposals, 177–79

Y

Yellow Pages, prospecting in, 99
"Yes" momentum, questions
  building, 105
Yesterday, investigating, 253